Inter-sections

Essays on Indian Literatures, Translations and Popular Consciousness

Rana Nayar

Orient BlackSwan

ORIENT BLACKSWAN PRIVATE LIMITED

Registered Office
3-6-752 Himayatnagar, Hyderabad 500 029 (A.P.), India
e-mail: centraloffice@orientblackswan.com

Other Offices
Bangalore, Bhopal, Bhubaneshwar, Chandigarh, Chennai, Ernakulam, Guwahati, Hyderabad, Jaipur, Kolkata, Lucknow, Mumbai, New Delhi, Noida, Patna

First Published by Orient Blackswan Private Limited 2012

ISBN: 978 81 250 4554 0

Typeset in Aldine 10.5/13 by
Techastra Solutions (P) Ltd
Hyderabad

Printed in India at
Yash Printographics
Noida

Published by
Orient Blackswan Private Limited
1/24 Asaf Ali Road, New Delhi 110 002
e-mail: delhi@orientblackswan.com

Dedicated to

Ganesh N. Devy
a nativist
who gave some of us
the courage and the confidence
to ask the right kind of questions
in our hyphenated times

Contents

Preface vii
Author's Acknowledgements xxvi
Prologue: Notes towards the History/Theory of Genres 1

Reading Indian and Indian English Literatures

1. Locating/Dis-locating Indian Literatures: A Metacritical Narrative 21
2. Re-contextualising the Post-1980s Indian Novel in English 36
3. Emerging Trends in Post-Independence Indian English Drama 46

Punjabi Literature: Some Contexts and Texts

4. Punjabi Literature through the Prism of History 65
5. The Novel as a Site of Cultural Memory: Gurdial Singh's *Parsa* 81
6. Atamjit Singh's *Kamloops Dian Macchian*: Polyphonic Discourse and Dramatic Art 110
7. Narratives of Dispersal: Reading Raghbir Dhand's Stories 122
8. Postcolonial *Katha*: Continuities and Ruptures in *Videshi* Punjabi Short Fiction 139

Reading Translation(s)

9. Author as Translator: Paradigms and Possibilities in the Indian Context 161
10. Punjabi and English: Mediating the History of Language, Literature and Translation 175
11. Bhisham Sahni's *Tamas*: Multiple Historical Perspectives and Literary Art 195
12. Mahasweta Devi's *Hajar Churashir Ma*: A Narrative of Healing 216

Power, Hegemony and Mass Media: Case Studies in Popular Consciousness

13. Of Language, Consciousness and Mass Media 227
14. Of Influence, Power and Empowerment 238
15. Of Little Magazines in Punjabi: A Historical Overview 245
16. Class, Ideology and Politics of Globalisation: A Case Study of Aravind Adiga 253

Epilogue: Rediscovering Humanities in Life and Literature 262
Index *273*

Preface

In our postcolonial, postmodern world, it has become fashionable to hyphenate words, and even bracket them into smaller segments. Those of us who have fed ourselves on a rich diet of theory find it almost impossible to resist this tendency to put words under erasure. In a way, language has become so self-reflexive that it constantly nudges and teases us into playing with it, just the way a child plays with toys. To my mind, it is the consumerist streak in our postmodernity that makes most of us regress into such child-like postures—insistently demanding, perpetually dissatisfied and constantly mulling over a new prank. After all, there is something about the very nature of language that almost demands that we use it in a certain impish, playful way. Having lost its transparency and communicability, language has acquired layers upon layers of sedimentation, making our task as communicators, at once, both frustrating and challenging. In my search for a book title—which, for me personally, is not just another name but a loaded signifier—if I have settled for a hyphenated version of 'Intersections' ('Inter-sections'), it is not a quirky decision, but a careful one; as it instantly helps us focus on the interdisciplinary nature of this volume. Besides, it also draws attention towards the diverse body of ideas that this collection engages with.

This title also has a personal significance for me, as it, at once, puts me on the crossroads of life and career, from where I may be able to cast a tangential look at the road receding into the past and stretching beyond the immediate. It was perhaps Sudhir Kakar, the famous psychoanalyst, who once said that as one approaches one's middle age, one tends to become less of a 'hunter' and more of a 'fruit gatherer'. One of the conscious symptoms of this 'enigmatic arrival' is that one begins to gather all the disparate, scattered work one has compulsively been doing over the years, without being aware of its future possibilities. Shorn of all vain hopes and false expectations, it is only in middle age that one tends to develop a very different perspective on life that often compels an honest, searching and realistic self-appraisal. Standing atop a plateau and grappling with the reality of what one really *is* and what one *is never likely to become*, one does begin to discern an identifiable, recognisable pattern in one's life as well as work. It was this recognition of a definite pattern in the essays written over the last eight years or more that gave me both confidence and courage to put them together in this collection.

All through my academic career, I have self-consciously resisted the tendency (which may also be a professional hazard for some) to produce books only because I was expected to. Somehow, ever since the University Grants Commission (UGC) started insisting that university teachers *must* produce a certain number of papers to earn their next promotion, academic writing has become an industry, driven by the principle of mass production. Books and articles are churned out a dime a dozen, and that too, at an amazing speed, as though straight off the conveyor belt. While it may have led to an unprecedented quantitative growth of academic publications across university departments, it has certainly not helped the cause of qualitative growth. In our postmodern world, where surface reality is all that matters, perhaps it is not just difficult but almost impossible to set up an equitable equation between quality and quantity—something that Karl Marx had sought to do in the nineteenth century. It is no wonder that so much of eminently unreadable and unpublishable material gets produced ever so often that it hardly profits those who read it, and of course, much less those who produce it. All this brouhaha apart, our universities have so far neither produced, nor are likely to produce in the near future, a great scientist or an economist, a potential or an actual Nobel Laureate!

I honestly believe that a book must be created out of our intellectual and emotional convictions, which are not easy to come by, and certainly take a long time to grow and develop. At some point in my academic career, I made a conscious decision to sidestep my primary duty of pursuing active research and focus instead on translation, which had, for a variety of reasons, begun to appear much more meaningful and intellectually stimulating. Around this time, I had increasingly begun to feel that most of the research being done in our universities was neither momentous nor authentic enough. Somehow, being a student of the humanities, I was constantly in search of a more humane way of connecting with my own people, my own language and my own social/cultural context. Every time I thought about English, I found it hard to shed this consciousness of it being a historical burden, a legacy of the colonial rule and hegemony. With time, it became increasingly difficult to shake off this burden, as it slowly became an inseparable part of my professional responsibilities, even my breath and being. So, translation seemed to be the only natural way out of this bind, the only way of harnessing professional knowledge of English in service of my own language and culture—Punjabi.

Though at a superficial level, 'research' and 'translation' may appear to be two distinctly dissimilar and diametrically opposed discourses, both have more in common with each other than is often recognised. Both demand passionate commitment, rigorous mental discipline, a strange amalgam of creative and critical faculties, and above all, a definite sense of purpose and meaning. Perhaps, more than anything else, it was this 'temporary absence of meaning' that had actually put me off research for some time, propelling me towards translation, almost with a vengeance. Thereafter, I spent years together, seeking both personal satisfaction and professional expertise through my several forays into, or should I say, skirmishes with, translation. I must confess that translation is something I learnt as an apprentice and that too, on the job, by testing out my skills on other people's works. It certainly is no mean task to walk in step with another writer's idiom and idiolect, syntactic oddities and ideological preferences. One has to have a fairly high propensity for self-negation, a readiness to examine and interrogate, and if need be, even set aside one's own linguistic preferences and belief systems. Translation is a highly self-reflexive act, a pretext for excavating layers upon layers of sedimentation surrounding the two linguistic systems that are involved. It may, therefore, be perceived as a definable/indefinable point of 'intersection' between two languages and/or cultures.

There is no denying that despite all the challenges it poses, translation does reserve its just rewards for anyone who chooses to devote the better part of her/his professional life to it, the way I have done. Though I have absolutely no regrets about the choice I made, somewhere down the line it had begun to dawn on me that I was simply rewriting someone's 'already-written' text. Somewhere in the process of honing my skills as a translator, I had negated myself to such an extent that it had begun to threaten my sense of subjectivity. It is ironic that it was translation that had initially helped me constitute my identity as a translator or reclaim my subject position or subjectivity, but it was translation again that, through all those years, slowly submerged my identity as a researcher. It was almost as though I was on an undeclared academic holiday or a temporary hibernation for a whole decade and a half, the time I devoted to translation. In a way, like all acts of writing, translation too forces upon the practitioner a mendicant's tactical withdrawal from the temporal, material world and the extent to which it does, it becomes a lonesome journey, a solitary enterprise. Looking back, however, I can say that I have both lost and found myself in, and through, my several works of translation.

All through those years, I somehow managed to retain my filial connection with research, but for all practical purposes, this remained both fitfully sporadic and tenuous. However, when I finally did return to research, it was more like a homecoming, and it happened in a somewhat fortuitous manner. Wrestling with real, material problems of translation, I felt a strong urge to return to theory, to seek answers to some of the nagging questions that had teased or irritated me in my practice. It is my conviction that anyone who wishes to take up translation as a semi-professional vocation (as total professionalism is simply not possible in our situation for a variety of reasons), must treat theory as *a posteriori*, and not *a priori*, to his/her own practice. There are several cogent reasons for it. One, the surplus of theoretical baggage often suppresses the instinct for translation. Two, most of the time, a translator has to look for contextual solutions for situational problems, not just pre-given solutions. Three, the narrative structured around the practice of translation always has an inherent theoretical edge to it. In a way, no practising translator worth his salt can actually escape or resist the compulsive theoretical itch for long. Sporadic acts of theorising about translation that surfaced in the introductions, prefaces or overtures I wrote for the texts I translated made my return to research easier.

And yet, it was the return of the 'prodigal', someone who had exhausted—though not necessarily dissipated—all his creative and critical potential. Research was a way of re-energising those lost potentials, a way of reclaiming a professional identity and ironically, once again it happened at the intersection of the practice and theory of translation. It is no wonder that I have chosen to include several essays in this volume that either deal directly with my 'translating consciousness' or have emerged out of my engagement with its theoretical implications. Significantly, my reasons for choosing the 'discursive essay' for articulating my thoughts go a long way towards underlining a certain strategic essentialism built into them. Despite its waning popularity, I do look upon this genre as the best form of self-expression, which must somehow be kept alive, if it has to ensure the ultimate survival of the dialogic tradition in our culture. Situated at the conjuncture of its argumentative and philosophical variants, a discursive essay combines the best of both. It communicates without overwriting itself and often goes straight to the heart of the matter, without offering any apologies. Ever since theory invaded our academia, it has become fashionable to regard heavily jargon-ridden critical discourse as a preferred mode of expression. I have always maintained that jargon never facilitates, only disrupts; it never makes discourse accessible, only stifles it.

However, these 'inter-sections' become real only to the extent to which they become effective interventions into the existing body of knowledge. While some may think that these interventions are a direct consequence of an overvaluation of my own work, the others may treat them simply as gratuitous acts of self-glorification. It is true that some amount of overvaluation is necessary for any author to sustain the illusion of being in the profession. It is also a fact that writing invariably draws its 'life' or its 'afterlife' (to borrow Walter Benjamin's famous phrase) from the involvement of the reader. In its simplest form, writing is a form of social contract between a writer and a reader, a leap of faith between two individuals that easily posits unlimited dialogic possibilities. Now, this is regardless of whether or not two individuals in this social contract actually believe in the reality of each other's existence. After the famous pronouncement of Roland Barthes about the proverbial 'death of the author'—both in the literal and metaphorical sense—it has become increasingly difficult to argue that 'author' has any substantive 'reality' or 'subjectivity' of her/his own. While the author's reality may always remain suspect or simply inaccessible, the reader may still be able to recover or reclaim her/his identity through volitional and involved acts of reading.

At this juncture, a word about the methodology and conscious (or unconscious) aims of this particular collection, by way of an overture to my readers, would certainly be in order. This volume is neatly divided into four (inter-)sections—Reading Indian and Indian English Literatures, Punjabi Literature: Some Contexts and Texts, Reading Translation(s), and Power, Hegemony and Mass Media: Case Studies in Popular Consciousness. The essays have been arranged thematically, keeping in mind the quintessential requirements of the areas of study, their distinctive operational logic as well as their distinctive constraints. This has been done with the consciousness that areas of overlap and interpenetration are bound to emerge as the essays unfold slowly across the four sections. While selecting essays for each section, my effort was to put together pieces that reflect a broad range and spectrum of issues falling within each category, thus enabling me to cover as much theoretical ground within that specific category as possible. Though each essay offers an understanding of a distinct idea, issue or problem and so is discrete, it does ultimately fit into the larger frame of each section, by virtue of its emphases, ideological imperatives and perspectival values. This internal logic of each micro-section may just as well be applied to the larger macro-frame of the volume, too.

This volume begins with a Prologue—'Notes towards the History/Theory of Genres'. It was delivered as a keynote address in a seminar on the history of genres organised by the Department of Punjabi, Punjabi University, Patiala, in March 2008. Though I do not have much expertise in the area of genre studies, this essay is a collocation of random thoughts I could be said to have gathered along my way. This tentativeness is definitely reflected in the way the essay is diffidently or self-consciously titled. Of course, I was consciously thinking of Eliot's *Notes towards the Definition of Culture* (whose resonance is found in the title) as a model for working out my own framework, but inspiration for the ideas came primarily from my occasional readings and, of course, long hours of teaching. In this Prologue, I have tried to demonstrate that the history of genres is as old as the history of human thought itself. Further, I argue that the principles of differentiation, classification and/or segmentation began to be applied around the time that the need was felt to separate the 'secular' from the 'religious'. Since the advent of theory, we have moved into a phase where either the history of different genres is being rewritten or the rigid boundaries across genres are gradually being pulled down, making way for the interpenetration of these categories.

The first section begins with the essay 'Locating/Dis-locating Indian Literatures: A Metacritical Narrative', an attempt to look into the problematic of how and where Indian literatures could possibly be located vis-à-vis Indian English literature. More than a mere superficial exercise in comparative literature, the essay addresses several theoretical problems that the Indian context throws up in this regard. At the same time, an effort has also been made to incorporate some empirical observations to give the necessary cutting edge to these theoretical problems. Though this paper emerged largely out of a national seminar on Indian English literature hosted by our department at ICSSR Chandigarh in 2000, it shows a definite imprint of how postmodern theories have influenced our lives and thought. In the postmodern context, the term 'location' has come to enjoy a very loaded, multiple signification. In a way, if any single development is to be linked to the historical twist from the 'modern' to the 'postmodern', it is the 'spatialisation' of our narratives. In this situation, we are often compelled to examine the contesting/competing claims of the local vs the global, the native vs the immigrant, the citizen vs the state. If this framework has been preferred, it is only because it permits us to interrogate some of the well-known institutional practices, operating both inside and outside the academia.

In 'Re-contextualising the Post-1980s Indian Novel in English', first delivered as a keynote address in a national seminar at HMV Jalandhar in September 2007, the effort has been to create a new context within which some of the recent Indian English novels, especially those produced after Salman Rushdie's *Midnight's Children*, could possibly be read or critiqued. Over the years, it has become fashionable for the West to hail every other work of an Indian English novelist as a unique literary experiment. This has somehow coincided with the ever-growing shrillness emanating from the 'end of history' rhetoric. Somehow, this whole argument surrounding the 'end-ism' seems unacceptable, as one must, following Frederic Jameson, 'always historicise'. Following this logic, I have tried to historicise the re-emergence or revival of Indian English fiction of the early 1980s, perceiving this development within the larger frame of what was happening in Europe or the US in the late 1960s or the early 1970s. Perhaps, the novels of Salman Rushdie and others of his tribe deserve to be seen against the backdrop of Gunter Grass and Gabriel Marquez, who had introduced 'magical realism' in fiction much earlier. In a way, the purpose of this essay is to create a counter-discourse, thereby offering a corrective to the perspective of the Western reader and critic, who often deny Indian English fiction the sense of history it certainly possesses.

'Emerging Trends in Post-Independence Indian English Drama' is another one of the historical gestures of the kind that I have already mentioned. The only difference is that this time round, my focus is not so much upon fiction as on drama. This essay is a reworked version of a seminar paper presented at GGS Khalsa College, Ludhiana, in January 2008. My argument here is that Indian English drama has remained, for a variety of reasons, a neglected area within the larger domain of Indian English literature. While both fiction and poetry in Indian English show a definite propensity for identifiable trends and movements, the same cannot be said about drama with equal force and conviction. Apart from mapping out the major developments that have emerged in this particular field since Independence, this essay also casts a tangential look at the logistics of why this particular genre has remained peripheral and/or neglected. There is also an attempt here to contextualise some of the early developments in this field within the broader frame of Parsi theatre, which is said to have influenced the whole range of urban theatre forms in various regional Indian languages, especially in the pre-Independence phase. In a way, my effort is to identify and delimit the points of intersection between regional urban theatres and the English theatre in India with its specific metropolitan orientation and bias.

In the second section, the focus of the volume ostensibly shifts away from Indian and Indian English literatures to Punjabi literature, but the main objective of this section is to explore the points of conjuncture between these two discourses. The essays here deal with Punjabi literature from the perspective of an outsider. Whether it is the question of mapping out the history of Punjabi literature or deconstructing the ideology behind the Indian variants of postcolonialism, these essays invariably lack the 'inwardness' often associated with an insider. As I have functioned all along within the Western paradigms and/or critical frameworks, my perception of Punjabi literature is bound to be qualitatively different from that of a Punjabi teacher/scholar. If, on the one hand, it has enabled me to locate Punjabi literature within a much wider frame of world literatures, on the other, it has helped me step out of the self-enclosed world of Punjabi scholarship and re-formulate my critical hypotheses on very different terms. To an extent, this is reflected in the way in which I have been able to read Gurdial Singh's *Parsa* from the perspective of cultural memory or discover an entirely new semantics for Punjabi diaspora literature in the form of a less popular notion of 'dispersal'. The last essay in this section, which seeks to locate the conjunctures and dis-junctures within Punjabi diaspora literature, again, falls in this category.

In the first essay, 'Punjabi Literature through the Prism of History', the original version of which was published in *The Book Review* (August 2007), the attempt is to provide a synoptic view of the history of Punjabi literature, spanning a thousand years or more, in less than twenty pages. Apart from the compactness of style and economy of expression, what really marks out this essay is its critical sharpness and wealth of historiographical material. Though it does not really emerge as a conscious aim in the construction of this essay, one of its avowed purposes is to interrogate the all-too-familiar notions of historiography that Punjabi literary traditions often foreground. Inured to the changes in the realm of historiography, most of the literary histories in Punjabi appear to follow the foundational notions of history as an objective science, based upon the twin principles of chronology and factual documentation. In my essay, I have consciously tried to escape this tyranny of conventional modes of recording history by foregrounding the notion of 'cultural history'. More than the discipline of history, it is 'literary history' that must aspire to become 'people's history' by recording their struggles, hardships and dilemmas emerging out of their contact with, or contestation of, historical forces. The extent to which this essay succeeds in doing so, it becomes a tour de force in anti-foundational views of history.

From the notion of cultural history to the concept of 'cultural memory', the progression is both natural and inevitable. Though I had translated Gurdial Singh's famous novel *Parsa* way back in 1999, it took me several years to read the inscriptions of cultural memory in this particular novel. It was an invitation to participate in an international conference on the theme, 'Punjabi Literature and Its Worlds', held at the University of British Columbia, Vancouver, in April 2008, which finally enabled me to crystallise my thoughts on this subject. This paradigm of cultural memory came into critical focus in the post-World War II context, especially when systematic attempts were being made to recover the traces of collective memory from the individual writings of German Jews who had suffered persecution at the hands of Hitler and his allies. It was through such exercises that the repressed contents of history came to the fore, thus deconstructing the conventional modes of 'history-making'. The retrieval or reclamation of cultural memory, therefore, becomes an act of individual as well as social/collective catharsis and responsibility. Of late, the genre of novel is increasingly being used, especially in Latin America, Africa and Asia, as a site for excavating the archaeology of repressed human knowledge. It is against this backdrop that I have attempted to re-read Gurdial Singh's *Parsa*.

In the third essay of this section, titled 'Atamjit Singh's *Kamloops Dian Macchian*: Polyphonic Discourse and Dramatic Art', I have taken recourse to Bakhtinian ideas to interpret a Punjabi play that deals with the eternal dilemmas and conflicts of Punjabi immigrants in Canada. Though Bakhtin has largely theorised about the novel and the novelistic discourse, his ideas such as 'polyphony', 'carnival' and 'heteroglossia' have much wider applications. For instance, more than the novel, it is drama that could be seen as an effective location for polyphony and heteroglossia, as also for defining the limits of the dialogic discourse. His deft and creative use of various Punjabi dialects makes Atamjit's play most appropriate for the application of Bakhtinian ideas. He mainly uses three different dialects—*Majhi, Malwai* and *Doabi*—in the speech rhythms of his characters—apparently, an interesting experiment in heteroglossia. The polyphonic effect achieved through the orchestration of different voices has further implications for the multi-lingual character and the identity politics of the Canada-based Punjabi diasporic community. It also has far-reaching consequences for the ways in which multiple dialogic possibilities have been projected—both within the community, and also in relation to the Canadian brand of multiculturalism. This essay establishes, rather unambiguously, how all of this ultimately has a cascading effect upon the construction of the play.

In 'Narratives of Dispersal: Reading Raghbir Dhand's Stories', I return to a deconstructive reading of Dhand's stories, preferring Robert Cohen's notion of 'dispersal' over the notion of 'diaspora' (a more widely used term in postcolonial discourse) for analysis. Over the years, the term 'diaspora', by virtue of its archaeological thickness, has become hegemonic, foregrounding the twin notions of 'forced exile' and the 'scattering of the Jews across the globe'. However, in the case of Jews, the notion of 'homeland' has a fixed centre and fairly stable boundaries, something that is not necessarily the case with Punjabis. For them, 'homeland' has been a mythic, 'wished-for' land and much less a real, historical or geographical space and/or territory. In fact, the configurations of the Punjabi homeland have constantly been shifting, so much so that it is practically impossible to draw even a rough map of its boundaries. This process of constant 'mythification' of homeland coupled with the idea of 'voluntary exile' is what sets the historical process of the Punjabi immigration apart from that of the other communities and/or races. So, one of the effective ways of exploring the diasporic tensions in Raghbir Dhand's stories is to read them as narratives of dispersal. It is the notion of dispersal that captures the endless process of decentring that the Punjabi community has experienced right through its history.

The last essay included in this section, titled 'Postcolonial *Katha*: Continuities and Ruptures in *Videshi* Punjabi Short Fiction', offers some very interesting points of intersection endorsed by our contemporary discourse. Most of these may be outlined in such apparently dichotomous though problematic terms as 'colonial' and 'postcolonial', 'theory' and 'narrative', 'English' and 'Punjabi', 'continuity' and 'rupture', 'native' and 'immigrant', and finally, '*desi*' and '*videshi*'. The essay is structured around different sets of polarities, with a conscious aim of turning them inside out or upside down. Proceeding on the assumption that *katha*, an Indian variant of narrative, is a significant tool of theorisation (following the lead of Barbara Christian, who, as a Black American scholar, perceives Western critical theory as an expression of White supremacy), I have sought to create a discourse of resistance in this essay. Rather than turn to the pre-given, critical framework of postcoloniality supplied by the Western academia, my effort has been to build up a sustained critique from below. For this purpose, I have also looked searchingly into the problematic of how human knowledge is first constructed and then circulated, disseminated or legitimised, both inside and outside the academia. This is what provides me with an alternative frame of reference within which I have tried to situate and/or critique a fair sampling of diasporic Punjabi short fiction.

The third section has four essays selected and arranged in such a way that the section reflects its concern with both the theory and practice of translation. The essay, 'Author as Translator: Paradigms and Possibilities in the Indian Context', was originally delivered as a valedictory address at a national seminar on 'Author as Translator', hosted by Jamia Millia Islamia, New Delhi, in March 2008. More in the nature of a speculative essay, it provides us a sketchy outline of various paradigms and possibilities that tend to emerge out of the dialogic interaction between the author and the translator. Some of the possibilities debated in this essay are as follows: an author translating his own work or that of another author, an author translating from one Indian language into another or from one Indian language into another European language and vice versa.

Each possibility apparently has its own distinctive rationale and logistics. The second part of the essay directs my search towards some indigenous tropes of translation to be found in the form of metaphors, legitimised by narratives that may ultimately help us redeem the Indian discourse on translation. Once again, my effort has been to escape the tyranny of the dominant discourse by resisting Western theories of translation and consciously moving towards a discourse of alterity.

The second essay, 'Punjabi and English: Mediating the History of Language, Literature and Translation', was originally written for a seminar organised by the Sahitya Akademi, New Delhi, in January 2006. It seeks to map out the historical relationship between Punjabi and English in terms of language, literature and translation. It needs to be pointed out here that I have self-consciously chosen not to construct this understanding of history in orthodox, conventional terms, but instead foregrounded the Foucauldian gaps and fissures, while exploring the rich terrain of literary and cultural archives and/or the popular folk consciousness inscribed in the local idioms, phrases and proverbs. The contours of this historical frame inevitably coincide with the extended phase of British colonial rule in India, when most Indian languages and literatures, including Punjabi, had begun to develop their multiple points of conjuncture and disjuncture with the English language, literature and culture. Building up on the asymmetrical transactions between Punjabi and English, this essay also externalises the 'politics of translation' that often results from it. This point is further corroborated by examining the manner in which two of the seminal texts of Punjabi culture, one religious and the other secular—*Sri Guru Granth Sahib* and Gurdial Singh's *Marhi Da Deeva*—have been translated into English. This essay throws up a wide range of questions about the theory and practice of translation that deserve our attention, particularly in the Indian context.

The third essay—'Bhisham Sahni's *Tamas*: Multiple Historical Perspectives and Literary Art'—was originally commissioned by the editor of *Desh Pardes*, a well-known Hindi literary journal, sometime in 2002, for a special issue on Sahni. So, it was originally written in Hindi and much later, it was translated into English and published elsewhere. Like all other translated texts, this essay too is twice-born, and so is an interesting study of how the problems pertaining to the theory and practice of translation must always be discussed in relation to each other. This makes this essay an ideal piece to be included in this section, although its real focus is not translation, but the new trends in historiography and its multiple implications for *Tamas* as well as other works of Hindi fiction. My concern here is with the question of 'how' and 'how successfully' has Sahni managed to depart from the conventional ways of representing history. In the process, I have also tried to establish linkages between Sahni's fictional strategy of multiple perspectivism and his art of writing. His ingenious and creative use of fictional strategies transforms this novel from just another 'historical fiction' into a well-crafted 'writerly text' (to borrow Roland Barthes' phrase), complete with its penchant for religious openness and linguistic plurality.

The last essay included in this section, again, does not necessarily deal with the trope of translation, though it does use a translated text for the purposes of analysis. In 'Mahasweta Devi's *Hajar Churashir Ma*: A Narrative of Healing', originally presented as a seminar paper at G.G.S. College, Ludhiana, in 2004, I have discussed four different types of narratives which may also be treated as paradigms for historicising the feminist discourse. My main focus in this essay, however, is upon the intermediate form of 'narrative of healing' which could be said to become a bridge, as it were, between a 'narrative of oppression' and a 'narrative of self-liberation'. My argument is that before a woman is able to attain a measure of autonomy or reclaim her 'subjectivity', she has to go through an extended phase of actual or mythopoeic (as may be the case) process of self-healing, enabling her to recover from the multiple inflictions of oppression. Drawing upon my understanding of Mahashweta Devi's oeuvre that appears to vacillate between the twin extremities of the 'primitive' and the 'civilized', the 'tribal and the 'bourgeoisie', which she negotiates apparently with an ideological aim of re-constituting them, I have offered an existential–aesthetic and political reading of one of her well-known works. By reversing the popular dictum that 'the personal is political', I have argued how *Hajar Churashir Ma* is about the politicisation of Brati's mother, a process that first helps her recover her subjectivity, her humaneness, and then provides her with inner, spiritual healing, a necessary pre-condition for self-liberation.

In the last section of this volume, the focus shifts away from literature and translation to the ideological influences of mass media and their implications for popular consciousness. Over the years, I have done substantial amount of journalistic writing in the belief that as teachers, it is our duty to communicate not only to our students inside the classroom, but also to the general public and the society at large. If, on the one hand, it is simply not possible for us to impose any definite limits on the process of communication in this globalised world, on the other, a teacher is always conscious of her/his role as a 'thinking being', who must rarefy, clarify and also circulate ideas, wherever s/he possibly can. One of the good things about journalistic writing is that it imposes a very rigorous mental discipline upon all those who practise it. Above all, it teaches the virtues of brevity, compactness and economy to a teacher who may otherwise be given to this sin of 'over-writing'—more of a professional hazard than anything else. In my case, incursions into journalism have helped me develop sensitivity towards the invisible reader out there (who always remains anonymous in all known forms of mass media). Besides, it has enabled me to look at the complex processes of communication in a more self-conscious and self-reflexive way. To some extent, this is reflected in all the essays I have selected for inclusion in the present volume.

The first essay in this section, 'Of Language, Consciousness and Mass Media', is an attempt to look into different ways of negotiating the complex relationship among three discrete though interdependent categories—language, consciousness and mass media. First, I have tried to build on the ideas of Martin Heidegger and Karl Marx to identify two distinct philosophical and historical ways of negotiating the relationship between language and consciousness. In the process, I have identified two theoretical configurations of this relationship—the phenomenological and the materialist. My purpose in conceptualising these two categories is to theorise on the changes that have come about in the print media, one of the prominent organs of mass media, especially in the Indian context. My contention is that after liberalisation, Indian newspapers have gone through a phase of restructuring their role and function—from the role of 'opinion-makers' they have fast turned into products of consumption. It is this commodification that is the real source of the crisis of credibility in our print media. Here, my main effort is to unmask various dimensions of this crisis and also establish how newspapers have largely become purveyors of mass culture. This argument has also helped me understand the manifold contradictions inherent in mass culture, and its subversive ideological implications for both language and consciousness.

In the second essay, 'Of Influence, Power and Empowerment', which was first published in the *Economic and Political Weekly* in November 2007, I look at the nature and content of media projections and argue that such projections have to be viewed with a great deal of scepticism, caution and care. This is all the more important when such projections have to do with issues as complex as women's empowerment or gender politics. When Indra Nooyi was named the CEO of a multinational company based in the US, the media hailed her elevation as a major victory for the cause of women's empowerment. What really intrigued me was the fact that a simple, somewhat naïve, equation was being set up between her personal success and women's empowerment. This is what prompted me to critique the whole idea of media projections as a subversive strategy that enters into a silent collusion with capitalist forces which ultimately control, manipulate and regulate the media in more ways than one. My contention is that women's empowerment becomes possible only if an individual uses her personal influence or power or both to either initiate women-friendly schemes/policies or offer greater opportunities to women within the organisation, thus widening the base of their collective influence and power. Individual success is dependent upon a number of incremental factors, all of which may not have anything to do with gender politics or women's empowerment.

'Of Little Magazines in Punjabi: A Historical Overview' is more in the nature of a survey essay, as it offers a bird's-eye view of the ways in which literary journalism has developed in Punjabi over the last hundred years or so. Though the first printing press in Punjab had been set up as far back as 1835, literary journalism in the language began to flourish only under the influence of the Singh Sabha Movement, around the 1870s. It was Bhai Veer Singh who played a pioneering role in this respect by starting *Khalsa Samachar*, which gave a definite direction to Punjabi literary journalism by shaping it into a full-fledged movement. Close on the heels of this development, other equally successful experiments such as Labh Singh's *Pritam* (1923), Heera Singh Dard's *Phulwari* (1924) and Gurbaksh Singh's *Preetlari* (1933) appeared in quick succession. If Lahore and Multan were the centres of Punjabi literary journalism in the pre-Independence phase, it spread largely to places like Amritsar, Ludhiana, Jalandhar and Delhi after Independence. During this period, *Aarsi*, *Kahani*, *Sirjana* and *Nagmani*, among others, became some of the more popular organs of Punjabi literary journalism. Not only did they help in shaping the spirit of Punjabi imagination, but they also reinforced a degree of self-consciousness and pride among the Punjabi people about their literature, history, religion and culture.

The last essay included in this volume—'Class, Ideology and Politics of Globalisation: A Case Study of Aravind Adiga'—was originally commissioned by *Hindustan Times* (Sunday Edition) as one of its lead articles. The essay deals with Aravind Adiga's *The White Tiger* which won the prestigious Man Booker Prize in 2008. Most of the media critics have praised Adiga for projecting the question of the 'underclass' or the 'underdog' in Indian English writing, perhaps, for the first time ever. In my essay, I have tried to question such naïve, ahistorical assumptions about Indian literature and so have sought to contextualise these two questions of class and ideology within the frame of Indian literature in general and Punjabi literature in particular. I have argued that what is being projected as a 'literary first' by media critics is an old hat that writers of all persuasions—right from Mulk Raj Anand in English to Premchand in Hindi, from Dalit writers in Marathi to Punjabi novelists like Gurdial Singh—have worn from time to time, and that too, with much greater panache and self-assuredness. Often, in our assessment of contemporary literature, we neglect the pressing claims of history and tend to view each new work as a 'great, never-before-seen, media event'. Not only does it go against the very grain of literary criticism, but it also tends to de-historicise Indian English writing. Further, both these responses are equally subversive, as they are closely tied to the politics of globalisation.

The volume concludes with an Epilogue that, in a way, serves to bring together some of the issues and concerns that have been raised in the earlier four sections. One of the concerns that the overbearing, almost intrusive 'presence' of theory has thrown up for our consideration is whether or not it is possible for us, at this juncture, to reclaim the 'human subject' from the debris of history. Not only has this created a serious crisis for the continuation of our belief in humanistic philosophy, but it also is threatening to sever the inalienable connection between life and literature, almost irreparably. The Epilogue titled 'Rediscovering Humanities in Life and Literature', emphasises, rather categorically, the imperative of redefining and resurrecting a new brand of humanism, especially in the Indian context. For this purpose, the essay seeks to re-locate the Indian concept of *dharma* within the larger frame of cultural pluralism. While reiterating the nativists' position of seeking 'local solutions for local problems', this essay also warns against the overwhelming tendency towards succumbing to the multiple pressures of globalisation or the hegemony of Euro-centric theories/constructs.

Though much of my focus and emphasis in these essays, as outlined so far, has been explicitly theoretical in nature, in the process of reading them, you may get the sense that these are being read out to you by an absent narrator. The essays definitely do possess a certain oral/aural quality, which, I must confess, was built into the way these were structured, and so must be accepted as *fait accompli*. I could have structured them in a much more formal and objective manner, but I have chosen not to do so. As a matter of fact, my decision to retain an egregiously personal tone (which I recognise to be the main strength of these essays), was a self-conscious strategy, a ploy that helped me set up the mise en scène for the reader in a more effectively intimate manner. This was my way of inviting you, dear readers, into a dramatic act of listening, or should I say, eavesdropping on some of my most private thought processes. If I may say so, you would literally get to scour my mind, sharing my personal, social and cultural meditations through this unique process that tends to combine reading with listening, and yet appears to transcend both.

Though these essays have been neatly divided into four sections and deal with a whole range of issues and problems, there is a common thread running through all of them. In its own distinctive way, each essay becomes an undeniable act of protest and resistance, a way of articulating and legitimising the discourse of alterity. Needless to say, such an alterity could have only been positioned at the 'inter-sectional' points of conjuncture and departure. Often, it is at such points of 'inter-section' that the acts of resistance become both alluringly desirable and potentially real. For 'inter-sections' offer that transgressive site where the status quo begins to appear, at once, both seductive and threatening. Now that I have brought these essays into the public space, I can see yet another point of 'inter-section' heaving into sight. This one is between you and me, dear reader, where we might ultimately come face to face with two equally compelling choices—of connecting with each other through a meaningful dialogue or just going our separate ways, without so much as batting our eyelids. My hope and belief is that you would, after all, find at least some of the ideas in this collection well worth your attention and by engaging with them at some level, reward the pains I have taken in stitching them together.

January 2012 **Rana Nayar**
Chandigarh

Author's Acknowledgements

I express my sincere thanks to all the colleges, university departments and academic institutions in and outside Punjab that expressed confidence in my ability to reflect on serious issues by inviting me to participate in seminars/conferences on a wide range of themes. This is what gave me an opportunity to dig deep into my mind and/or reading, enabling me to explore my ideas on a variety of subjects. Without this, it would have been well-nigh impossible for me to put my thoughts together, in the first place; and perhaps, this collection of essays would not have been born at all. Having looked upon seminars/conferences somewhat sceptically all my life, I have finally come round to believe that more than just necessary forms of 'academic socialising', these events do promote some individual and/or institutional academic good.

I must express my deep sense of gratitude to Mr Tanmoy Roychowdhury and Mr Vinit Mehra of Orient BlackSwan, who took the initiative to pass this manuscript on to Dr Madhavi Menon, Senior Editor, Orient BlackSwan. Dr Menon was kind enough to get this manuscript evaluated on priority and give her magisterial, final nod for its publication. Mr Sreenath Sreedharan has worked tirelessly to give final shape to this book, in which it will ultimately get to the readers. It was an exhilarating experience for me to work in close coordination with Mr Sreedharan, as he pored over every word on each page, making some invaluable suggestions for improving the quality of the final product. This book owes a great deal to the extraordinary editing and proof-reading skills of Mr Sreedharan, much more than he would be willing to acknowledge or concede.

My publishers, Orient BlackSwan, Hyderabad, deserve full credit and appreciation for bringing out this book in a record time of less than a year. Of course, my wife Aruti, who has always been the first reader and the most unsparing critic of whatever I write, was, as always, generous with her time and patience, and so deserves rich kudos. An occasional nod or a smile from my children Mayank, Megha, Kriti and Madhav, spurred me on, especially in my fallow moments, to finish this book in double quick time.

My special thanks to Dr Shelly Narang and Ms Ashima Thakur, two of my very competent young scholars, whose incisive reading of the 'Preface' made it what it has now become.

Above all, I am grateful to God Almighty, without whose blessings no task can either be undertaken or accomplished, and whose gracious presence I palpably sense in each thought I articulate or decipher.

Rana Nayar

The author and the publishers would like to acknowledge that some of the chapters in this book have appeared in modified forms in earlier publications as per the list below. However, copyright for all the articles mentioned here rest with the author, and there has been no need to obtain permissions. Even so, as a gesture of goodwill, the author has written to all the publishers of the journals/newspapers mentioned below, informing them that he is reproducing altered versions of these in the present publication by Orient BlackSwan.

'Novel as a Site of Cultural Memory: Gurdial Singh's *Parsa*', *Summerhill IIAS Review* XVII, no. 1 (Summer 2011): 56–67.

'Rediscovering Humanities in Life and Literature', *Dialog* 20 (Spring 2011): 1–10.

'Class, Ideology and Politics of Globalisation: Story of Adiga's Success', *Dialog* 18 (2008): 35–43.

'Of Little Magazines in Punjabi: A Historical Overview', *Dialog* 17 (2009): 17–24.

'Trends and Techniques in Contemporary Indian Fiction', *Dialog* 15 (June 2007): 33–48.

'Punjabi Literature through the Prism of History', *The Book Review* XXXI, no. 8 (August 2007): 16–19.

'Mahasweta Devi's *Mother of 1084*: A Narrative of Healing', *Dialog* 13 (Spring 2005): 87–96.

'Post-Colonial *Katha*: Continuities and Ruptures in *Videshi* Punjabi Fiction', *Studies in Humanities and Social Sciences* XI, no. 1 (Summer 2004): 57–74.

'Reflections on Language, Consciousness and Mass Media', *Studies in Humanities and Social Sciences* X, no. 2 (Winter 2003), 89–98.

'Bhisham Sahni's *Tamas*: Multiple Historical Perspectivism and Literary Art', *Creative Forum* 15, no. 1–2 (January–June 2002): 5–22.

'Locating/Dis-locating Indian Literatures: A Story of Hits and Misses', *Summerhill IIAS Review* VII, no. 1 and 2 (Summer–Winter 2001): 7–10.

'*Kamloops Dian Macchian*: Polyphonic Discourse and Dramatic Art', in *Kamloops Dian Macchian: Samvad Te Samikhiya*, ed. Sukhdev Singh (Chandigarh: Lokgeet Prakashan, 2002), 210–21.

'Of Influence, Power and Empowerment', *Economic and Political Weekly* 42 (49): 16–18.

Notes towards the History/Theory of Genres

'In the beginning was the Word [the undifferentiated "logos"].' Then the 'Word' became flesh. This is what created a variety of sounds, music patterns, colours and differentiated images. This is how multiplicity and plurality resulted. This is how the 'Word' became the Tower of Babel.

This is *not* the way in which the story of John (1:14)[1] of either the 'world' or the 'Word' is recounted in the Bible. (Here, I am not going into the question of whether or not and to what extent, if so, the Bible could actually be regarded as a work of literature. This question, debated extensively in the late nineteenth and early twentieth century, is best left to the historians of religion.)[2] However, I have adapted, modified and subverted this Biblical story, to focus our attention on the question of how a differentiated, classified understanding of literary genres emerged through the ages. This begs another question: In the process of doing so, are we, by any chance, returning to the 'originary myths' (all of which have already been debunked and deconstructed by Derrida and other poststructuralist theorists)?[3] In a way, we are, and perhaps there is no escape from these originary myths, especially when we probe into the history of literary genres. Located as we are in a poststructuralist context, all attempts at constructing knowledge (of whichever kind) tend to become somewhat self-reflexive. For this reason, we need to raise another related question here: What are the different ways in which this knowledge about the history of genres can possibly be constructed? There are two antithetical and, perhaps, divergent ways of constructing this knowledge: 1. to mediate the knowledge directly (not necessarily chronologically or sequentially) and look through the prism of literary history of a particular language/culture and, 2. to mediate the knowledge indirectly and look at it through the multiple perspectives of literary theory.

The history of literatures is, strangely enough, implicated in the history of religions. The early literatures in all cultures, without an exception, emerged out of religion, and in more ways than one, even today, religion continues to constitute the mythical substratum of literatures across the world.[4] Perhaps for this and several other related reasons, it is important to look into the cultural archives, to dig deep into the 'archaeology of knowledge' (to borrow the title of Foucault's fascinating book), if we are to understand the ways in which literary genres have slowly evolved over the centuries.

As the story of creation from *Genesis* shows, in the beginning, just as we, human beings, existed in a primeval, embryonic state of undifferentiated mass—indistinguishable from lizards (and regardless of whether we go along with the Biblical premise of 'divine creation' or the Darwinian notion of 'biological evolution')—there was no differentiation among the genres of poetry, prose, narrative, drama and novel. All of these existed in an undifferentiated, archival form in religious rituals, conventions, ceremonies, myths, legends and folk tales. This was the time when the separation between the spiritual and the secular—the divine and the human—had not yet taken place. One can argue that the 'epic' as a subgenre of literature emerged at a point of historical (dis)juncture where this separation came into effect. The contemporaries of Vyasa or Homer understood and categorised their own works as 'poems'. They did not anticipate that these 'poems' would later be labelled or categorised as 'epics'. It is only when the narrative had begun to separate itself from the dramatic, and the poetry from the prose—that too, in the times of Aristotle (384–22 BCE)—that the notion of the epic emerged in the West and came to be applied to the *Iliad* or the *Odyssey*.[5] (*Poetics* offers such a classified and differentiated understanding of literary forms/types/genres.)

The case of the *Mahabharata* is somewhat different. Right through history, until the eighteenth century when the orientalists arrived on the scene, Indian scholars continued to describe the *Mahabharata* as *itihasa*, *purana* or *kavya*. Orientalists were the ones who, under the influence of their canonical tradition, chose to impose—that too, somewhat violently—this European notion of the epic upon the *Mahabharata*.[6] This analysis does not have the space to go into the ramifications of this debate. Yet, this tentative survey of two great poems prompts us to draw the most obvious inference: In the preliterate, tribal stage—when literature was mainly 'orature' and had not yet become 'ecriture'—if the generic distinctions did not exist, it is only because these were largely considered unnecessary, and even irrelevant. To put it differently, human beings' search for a classified, differentiated understanding of literary genres/forms was the result of a slow evolution of their intellectual and cultural history. It is only when they found themselves surrounded by a complex and bewildering network of social, historical and cultural forces that they felt compelled to invent, discover and evolve structures of knowledge commensurate with this complexity. This makes one thing very clear: The need to articulate this complexity or make finer distinctions is not so much of an individual choice as a historical necessity, and such a necessity is felt not only when the society is in the upswing but also when it is on the downslide. In other words, the thinkers and sages such as Bharata Muni or Aristotle felt the need to construct elaborate systems of classification and knowledge in two different situations: when a society, culture or civilisation was either poised for a big leap forward, and when it was on the brink of a virtual collapse.

To put the same idea differently, in both these apocalyptic situations—i.e., at the points of historical 'conjuncture' and 'disjuncture'—the social or cultural situation demands that rarefied distinctions be made, or classified, differentiated structures of knowledge (of literary forms or otherwise) be created or constructed. If on the one hand, the advances in Greek and Indian thought are a thesis—a direct outcome of the civilisational complexity—on the other, the massive proliferation and even 'dismantling' or 'decentring' of thought in Europe and outside in the twentieth century is its clear obverse—an antithesis. It is in this sense that Nietzsche, Heidegger, Barthes, Foucault, Bakhtin and Derrida could be seen as the 'antichrists' of our age, as much as Plato, Aristotle and Bharata Muni could be perceived as the 'Christs' of their own.

From the observations above, it also follows that the 'structures of knowledge' follow the structures of social or cultural organisation rather closely.[7] (Raymond Williams makes precisely this point in several of his writings.) In an age that supports monarchy or feudal social order based on hierarchical social stratification, it is somewhat difficult to conceive of a situation where the internal ordering of the genres/subgenres is attempted along more equitable and democratic lines. In such a situation, it is inevitable that the unconscious, archival principles of hierarchy shall provide the necessary conceptual framework, within which the structures of knowledge shall ultimately be constructed.

By the same logic, it would be anachronistic to expect the nation-in-infancy ideology of an epic to gain wider acceptability in an age characterised by—as Frederic Jameson puts it—the 'cultural logic of late capitalism'.[8] It is pertinent to mention here that the epic, as a subgenre, is historically tied to the ideology of 'nation-in-the-making', a point that Hegel made in his famous interventions in that great debate that raged in Germany in the late eighteenth and early nineteenth century.[9] If the novel has, today, replaced the epic, thus becoming the genre of our age, it only marks the triumph of the ideology that it is essentially located in. And interestingly, the genre of the novel has become, in the past hundred years or so, a site of formal, aesthetic, structural and ideological experimentations, thus becoming not just another hybridised form in the process, but, in Bakhtin's famous phrase, 'a complete novelistic discourse'. At this point, it is important to emphasise that just as each subgenre has its own 'specific ideology', it has its own distinctive 'ontology' and 'epistemology' as well. It would be extremely productive, if not challenging, to face some of these questions, especially when we sit down to reflect upon the history of genres or attempt to construct or reconstruct it in any specific cultural context. That the study of genres is both context-specific and culture-specific is another inference that could logically be drawn from our analysis so far.

We can discern several important trends in the history of genres in the West. However, the Western context is not being used here as a frame of reference or being set up as a paradigm, but only as a point of departure, because it lends itself rather easily to a more systemic or orderly critique. In fact, as we analyse European history, various stages in the evolution of its literature emerge, almost as distinctively as they do in the study of its economy or society, á la the notion of 'dialectics' envisioned by Karl Marx.[10] However, this analysis will not invoke the critical apparatus of Marxist thought or theory for the purpose of building a critique. The purpose here in outlining such a critique is to reinforce the fact that at different stages in the evolution of literary genres and subgenres, we tend to deal with different sets of theoretical, critical and philosophical issues and problems.

The first stage in the development of literary genres and subgenres is marked by the emergence of the category of 'religious literature'. As T.S. Eliot has pointed out in several of his essays, 'religious literature' is essentially a misleading term, a problematic category, as it could mean both 'sacred literature' and 'literature infused with religious consciousness'. Eliot developed this argument in 'Religion and Literature' and several other essays.[11] This analysis uses the term 'religious literature' with this double emphasis, and we shall start our exploration of the history of genres with a discussion of this category.

In its first phase, as pointed out earlier, literature was closely tied to religious consciousness, and it ran a course that was almost parallel to the history of religion. This stage can be characterised as the pre-literate, tribal, mythical or oral stage, when the concept of authorship was not really an issue—for instance, the authorship of the Vedas, the Bible, the Koran or the Guru Granth Sahib.[12] Moreover, it is difficult to say whether these sacred texts in different cultures are to be treated as poems/hymns, parables/stories, series of anecdotes or a combination of all these.[13] (Confusion regarding the formal character of these texts prevails, despite the wider consensus on their content and concerns.) At this point of time, literature was considered to be the collective heritage of a community, a collectivity or a cluster of people—not always a tribe. As the 'Word' or 'logos' existed as a manifestation of the 'sacred', the 'magnified poem' always had a more diffused, amorphous and eclectic form, and failed to acquire a specific identifiable face, character or identity. This also explains why the 'poem' was considered more important than the 'poet', who was regarded as no more than a medium, an anonymous non-entity. This is the reason why the question of 'authorship' receded to the margins.[14] It was during such a phase that most of the sacred, scriptural or sacramental literature emerged in different cultures across the world.

In the second phase of the development of literary genres, it is the other type of literature—strongly infused and tempered with religious consciousness—that began to emerge. Moving out of the mythical stage, literature took the first few halting steps towards historicising itself, as the separation between the divine and the human, or the religious and the secular, finally came into effect. This process of historicisation also resulted in the separation of literary forms and the slow evolution of a classified, differentiated and more structured understanding of genres/subgenres. For instance, in the case of Western drama, though such a process had been underway for close to four hundred years or more (from the choral hymns in the eighth century BCE to the times of Sophocles and Euripides, i.e., the fourth century BCE, when distinctive forms of drama such as tragedy or comedy began to emerge), its theorisation did not begin until much later when Plato and Aristotle came on the scene.

While in his *The Republic* Plato had only talked about the distinction between the narrative and the dramatic, rejecting dramatic poetry for its baneful influence, Aristotle in *Poetics* went far beyond the limited framework of his predecessor. Developing a more sophisticated theoretical framework based upon the distinction between the living/performing (music, dance, drama and poetry) and plastic (painting, sculpture, architecture) art forms or that between the mimetic and the non-mimetic forms, he constructed his theory of drama in general and tragedy in particular. That a clear differentiation between the genres of the epic and the drama or the internal hierarchical distinction between tragedy and comedy is unambiguously established by Aristotle is only too well known to be repeated here. Significantly, Aristotle used his understanding of nature to evolve a highly sophisticated structure of understanding of the human arts. To put it differently, the first principles that govern the classification of the human arts evolved directly out of scientific, empirical understanding and observation of how the natural order functioned or operated.[15] It was as though the unitary nature of religious thought had split itself into multiplicity and plurality, into variegated and differentiated nature of human beings and the art forms created by them.

Undoubtedly, some of the best ever works in humanistic literature, with their unique brand of universalism, belong to this second phase. It needs to be pointed out here that the history of humanism is discontinuous and that two distinct historical junctures could be seen as the starting points of humanism in the West: the first is located in ancient Greek literature (Plato, Aristotle, Sophocles and Euripides), and the other within the specificities of European cultural Renaissance in the fourteenth century.[16] This has been corroborated by many scholars, especially those who analyse the Western project of Enlightenment. Though this focus on humanism here might appear out of place, it certainly has wide-ranging implications for the question we are debating. Through this emphasis, I wish to make three points: 1. The order of classification and differentiation of genres is somewhat closely tied to the ideology of humanism. 2. The process of generic differentiation and its structured understanding was largely a byproduct of the first phase of humanism and the slow dissolution the result of the second. 3. The notion of 'authorship' and author's distinct individualism emerged as the major concerns of humanistic ideology, thus departing from the earlier phase where s/he was no more than an anonymous entity.

The only difference between the Greek and the Italian (or European) Renaissance was that while the former emphasised the purity of generic forms (segregation, distinctiveness and autonomy), the latter experimented with hybrid forms such as tragi-comedy (the hyphenated version, unlike the fused version that emerged in the twentieth century), romantic-comedy, dark-comedy, historical-tragedy, epic-romance, etc. If on the one hand, it had to do with attempts to fuse diverse strands of classicism and romanticism, on the other, it resulted from cross-cultural influences of a wide variety. However, the genre of poetry somehow resisted this kind of hybridisation and the purity of generic form continued to persist, reflected as it largely was in the distinctiveness of such subgenres as sonnets, ballads, lyric poetry, religious poetry, love poetry, court poetry, etc.

In the third stage, the process of hybridisation or dissolution of generic boundaries (which had apparently started during the Renaissance) came full circle at the height of modernism.[17] This also enables us to see the connections we sometimes fail to make between 'early modernism' (based upon mercantile capitalism) which we associate with Renaissance and 'late or high modernism' (based upon industrial capitalism) which we often associate with twentieth-century literature. Somewhere, this glosses over a very important development we often trace back to the late seventeenth or early eighteenth century, when the genre of the novel surfaced as a distinct literary form in response to a definitive set of social needs of a particular class. We will discuss the emergence of the novel in a later section.

Modernism was all about the interpenetration of various genres, as by then, the rigid boundaries/frameworks had begun to collapse. It is no wonder that we had *The Waste Land* (1922), a dramatic lyric (with a definite degree of interiorisation), classified either as an epic poem or as a play in five sections. We also had James Joyce's *Ulysses* (1922)—which subverted all the known conventions of the eighteenth- or nineteenth-century novel, and yet was labelled one—which became an epic novel, despite being an interiorised, personal narrative. In the same manner, we found the barriers between the genres of poetry and novel or those of poetry and drama slip away in Virginia Woolf's poetic conception of a novel, or in Eliot's return to the idea of rituals for reviving the ancient form of poetic drama.

The dissolution of generic boundaries gave rise to avant-garde, experimental literature in this phase of modernism. However, that does not really sum up the whole range of developments that characterised this movement. Apart from the non-mimetic forms, modernism did produce a good deal of mimetic literature, as has been pointed out by Auerbach in his famous work, *Mimesis*.[18] To put it differently, modernism was a magnetic field of pressures and counter-pressures, which sustained itself through a variety of self-contradictory impulses.

In a manner of speaking, postmodernism could be seen as a later, more self-conscious and more self-reflexive stage of modernism. If seen from this standpoint, postmodernism can easily be perceived as the next, logical step away from modernism, with a definite sense of continuity, even ideological affiliation, connecting the two. If modernism had dissolved the generic boundaries, postmodernism turned them inside out or upside down. The result was the subversion of forms and the emergence of a medley of styles. Eclecticism is the hallmark of this phase, with pastiche and other self-reflexive forms such as meta-fiction, meta-poetry and meta-theatre emerging as the preferred modes of expression. It is against this background that we need to understand some of the developments in the arena of European and/or American literature from the 1950s through the 1990s.[19]

So far, our focus has been on the history of genres, their gradual evolution and their equally imperceptible dissolution, with each process raising its own set of problems and issues. We began this discussion by outlining the two modes of constructing knowledge about genres—the direct mediation and the indirect one. Having mediated this question directly, we shall now attempt to reconstruct this history, very briefly, through a variety of critical perspectives offered by literary theorists, especially in the later half of the twentieth century. It is pertinent to mention here that regardless of what we take to be the starting point of 'theory', 1950 or 1967,[20] one of the most important developments in this regard was the emergence of 'genre criticism'. Supported mainly by critics located in various universities in the US, this school of criticism largely aimed at bringing back into circulation the entire canonical apparatus set up by Aristotle.[21] It was as if the history of genres was finally coming back full circle. Though it did not last very long, in the 1940s and the 1950s, when New Criticism and structuralism were the propelling forces in criticism, the emergence of such a phenomenon was extremely significant.

Northrop Frye's *Anatomy of Criticism* appeared in 1957, and it helped revolutionise the way in which we either thought or theorised about genres. Frye's main inspiration was the Bible and he sought to reconstruct his notion of literary history purely from within, in isolationist terms, without factoring in social or cultural forces. He sought to establish that the 'literary universe' is both self-contained and self-sustaining, with its own central hypothesis and coordinating/regulating principles. He looked at genres primarily as regulating principles, which were held together by a repertoire of myths, rituals, ceremonies and archetypes. This approach made him one of the leading exponents of archetypal criticism.[22]

In moving from Northrop Frye to Mikhail Bakhtin, we are taking a big leap forward from the structuralist to the poststructuralist phase. In several of his writings, especially in *Problems of Dostoevsky's Poetics* (1929) and *Discourse in the Novel* (1934–5), Bakhtin sought to historicise the concept of the novel, tracing its beginnings back to Homer and categorising some of the early developments in literature as 'pre-novelistic discourse'.[23] Not only did Bakhtin historicise the idea of the novel, but he also subsumed a variety of distinctions across the narrative-spectrum—such as the epic, the long poem, the story and/or the novel—into the single frame of 'a pre-novelistic' and/or 'a novelistic discourse'. This is where Bakhtin's position comes very close to that of other poststructuralists, who legitimise not only the internal ruptures of generic boundaries, but also the external frames across disciplines.

Another development in recent times which has challenged and interrogated the boundaries of disciplines can be found in the writings of theorists such as Dominick LaCapra, Hayden White, etc. Interrogating the assumptions of foundationalism, they have sought to renegotiate the relationship between 'history' and the novel.[24] Rejecting the notions of universalism, and grand and totalising narratives, they have questioned the limits of both 'history' and 'fiction', thus opening up unimaginable possibilities in 'fiction-making'. Of course, it is within such a frame that the writings of some of the postcolonial theorists and writers such as Chinua Achebe, Ngũgĩ wa Thiong'o, Gabriel Garcia Marquez, Salman Rushdie, Graham Swift, etc. need to be located or relocated. However, it is quite another matter that a theorist like Ngũgĩ wa Thiong'o has also looked into the related question of how the novel, essentially a 'Euro-centric form', could possibly be subverted through the infiltrations of African folk narratives, if one needs to expand the range, scope and magnitude of this genre for self-articulation.[25]

This prologue has attempted to locate a conceptual framework within which several critical questions regarding the history/

theory of genres could possibly be raised. One of the most obvious conclusions of this analysis is that the structures of knowledge (about literary genres or otherwise) are as inescapable as is the realisation that all systems/orders of classification are fluid, febrile and even porous. Moreover, if such modes of constructing knowledge about literature had once followed either the natural or the social order, in the twentieth century, 'thought' itself provided a self-reflexive frame for it, thus becoming the cause of its own 'framelessness'. Also, we conclude that regardless of how we choose to reflect upon this question—through direct or indirect mediation—one thing is clear that there is constant synergy between the theory and practice of literary forms, and it is this synergy that defines the course of literary genres.

All said and done, genres are somewhat like the name plates outside a house or the signposts on the road that simply announce the nomenclature. They do not necessarily provide us with points of entry, either into the house or into the road. At the end of this analysis, we may do well to remember what Shakespeare had to say in *Romeo and Juliet*, 'What's in a name? That which we call a rose/By any other name would smell as sweet'.[26]

Notes and References

1. The relationship between the 'world' and the 'Word' has been a subject of philosophical debate for as long as one can remember. It has been negotiated in the works of Socrates, Plato, Aristotle, and even the Vedas and the Upanishads. So central is this issue to the understanding of man's relationship to God, society, consciousness and language that it has been extensively debated in all world religions and religious texts. Besides, this question also figures very prominently in all the philosophical debates related to human culture and civilisation. The Bible raises this question in the Book of John (1:14), wherein it states, 'First there was the Word. And then the Word became flesh.' In a manner of speaking, this is a way of accessing the relationship between not only the sacred and the profane, but also that between language and materiality, or the creator and the created.

2. Two questions that have insistently plagued the Western historians of religion of the nineteenth and twentieth centuries, particularly in relation to the Bible, are: the question of historicity, i.e., whether the incidents

and situations that feature in the Bible are historically real or imagined, or both; and the question of its literary merit, i.e., whether it is to be assessed in terms of its spiritual message or its secular though sublime poetry and/or parables. Long after the Bible had been accepted as a canonical text in the Western–Christian tradition, the historians of religion continued to debate whether it should be conceded a special place as a revealed text or be incorporated into the canonical literary/secular tradition. It was Julius Wellhausen (1844–1918), a nineteenth-century German thinker, who first initiated and then promoted scientifically oriented 'historical–critical' approach to the Biblical Studies. His 'diachronic' approach, which largely dominated the nineteenth-century Biblical Studies, was gradually replaced by the 'synchronic' approach (New Critical/structuralist/deconstruction, etc.) in the twentieth century. Biblical 'hermeneutics' is an entirely different order of discipline, specifically connected to the problems of 'hows' and 'whys' of interpretation. In order to understand the contours of this entire debate, you may refer to the following: J. Wellhausen, *The Early History of Israel* (Philadelphia: Westminster, 1978); W.G. Dever, *Jerusalem and the Holy Land Rediscovered: The Prints of David Roberts (1796–1864)* (Durham: Duke Museum of Art, 1996); E.M. Meyers, ed., *The Oxford Encyclopedia of Archaeology in the Near East* (New York: Oxford University Press, 1997); D.N. Freedman, *The Bible Unearthed: Archaeology's New Vision of Ancient Israel and the Origin of Its Sacred Texts* (New York: Free Press, 2000); H. Geva, *Who Wrote the Bible?* (New York: Summit, 1987); R. de Vaux, *The Mythic Past: Biblical Archaeology and the Myth of Israel* (New York: Basic Books, 1999).

3. Jacques Derrida (1930–2004) and other poststructuralist theorists are suspicious of, and sceptical about, foundational ideas such as 'God', 'Man', 'History', 'Progress', 'Enlightenment', etc. For them, such foundational ideas often give birth to epistemological gestures that aim specifically at identifying their 'source' or 'origin'. By valorising the notion of 'metaphysics of absence' and consequently articulating vehement disapproval of all such epistemological gestures aimed at locating the unlocatable 'centre', Derrida has diminished the importance of all origin-related moves. For him, all such moves only lead to the falsification of knowledge, reducing it to the status of myths. 'Originary myths' is a term often used to describe such epistemological manouvres.

4. In order to understand this equivalence between the history of literary forms and the history of religion, all one has to do is to look at the development of the genre of 'drama' in the Greco-Roman or Indian context. In both the cases, 'drama' is said to have originated in the form of religious rituals, located in respective cultures. In the Greco-Roman context, the origin of the genre is closely tied to the enactment of multiple rituals associated with Dionysus, the Greek God. The same can be said

about the origin of poetry, one of the earliest forms of literary expression. Democritus, the Greek philosopher, is believed to have suggested that man learnt the art of music and poetry from nature, by first listening to the sounds of nature and birds and then imitating them. It is in this respect that the history of religion runs quite close, or even parallel, to the history of the literary forms.

5. Though Homer is said to have composed the *Iliad* and the *Odyssey* around the eleventh century BCE, it was initially known as a long poem, not as an epic. It came to be known as an epic only after Aristotle theorised about it in his *Poetics*, making this important distinction between the genres of tragedy and epic. He was the one who pointed out that despite the commonality of subject matter and content, an epic was different from tragedy in terms of its scale, magnitude, temporal sequencing and modes of presentation. In a way, this was the first step, in the Western tradition, towards evolving a finely differentiated and classified understanding of literary genres/forms.

6. That the *Mahabharata* is history, a historic and historical text, is attested to by the tags '*itihasa–purana*' and '*pancham-veda*' which is further corroborated by *Chhandogya Upanishad* (900 BCE). It is referred to as the '*itihaasa-veda*' in Kautilya's *Arthashastra* (400–300 BCE). The *Mahabharata* is referred to directly in *Asvalayana Grihya Sutra* and indirectly in *Satapath Brahmana, Atharva Veda, Manu-Samhita* and *Brihadaranyaka Upanishad*. The *Mahabharata* is a highly self-reflexive text, as it offers not only a self-description of itself as *kavya, itihasa* and *purana*, but also talks about its own processes of creation, reduction, expansion and transmission. In the pre-colonial context, Indian scholars primarily focussed their attention either upon the poetic/aesthetic features of this text or its didactic codes/messages. Scholars like Anandavardhana (820–90 CE) also deliberated over the question of the kind of '*rasa*' that pre-dominates this poem. He came to an interesting conclusion that though this text dramatises all the *rasas* that Bharata Muni's *Natyashastra* otherwise talks about, it ultimately privileges and foregrounds the '*shanta rasa*'. Significantly, nowhere in the writings of Indian scholars/critics do we come across the description of the *Mahabharata* as an epic, which is clearly a colonial construct—an imposition that emerged in the critical discourse through the efforts of the orientalists. Though the orientalists took a stand favouring a serious, scholarly engagement with the corpus of Indian literatures and Indian canonical texts, including the *Mahabharata*, as opposed to the adversarial position of the Anglicists, they too, were unable to resist their own worst prejudices of inferiorising some of the best among the Indian literary/cultural texts. Edward Said's pejorative notion of 'orientalism' is very much at work in the way the orientalists chose to respond to some of the foundational Indian texts including the *Mahabharata*. For a more detailed

discussion, see V.S. Sukhthankar, *On the Meaning of the* Mahabharata (Bombay: Asiatic Society of Bombay, 1957).

7. The phrase 'structures of knowledge', as deployed in the present context, is derived from Raymond Williams' famous phrase 'structures of feeling'. It needs to be pointed out here that while the focus and ideological underpinnings of this phrase are largely that of Williams, the extensionality and modification of meaning is entirely mine. For a more detailed discussion of the original phrase, see Raymond Williams, *Culture and Society* (London: Chatto and Windus, 1957); *Idem.*, *Keywords*, Fontana Communications Series (New York: Oxford University Press, 1984); *Idem.*, *Marxism and Literature*, Marxist Introductions Series (London and New York: Oxford University Press, 1977); *Idem.*, *Modern Tragedy* (London: Chatto and Windus, 1966).

8. F. Jameson, 'Postmodernism, or the Cultural Logic of Late Capitalism,' *New Left Review* I, no. 146 (July–August 1984). In this essay, Jameson offers a sustained critique of the postmodern culture and talks about its emergence in the context of multinational/transnational, late capitalism. In his discussion covering a whole range of ideas and art forms, he also emphasises both the continuities and the ruptures between the modern and the postmodern conditions, extending, expanding and redefining the scope and function of both.

9. G.W.F. Hegel, *Aesthetics: Lectures on Fine Arts*, 3 vols, trans. T.M. Knox (Oxford: Clarendon Press, 1975). In this work, Hegel postulated that in different historical epochs, the world view or *weltanschauung* and its expression in art is likely to be materially different, depending upon the religious world view that circumscribes it. Regarding the epic and its ideology, he writes, 'The content and form of the epic proper is the entire world-outlook and objective manifestation of the national spirit presented in its self-objectifying shape as an actual event' (1:603). Here, he clearly suggests that there is equivalence between the dominant ideology of nationalism and its literary expression through the content and form of an epic.

10. The Marxist idea of 'historical materialism' has essentially been used to understand the evolutionary processes of the Western/European society. In fact, Marx, too, had realised the limitations of his own ideas and his inability to extend them to understand the operations of a society other than a Western one. Perhaps, this is what motivated him to conceptualise a discrete mode of sociological enquiry known as the 'Asiatic Mode of Production'. Often, we extend Marx's ideas to understand the sociological processes governing societies other than those of Europe, without realising that even Marx would not have approved of such transgressions.

11. In his essay, 'Religion and Literature' in *Selected Prose of T.S. Eliot*, ed. Frank Kermode (London: Faber and Faber Ltd., 1975), 97–106, T.S. Eliot has made an interesting distinction between 'sacred/theological literature' and 'religious literature'. Though in his earlier writings, it is the liberal, modernist Eliot we encounter, in most of his later writings, we find him taking a very conservative and orthodox position as a literary critic. His decision to embrace Anglican Church in 1927 and his subsequent religious conversion definitely had a shaping influence on his critical approach and ideas on literature, much of which is reflected in his later writings. According to him, 'sacred/theological literature' is canonical in nature, while the best literature in any given period of time, regardless of the presence/absence of religion or ethics in public life, is invariably fused with the spirit of ethics and religiosity. According to him, literary criticism must necessarily assess a literary work from this standpoint, even if it is not written from this perspective. This is how literature could possibly reclaim its religious function, more so, at a time when the role of religion in public life is, otherwise, circumscribed. This is an extension of Matthew Arnold's position with respect to the role and function of literature/poetry articulated in his famous works, *Culture and Anarchy, Literature and Dogma, God and the Bible, Essays in Criticism,* etc.

12. For a more detailed discussion on this subject, particularly in relation to the *Mahabharata*, please refer to the first chapter ('Author and Authority') of Bruce M. Sullivan, *Kṛṣṇa Dvaipāyana Vyāsa and the Mahābhārata: A New Interpretation* (New Delhi: Motilal Banarasidass, 1999), 1–26.

13. Apart from the question of authorship, another question that has insistently been raised in relation to all the scriptural texts, regardless of the cultural context in which they are found, is whether or not, while reading or interpreting them, it is necessary to make the generic distinctions in terms of poetry, narrative, parable, epic, etc. Some scholars are of the view that the scriptural texts offer undifferentiated view (even synthesis) of a large variety of literary subgenres, as such demonstrating the principle of 'unity-in-diversity' in their structuring. For a more detailed discussion, see, Paul R. House and Scott J. Hafemann, ed. *Central Themes in Biblical Theology: Mapping Unity in Diversity* (London: Apollos, 2007).

14. Roland Barthes points out in his well-known essay 'Death of the Author' that the idea of the 'author' is a byproduct of the capitalist ideology and thus came into existence during the Renaissance. Before that, the author was regarded as an interlocutor or a shaman (especially in the primitive societies) and now, after the advent of the 'automatic writing', promoted by modernity and surrealism, the idea has become eminently dispensable. He is emphatic that the changes in the way the language is now expected

to function are largely responsible for this paradigm shift. In his essay, 'What is an Author?' Michel Foucault refers to the author as 'a function of language, who exists as a product of his text and/or language'. Both these positions reiterate the poststructuralist notion of how the text has ceased to be author-centric, and become reader-oriented.

15. It is a well-known fact that Aristotle's entire schema of generic differentiation and classification, as envisioned in *Poetics*, draws heavily upon his empiricism and/or his scientific understanding of nature. He was the one who, first of all, proposed a synthesis of art and nature in his construction of epistemological categories.

16. Earlier, our discussions on humanism usually referred to the ideology in universalist terms. Of late, the scholars of humanism are beginning to emphasise the cultural specificities of this ideology and are thus talking in terms of 'early humanism' and 'late humanism', 'their humanism' versus 'our humanism'. There has also been an attempt to historicise this notion by extending it beyond the frontiers of Renaissance to the Greco-Roman period. Regardless of how we perceive it, humanism is now largely regarded as a Euro-centric ideology. For detailed discussion, see, Richard Norman, *On Humanism: Thinking in Action* (London: Routledge, 2004).

17. Malcolm Bradbury and James W. MacFarlane, eds., *Modernism: A Guide to European Literature 1890–1930* (London: Penguin, 1978).

18. Erich Auerbach, *Mimesis: The Representation of Reality in Western Literature*, trans. Willard R. Trask (Princeton: Princeton University Press, 2003).

19. For a detailed discussion, see, Richard Gray, *A History of American Literature* (London: Blackwell, 2004).

20. Historians of literary criticism and theory are of the view that the separation between criticism and theory first came about either in 1950 or in 1967. These two dates are often treated as two distinct points of departure in any discussion on the break between criticism and theory. While some prefer to give credit to Derrida for formally inaugurating the historic moment of theory in 1967, others trace it back to Rene Wellek and Northrop Frye, who did most of their writings in 1950s. In a way, theory began with Rene Wellek and Northrop Frye but its politicisation did not begin until 1967.

21. Variously described as 'Chicago School of Criticism' and 'Neo-Aristotelianism', 'genre criticism' surfaced in the US in the 1960s, essentially as a reaction against the excessive subjectivism of New Criticism. Genre critics were of the view that a return to the classical, objective ways of literary evaluation, as enunciated by Aristotle, was absolutely necessary if evaluation of literature was not to become a

purely subjective enterprise. R.S. Crane, Elder Olson, W. R. Keast, R.P. McKeon, among several others, were the main exponents and adherents of this school.

22. Northrop Frye, *Anatomy of Criticism: Four Essays* (Princeton: Princeton University Press, 1957).

23. Mikhail M. Bakhtin, *Problems of Dostoevsky's Poetics*, trans. Caryl Emerson (Minnesota: University of Minnesota Press, 1984).

24. For a detailed discussion, see, Hayden White, *Metahistory: The Historical Imagination in Nineteenth-century Europe* (Baltimore: John Hopkins University Press, 1973); Fernand Braudel, *On History*, trans. Sarah Matthew (Chicago: University of Chicago Press, 1980); Dominick LaCapra, *History and Criticism* (Ithaca: Cornell University Press, 1985); Keith Jenkins, ed., *Postmodern History Reader* (London: Routledge, 1997); Michael Bentley, *Modern Historiography: An Introduction* (London: Routledge, 1999).

25. Ngũgĩ wa Thiong'o, *Decolonising the Mind: The Politics of Language in African Literature* (Nairobi: East African Educational Publishers Ltd, 1978).

26. William Shakespeare, *Romeo and Juliet*, ed., Jay L. Halio (New Jersey: Associated University Press, 2008), 38.

Section One

Reading Indian and Indian English Literatures

Chapter One

Locating/Dis-locating Indian Literatures: A Metacritical Narrative

This essay discusses, in some detail, one of the important issues the Indian academia has been wrestling with, especially since the introduction of the postcolonial thrust in our critical and pedagogical practices: whether to 'locate' and read Indian literatures within the existing critical paradigms or create new structures of thought for studying it? Further, it raises some basic questions about the nature of the relationship between the critical and the creative traditions in any given society, arguing that these do not necessarily develop independently of each other, but tend towards a symbiotic relationship. Going beyond these questions, it also offers a brief survey of the several attempts Indian critics have made over the years to redefine the existing canon in English studies, with its own share of attendant problems.

The concept of 'location' is essentially a postmodernist idea and it entered our lexicon around the 1960s. The idea had its origins in the discipline of architecture and soon enough, it found its way into literary and cultural studies.[1] This process of interrogating, overturning, breaking down and dissolving the artificial boundaries of disciplines laid the groundwork for the various interdisciplinary approaches that we often use as critical or methodological practice. Postmodernism came into existence in the US, specifically in response to the cultural/literary/artistic practices that had emerged there as a result of a nagging discontent with, or a perceived demise of, the modernist agenda.[2] It is quite another matter that any attempt, deliberate or strategic, that seeks to drain away the specificities of postmodernism is likely to turn it into yet another liberal humanist, universal myth or fiction. It is a well-documented fact that, among other things, it is the 'localism' of postmodernism that is supposed to make it ideologically different from the 'universalism' of liberal humanism.

In the past few years, a number of scholarly books have appeared on Indian society, literature and culture that have tried to de-historicise 'postmodernism' as a cultural phenomenon, thus emphasising its universal character.[3] It is this absence of historical and cultural specificities of postmodernism that often reduces it to a popular catch-phrase, depriving it of its inherent critical potential as well as thrust. The underlying assumption in most of these books is that what is true of the US or the European society is equally true of the African and Asian societies, too. To assume that the Indian society stepped into the postmodernist phase in the 1970s simply because this was a dominant cultural movement/trend across Europe, US and elsewhere is not only to deny 'the principle of difference' that often governs societies (in their constitution, evolution and character) but also to denounce 'the principle of identity' that makes them distinct from each other. And both these principles, we know, are uninhibitedly celebrated and cherished by the postmodern thought.

One may raise another related question, along with Frederic Jameson, regarding 'the cultural logic of late capitalism' and the possibility of conceptualising and hypothesising its variant in the Indian context. One may also like to ask: When did we in India experience this stage of 'late capitalism'? Or for that matter, do we ever pause to think in terms of setting up a correlation between our 'modes of production' and the concomitant 'cultural formations' they often give rise to? Though postmodernism may be said to thrive on easy, free and uninterrupted circulation and/or dissemination of the 'cultural formations' across the globe, does it mean that these cultural formations circulate within each society at the same pace, urgency and accessibility as they do in some other societies? All these are important questions, and admittedly, there are no easy answers. However, as the present analysis does not allow us much scope for a detailed discussion on this subject, for the time being, we shall have to stay content with merely a statement of intent in this regard. All that deserves to be emphasised at this stage is that in our sociological/cultural and even literary studies, we must recognise and factor in the urgent need to question, interrogate and problematise the specific ideology behind our efforts at teaching, popularising and circulating postmodernist ideas in and outside our classrooms.

The use of the idea of 'location' also points to some interesting insights into the way we have approached the issue at hand. We often tend to pay more attention to the problem at hand than to the language in, or through which, it is articulated or expressed. But the language used for positing any problem, being a matter of conscious, subjective choice, is often reflective of an ideology we subscribe to. Careful consideration of our ideological moorings will reveal the nuances of our approach to the problem. In this context, it would be interesting to note whether it would have been possible for teachers and scholars in English departments, say fifty years ago, to posit the problem of locating/dis-locating Indian literatures in the manner in which the new generation of scholars has.[4] This is not to suggest that we are fifty years too late in positing this problem (though that is not entirely a false position) but that the previous generation of scholars could not have possibly done so without the benefit of the postmodernist jargon that we now find ourselves implicated in. In other words, the whole idea of 'location' is a by-product of postmodernist and postcolonial interventions. Among other things, one of the most contentious issues debated in all serious engagements with 'postmodernism' as well as 'postcolonialism' is whether or not both these terms should be hyphenated.

Now, let us come back to the central question that we had posed at the beginning of this essay. Our ideology is often reflected in our choice of language as well as in our perception of its special role and function. The manner in which we have articulated the problem becomes dubious, even suspicious, for a variety of reasons: 1. We have used the postmodernist language to reflect on the status/function/relevance/positioning of Indian literatures, assuming that Indian literatures and Indian society have already entered the postmodernist stage of what Fredric Jameson calls the stage of 'late capitalism'. 2. This question has been posited within the discipline of English studies which, for several years now, has been advocating the cause of the Anglo-Saxon canonical tradition. 3. The fact that appears most anomalous, and rather anachronistic, is that we are discussing the fate of Indian literatures in a language which, in a genuine postcolonial sense—granting that there might be a false variety of it too—could only be seen as a disruption, not a continuity in consonance with our historical experience.[5] These three factors will unmask the ideological contradictions that are likely to surface each time we talk of 'locating' Indian literatures.

Let us now move on to another set of problems that we might encounter in our discussion of the location of Indian literatures. These are not so much 'ideological' as 'methodological' in nature. Any attempt at locating Indian literatures throws up the essential question: Where and in relation to what? Location is, after all, by its very nature, a relative, spatial category. So we need to ask ourselves: Are we talking of locating Indian literatures within the departments of English? If we locate them within the canonical Anglo-Saxon tradition, it will mean displacement of the canon and emergence of a 'counter-canon'. Going by the history of canonical shifts in the past or our own efforts at opening up the canon, all one can say is that it is a very dismal scenario, indeed, offering little encouragement and very little hope. Whatever anyone might say in defence of such experiences, the fact remains that we have only succeeded in exoticising, fetishising and showcasing Indian literatures in our departments of English.[6] At its worst, it is only a form of tokenism as despite our best efforts, Indian literatures continue to have only a marginal presence in relation to English literature, whose fossilised centrality is almost an undisturbed, undisputed fact. Even after sixty years of Independence, we find it nearly impossible to initiate any major paradigmatic shift from Macaulay's agenda which we have followed so scrupulously and religiously for over hundred and fifty years. Our affiliation to the canon has been persistent and continuous. Most of our efforts to redefine the canon have either been aborted prematurely or carried out most half-heartedly.[7]

Perhaps, English studies in India needs to take the route that Ngũgĩ took some forty years ago in Nigeria. His campaign was not against English literature per se, but towards the revival and resurgence of African literatures. This ultimately resulted in the closure of the English department in the University of Nigeria and its replacement by the Department of African Languages and Literatures.[8] One wonders whether our departments of English are prepared for this kind of radical or revolutionary step that demands not merely locating, but re-locating or rather re-placing of Indian literatures vis-à-vis English literature. If it sounds a little too revolutionary or forbidding, perhaps we could think in terms of an alternative. This would mean creating a space within which attempts at de-hegemonising and de-centring English departments could effectively be made. As a first step, we may think in terms of completely doing away with a set of compulsory courses, which often hinge around British literature, drawing strength from a false assumption that no course on English literature can possibly be conceived without a major/compulsory/significant content from British literature. The space created by the absence of British literature may be offered to Indian English literatures and Indian literatures in English translation, thus Indianising and nativising the content of the curriculum, to a large extent. This would effectively mean turning the canon right on its head, so that what is marginal right now becomes canonical and what is of central importance is strategically pushed into a state of marginality. In actual practice, it would mean that Indian literatures in translation are accorded the centrality that has been denied to them so far, while English (read British) literature, would be 're-located' in our textual/literary practices only as a marginal presence within the larger realm of world literatures. After all, 'location' is primarily a matter of spatial displacements and spatial adjustments or readjustments, which ultimately work towards the making, unmaking or re-making of the literary culture within a society.

Apparently, if our students are taught courses with a preponderance of Indian texts (written originally in English and/or in translation), it shall create a very different literary culture than the one we have already succeeded in creating. The creation of a literary culture depends largely upon the kind of placement/positioning or spatial adjustments we often make within our curriculum design and pedagogical practices. In my own experience of teaching literature, I have often come across students who challenge the hegemonic notions of British literature, suggesting that they would much rather read their own cultural texts than the ones the canon has been forcing down on them for so long. The need to challenge, overturn and redefine the canon definitely has a groundswell of support among the users or the consumers of this product. It is another matter that we, the policy planners and teachers, continue to blink even in the face of a growing demand for change, thus demonstrating our wilful neglect of the 'local' and the 'contingent', in the process lending our covert as well as overt support to the hegemonic practices governing both the curriculum and pedagogy.

Now, let us turn to the next question (which in turn begs several others): Are we going to discuss the location of Indian literatures within their specific socio-cultural matrix? If so, who is going to perform this function, and where? Will the departments of Indian languages, operating within the hallowed precincts of the academia, perform this function? Or is it something that is, at best, left to the untrained, uninitiated critics outside the academia? The term 'amateur' or 'untrained' here covers the entire range of critical activities that takes place outside the academia. For instance, all journalistic writings would easily fall in this category. To my mind, all scholars within the academia, regardless of whether or not they choose to function in a professional manner, belong to the class of professional critics. Now, let us first look at this class of critics, those who work from within the academia. This particular class of critics has, for the last few decades, been labouring rather heavily under the influence of Western critical theory. It is almost as if they have developed, to borrow Harold Bloom's memorable expression, an acute 'anxiety of influence'.[9] One of the several forms this anxiety often takes is the constant worry shown by a majority of critics operating within the departments of Hindi or Punjabi literatures to keep abreast of the latest 'products' rolling off the 'knowledge production units' in the West. As soon as the metropolitan centres in the West 'offload' a new 'product', it is appropriated, circulated and canonised. Ironically enough, the reverse does not always happen. Also, the same kind of haste is certainly not witnessed when it comes to translating the very best that is available in our own literatures into other Indian languages, including English, for their inclusion in the canon. As a result, the balance of power often tilts dangerously against the production or reclamation of indigenous literary/cultural traditions, but settles rather favourably towards the wholesale, uncritical consumption of the 'goods' from the West. It is perhaps this mismatch between consumption and production that is responsible for our cultural deficit, the impoverishment of our own literary/cultural practices.

We live in a globalised space of high connectivity within which ideas tend to circulate with much more frequency and rapidity than was the case, say, a hundred years ago. Consequently, Western critical theory is readily available to any young researcher or critic operating in the field of Indian literatures. A situation may arise where an untrained researcher may be tempted to use Lacanian or Foucauldian strategies and/or hermeneutic practices to approach such texts as *Gurbani* (Sikh spiritual text), Baba Farid's (1170–1266) poetry, Waris Shah's (1722–98) *Heer*, or Kabir's (1440–1518) *dohas*, and his/her supervisor may endorse it in the name of novelty/innovation. Though there is much to be said in favour of eclecticism, it certainly cannot become a vehicle for uncontrolled, unchecked experimentation or completely de-contextualised reading. While in most of the cases, it may not be very clear as to how the application of Western critical paradigms/theory to a relatively modern or contemporary text in any of the Indian languages could become anomalous; in some specific cases already pointed out, the incongruity may become truly and glaringly conspicuous. For instance, it may be all right to study Mannu Bhandari or Krishna Sobti from the vantage point of feminism, Indian or Western, but it would be truly bizarre, if not downright obnoxious, to study Mirabai's poetry or her mysticism from the perspective of French feminism in general or '*ecriture feminine*' in particular. While approaching the French feminists, one has to be mindful of the fact that their entire discourse is based upon the critique of Greek mythology/culture, which may have some parallels with, but is certainly not coextensive with, Indian mythology/culture. The point being emphasised here is quite simple. Just as literary production is context-specific, so is critical production. Whenever a critical enterprise ceases to be context-specific and tries instead to transgress the boundaries of its specificities, it threatens to become a dangerous engagement, a self-defeating endeavour. It ceases to be a critical enterprise and becomes a non-reflexive form of satire or parody. It is this kind of 'anxiety of influence'—bordering on parody, if not mimicry—that is often very difficult to sympathise with.

An average critic of Indian literatures finds himself or herself caught up in a very peculiar dilemma, an inescapable bind. How to read contemporary texts in the absence of indigenous textual/literary practices, without sounding either archaic or obsolete, is the question. Sanskrit poetics is no longer serviceable and *bhashas* are yet to throw up 'poetics' suited to the intrinsic needs and requirements specific to each Indian language/literature. Western critical paradigms provide for this lack of indigenous critical material, which is often felt but is rarely ever articulated. Thus, Western critical/textual practices have come to occupy, through sheer default, a pre-eminent position within the departments of Indian literatures. It is obvious that our obsession with such practices has inevitably led to a gross neglect of the literary history/historiography of Indian languages and literatures.[10] How many of us, in our critical endeavours, actually locate works produced in Indian languages within the specificities of a language—its history, its literary tradition, its genealogy of forms/ideologies and the reading practices motivated by them?

Another related issue is that, having been fed on a heavy dose of Western metaphysics and epistemology, an average critic of Indian literatures has begun to harbour this mistaken notion that 'textuality' is all—that the real power flows from the barrel of 'discourse'.[11] This has created a situation, where he/she, like the Western counterpart, is now content to be the 'critics' critic'—someone who addresses all the questions pertaining to literature/language and textual/cultural practices only for the benefit of setting up a dialogue with his/her own community or fellow critics.[12] The direct outcome of this has been that the critic has virtually cut himself off from his roots and also from the people/masses outside the academia, towards whom he has a definite social responsibility. In the West, some of the best academic critics like Raymond Williams, Frank Kermode and George Steiner have been equally successful journalists too. Not only have they worked assiduously within the hallowed precincts of the academia to strengthen and nurture the canonical critical tradition, but they have been equally mindful of their obligation towards the lay readers, which they fulfilled successfully by promoting non-canonical traditions through their equally committed journalistic writings. One comes across a near absence of such a convention among our literary critics/stars. Somehow, they seem to harbour this mistaken notion that people only deserve to be the 'subjects' of literary works, and they do not necessarily have to be guided about how they could become efficient and active (not passive) readers of these works.

Perhaps, this is what 'creating' a discourse is all about. In a society like that of the US, where 'late capitalism' has already made its inroads—as Fredric Jameson suggests—the circulation and use of the notion of 'discourse' do make sense. But does it make as much sense in our society, which is hopelessly striving to catch up with different stages of economic and social evolution—be it feudalism, capitalism, modernism or postmodernism—all at once? While we do come across critics willing to make a literary work sound more mystifying than it actually is, we rarely ever come across ones whose efforts are directed towards communicating an understanding of literature to those to whom it rightfully belongs—the common people. Though we continue to bemoan the loss of the reading habit among the masses, what do we really do to locate our literatures where they belong—in the hearts of our people? In the past, those who did not have direct access to complex, overtly Sanskritised structures of pure Vedantic thought could take the help of the mediation of *Upanishadic* aphorisms or *Pauranic* narratives. Those who could not grapple with the complexities of *Gurbani* could turn to more accessible forms of *Japji Sahib* (universal song or *Mool Mantra* composed by Guru Nanak Dev ji, the first Sikh guru) or *Janamsākhīs* (literally, the birth stories or the hagiographies connected with Guru Nanak). Whatever remained inaccessible to people in pure thought was often conveyed through the medium of popular narratives. Narratives have traditionally been used in our context as vehicles of various theories or even for the purposes of theorising, almost as essential ancillaries to pure thought. In one of her acclaimed essays, 'The Race for Theory', Barbara Christian has made a similar observation about Afro-American women's writing.[13] Unfortunately, our critics have chosen to cut themselves off from the masses at a time when they ought to have made a conscious effort to engage with them.

The organic connection between the '*shastrachar*' and '*lokachar*', which has been one of the enduring aspects of our creative as well as critical traditions, has snapped irretrievably, leading to a disconnect between the critic and the people, the literature and society. The Western critic can afford the luxury of indulging in abstract notions such as 'discourse' and 'textuality', but a critic working from within a society still striving to make a mark cannot afford such indulgences. In our context, literature or literary practices, and writers as well as critics need to move towards the masses, not away from them. And it is this 'moving away' that really sums up the burden of 'anxiety' we had discussed earlier. Critics have ceased to be the mediating agents between literary practices and social/cultural practices. They have instead become self-indulgent, self-exhibitionist dilettanti. In such circumstances, critical enterprises produce very little of readable and useful material. Once this kind of mediation runs into an impasse, all attempts at locating Indian literatures within their specific socio-cultural contexts are bound to fail. And it is obvious that this question is far too serious to be left to critics outside the academia. What we need to inject into our critical tradition is perhaps a sense of metacritical consciousness.

We will also need to address the question of ideologies of languages/ literatures competing for space within the official, bureaucratised, institutional practices—the questions of relative status, function, and even the distribution of power among languages in our own practices. In 1952, around the time we were laying the foundations of our nation-state, English was accorded the status of an official language as we found the question of national language almost impossible to settle. This status was granted for a limited period of time (until 1963), but once the battle was over, the issue of a national language became bitter and even fiercer in the late 1960s and was deferred indefinitely. The present essay does not have the scope to narrate the history of how this issue had created a north–south divide in our midst, snowballing into a major crisis. But it is clear that the only winner in this battle has been English. In the tussle among regional languages, English emerged as the best choice. Hindi could not be declared as the national language, and Tamil did not find acceptability in the Hindi heartland. And it was through sheer default—owing to our total incapacity to settle this crucial question of national/official language—that English has marched on triumphantly to its present, sovereign, dominant position. The attempt here is not to disparage English, but one needs to be mindful of the ideology that is inscribed in it. For instance, as a teacher of English, I cannot help going back to the historical contingencies that prompted the introduction of English in India. To put it somewhat differently, it is fastened like a saddle upon our backs, something we have not been able to throw off. And within our globalised space, English has not only reasserted its pre-eminent, hegemonic position, but has increasingly been seen as the most dominant tool of self-empowerment. As a result, Indian languages, which had already lost the first round of the battle for linguistic superiority to English, are now threatened with a bleak prospect. Indian literatures will perhaps continue to jostle for space in our elitist, highly bureaucratised, hegemonic territories, without being able to find a perch.

There have been authors of Indian writing in English whose output has been sparse but since they have published in English, have sold millions of copies of their works and garnered international attention and adulation. At the same time, we have had writers who have devoted their entire lives to the development of Indian literatures, and yet continue to remain unnoticed by a wider audience. One does not have to mention any names here. All one has to do is to compare the fortunes of any second-rate Indian English writer with those of a first-rate Indian writer writing in any of our official languages, and perhaps the anomalies of the situation shall begin to fall into a neat, recognisable pattern. The inference is that our obsolete institutional practices and flawed notions of linguistic hierarchy have often worked to the detriment of our own literatures. The dice is always heavily loaded against Indian languages and literatures. We need to find a way to change this situation, and relocate these contesting linguistic and literary ideologies. We must strive towards, and also create, if possible, a genuine republic of languages/literatures. Our dream of creating a true democratic republic that offers equal opportunities, respect and dignity to all may have soured, but we can always hope to create a world where Indian languages/literatures do not have to struggle for survival, space or expression.

The location of Indian literatures, as we have seen, is an extremely problematic but not entirely unfamiliar territory. This essay has attempted to bring out some of the central issues with regard to the academia's approach towards the reading and propagation of Indian literatures. The attempt has been to initiate a dialogue necessary for restoring Indian languages/literatures to that pre-eminent position they have always deserved.

Notes and References

1. It was Homi Bhabha who, in his *The Location of Culture* (London: Routledge, 1994), posited 'location' as a theoretical problem. He suggested that in a multicultural society, the immigrants invariably have to negotiate two or more cultures, which they do by locating themselves in an alien culture and seeking their identity in terms of 'hybridity' and/or 'liminality', which, according to him, was one of the ways in which an immigrant could possibly escape the constraints of the 'either/or' binarism. He foregrounded and popularised the notion of 'location' in cultural context. However, it has been seen as a significant 'postmodern signifier', ever since it emerged in the discourse of architecture. Postmodernism, it may be mentioned here, started in architecture and then found its way into art, literature and culture. For a detailed discussion on the relationship between postmodernism and architecture or postmodernism and location, see, Charles Jencks, *The Language of Postmodern Architecture*, 3rd rev. ed. (London Academy, 1981); Hans Bertens, *The Idea of the Postmodernism: A History* (London & New York: Routledge, 1995); Robert Venturi, *Complexity and Contradiction in Architecture* (London: The Architectural Press, 1977).

2. One of the questions we often debate about in relation to postmodernism is whether or not there is continuity between modernism and postmodernism. In fact, the academia is vertically split over this question. Some scholars emphasise continuity, while others point out the ruptures and discontinuities, and there are still others who underline both. For details of this debate, see, Christopher Butler, *Postmodernism: A Very Short Introduction* (New Delhi: Oxford University Press, 2006); Linda Hutcheon, *The Politics of Postmodernism* (London and New York: Routledge, 1980); Walter Truett Anderson, *The Fontana Postmodern Reader* (London: Fontana Press, 1996).

3. In *Postmodern Perspectives on Indian Society* (Jaipur: Rawat Publications, 2008), S.L. Doshi argues that India is a postmodern society as it has already rejected all grand narratives of Marxism, Gandhism and rationalism. Emphasising that in the Indian context, modernity has created religious, academic and market fundamentalism, Doshi chooses to look at the main cultural markers of Indian society—family, caste, village, culture and religion—from the postmodern perspective. While Doshi's analysis may appear a little too sweeping and generalised in its approach, Bijay K. Das treats 'postmodern' in an entirely unproblematic manner. In his *Postmodern Indian English Literature* (New Delhi: Atlantic, 2001/2006), Das posits 1980 as a cut-off date for the emergence of postmodern literature in Indian English. He does not feel the need to make the necessary distinction between postmodernism and postcolonialism, as he happily uses the two interchangeably and then, for some inexplicable reason, chooses to leave Salman Rushdie out of the range of postcolonial/postmodern writers. Nowhere does he make any effort to define the term 'postmodernism' (upon which his entire thesis rests), nor does he talk of its relevance or otherwise to the Indian context. In his essay 'Facets of Postmodernism: A Search for Roots. The Indian Literary Scene' anthologised in Hans Bertens, *International Postmodernism: Theory and Literary Practice* (Amsterdam/Philadelphia: John Benjamins, 1997), Indra Nath Choudhuri describes the '*uttar adhunik*' (Hindi translation of the term 'postmodern') period in 'Indian literature' as a period when it was 'developing a sense of Indianness' (485). It is somewhat difficult to understand how postmodernism could possibly be understood as 'a return-to-the-roots' programme, except as parody or travesty. His argument is that this is the period when 'culture' (whatever that may mean) became a dominant factor in literature (we may ask: when was it not?) and that in the Indian context, '*shestrachar*' (elite) and '*lokachar*' (popular) versions of culture have always been complementary, never oppositional. If that is the way postmodern has to be mediated and understood, should we also presume that we have always been a postmodern society, an argument quite similar to the one conservatives often give with a sense of déjà vu, claiming, 'We are an ancient society, and so we have been there and done all that'. This logic is, apparently, naïve and simplistic, even facetious.

4. In the last twenty years or so, 'postmodernism' has become quite a buzzword within Indian academia. All our academic debates invariably hinge around it, one way or the other. However, while conceding that postmodernism certainly provides an effective critical apparatus for critiquing and interrogating contemporary reality, we must remember that this theory, like so many others that are now integral to our pedagogical and research practices, is not only Euro-centric, but also a

by-product of European modes of production and cultural practices. One must emphasise that critical theories, especially the postmodern ones, are culture-specific, not universal, as we often tend to believe them to be. Therefore, when we do use, borrow or draw upon such critical approaches, we need to problematise them with the material at hand. This essay attempts to emphasise the problematic nature of postmodern ideas and concepts and use them, with a degree of self-consciousness, as resistance strategies.

5. Some of these questions have been extensively debated over the years. For detailed discussion, see Gauri Viswanathan *The Masks of Conquest: Literary Study and British Rule in India* (New Delhi: Oxford University Press, 1998); Ganesh N. Devy, *After Amnesia: Tradition and Change in Indian Literary Criticism* (Hyderabad: Orient Blackswan, 1996).

6. In order to get a sense of the course scholarly debates have taken over this question of paradigm shift in M.A. English curricula in Indian colleges and universities, see Swati Joshi, ed., *Re-thinking English: Essays in Literature, Language, History* (New Delhi, Oxford University Press, 1991) and also Rajeshwari Sunderajan, ed., *The Lie of the Land: English Literary Studies of India* (New Delhi: Oxford University Press, 1992).

7. The first draft of this essay was conceived and written way back in 2002, when the radical changes in the English curricula had not yet begun to take place across the country. Of course, the debate on the nature of the proposed changes had already begun, but the ground reality had not changed much. In the past few years, most of the departments of English across the country have revised their curricula, expanding the scope of Indian English by bringing in Indian literatures in English (a more inclusive category) instead of the self-limiting notion of Indian English literature. In 2009, Panjab University agreed to a move initiated by the department to rechristen the Department of English as the 'Department of English and Cultural Studies'. This is how we were able to push through translations of Indian texts, courses on media, culture, etc., into our curriculum at the post-graduate level. Despite that, presently we have only two courses that could be said to constitute the counter-canon—Indian writing in English and Indian literatures in translation, both being compulsory, and not optional courses. However, it must be stressed that this paradigm shift had not yet taken place when this piece was conceived and written. Here, I have decided not to change or alter these formulations for two reasons. They are central to the arguments made in this chapter and, also, it has enabled me to retain a sense of the history of curriculum design in our context.

8. Ngũgĩ wa Thiong'o, *Decolonising the Mind: The Politics of Language in African Literature* (Nairobi: East African Educational Publishers Ltd, 1978).

9. This term has been coined by Harold Bloom. See his *The Anxiety of Influence: A Theory of Poetry* (New York: Oxford University Press, 1973). Bloom is of the view that a poet/writer constantly labours under the anxiety of the influence(s), s/he may have received and/or internalised from his/her literary ancestors in his/her journey towards creating, shaping a poetic self. Re-interpreting the myth of Oedipus in the poststructuralist terms, he emphasises that each poet must go through the ritualistic, symbolic act of 'killing his/her father' in order to emerge out of the paternal shadows and constitute his/her poetic self. I am simply extending this concept of Bloom to understand how the critics, too, engage in a similar act of parricide to come into their own and establish their credentials.

10. In order to corroborate this point, all one has to do is to go through various literary histories of regional Indian languages prepared and published by Sahitya Akademi, New Delhi. To illustrate my point, I would refer to Sant Singh Sekhon and Kartar Singh Duggal, *A History of Punjabi Literature* (New Delhi: Sahitya Akademi, 1992). Not only is the notion of historiography in this work rather old-fashioned and outdated, but the periodisation, thematic arrangement and valorisation of authors invariably follow the model often used for writing history of English literature. Our attempts at writing history, especially in the field of literature, have often remained flawed, though to some extent *A History of Indian Literatures* (in several volumes) by Sisir K. Das does break fresh ground.

11. 'Discourse' is a Foucauldian concept that admits no distinction between literary and non-literary forms of writing, and thus allows us to analyse similarities across a range of texts as the products of a particular set of 'power/knowledge' relations. Textuality, however, is a Derridean notion that de-emphasises power/knowledge relations and refers to a set of signifying or hermeneutic practices that constitute or reconstitute the text in a different way, by different people, in different time frames.

12. For an extended discussion of this idea, see Stanley Aronowitz, *Dead Artists, Live Theories, and Other Cultural Problems* (London and New York: Routledge, 1994). Aronowitz points out that, owing to a number of cultural factors, an academic critic in the US academia has become as much of a star or a cultural icon as Madonna is or Michael Jackson once was. For him, it is a direct outcome of the consumerist culture, a gesture towards commodification, and therefore, a sign of cultural depletion and impoverishment, not necessarily plenitude and enrichment. We find a similar trend emerging in the Indian academia, too.

13. Barbara Christian, 'The Race for Theory,' in *Gender and Theory*, ed. Linda Kauffmann (Oxford: Blackwell, 1989), 225–36.

Chapter Two

Re-contextualising the Post-1980s Indian Novel in English

This essay attempts to bring out some of the trends and techniques that have emerged in the domain of Indian writing in English in the past two or three decades.[1] However, before initiating this discussion—a veritable Pandora's box, with unlimited possibilities—one needs to address the question that would be crucial to this discussion: What does it mean to be 'Indian'? One needs to ask this question as a prelude to defining the category/genre that is under analysis here: What constitutes 'Indian writing'? However, these questions put forward here are not in the same mould as the stock-in-trade of the academic debates in our country through the 1990s. For instance, the discussion here will not focus on the urban orientation or the diasporic consciousness of Indian writing in English or question the basis of an Indian English writer's understanding of 'Indian reality' or the readership of such a writer. All such questions have been debated for long, and perhaps could legitimately be considered as settled, though somewhat inconclusively.

The unprecedented growth of translation as a 'culture industry' is perhaps one of the most significant developments that have taken place in the field of Indian writing in English in the last two decades. This phenomenal growth has thrown up a whole new set of questions that we may find rather hard to escape from. A great deal of regional literature, which was obviously not written or produced for an Indian English readership, has been extensively and competently translated into English. This has compelled some of us, who have spent a lifetime teaching/researching English canonical texts, to sit up and take notice, and even reorder our priorities as teachers and researchers, wherever we could.[2] Delhi University, for instance, has introduced major revisions in its syllabi (in terms of its course content and pedagogy), both for undergraduate and postgraduate levels. This is reflected in the way the University has consciously moved away from Milton, Shakespeare and T.S. Eliot. The syllabi are now oriented more towards writers such as Kabir, Kalidas and Keki Daruwala. This exercise towards de-canonising English Literature courses was initially undertaken by Delhi University in the first decade of the twenty-first century. Over the years, it has spread to other Indian universities, too. More and more departments of English across a vast spectrum of Indian universities have initiated moves towards 'indigenising' courses and syllabi. We may debate on whether this is a move in the right direction, but it is a fact that the exclusivity of English studies has been breached. And this has opened up more space for writers originally writing in Hindi, Bengali, Marathi, Kannada, Tamil, Telugu, etc. within the hegemonic domain of English studies.

These developments are so significant and influential that they cannot be dealt with in isolation. However, let us now return to the question we posed at the beginning of this discussion: What does it mean to be 'Indian'? This question has been raised from time to time, with all kinds of plausible and implausible answers. Right from Vedic times to the twentieth century, hundreds of scholars and intellectuals have addressed this issue, with varying effects and responses.[3] In recent times, Amartya Sen, along with Sunil Khilnani and Pavan K. Verma, has put this question back on our agenda.[4] Though Sen has raised this question in several of his previous writings, it is in *The Argumentative Indian* (2006) that he appears to have finally stumbled upon a convincing and cogent answer. Returning to the history of India, he searches for the answer in the durability and sustainability of the nation's 'dialogic tradition'. He argues that this 'dialogic tradition' has always been a part of our culture, right from ancient times. He goes on to suggest that to be an 'Indian' is to be a legatee and a possessor of multiple histories and identities, and the only way of mediating 'Indianness' is to acknowledge its pluralism in terms of languages, literatures, ethnicities and religions. Coexistence of these pluralities and diversities and their constant interface and negotiation has been a permanent feature of our cultures and the reason for their sustenance and survival.[5]

If we go along with Sen's thesis, 'cultural pluralism' can easily be perceived as one of the defining characteristics of 'Indianness'. Even at the risk of sounding simplistic and naive, one may suggest that this 'cultural pluralism' is one of the greatest strengths of contemporary Indian writing in English. Moreover, it is within the extended space of 'cultural pluralism' that we can possibly hope to situate, negotiate or understand some of the new experiments and developments that have surfaced in the realm of Indian writing in English in general, and the Indian novel in English in particular.

To begin with, let us put forward a few tentative formulations about the Indian novel in English. Somehow, whenever we analyse the state of the Indian novel in English, we tend to restrict ourselves purely to the Indian context. This, as this essay will go on to argue, is essentially a fallacious position, which one can take only at the risk of sounding over-reactive and gratuitously constrictive. We often take recourse to such analyses on the assumption that despite being a Euro-centric form (Who can deny that the genre of novel first originated in Europe and then travelled to other parts of the world before surfacing in the Indian context?), the novel has, in its long journey through various Indian languages over the past hundred and fifty years or so, 'indigenised' itself and even acquired a truly Indian identity and character. By all accounts, Bankim Chandra Chatterjee's (1838–94) *Durgeshnandini* (1865), in Bangla, was one of the earliest attempts at writing a novel, an effort that preceded Raja Rao's *Kanthapura* (1940) by about seventy-five years. This is proof that the novel had already become an established form in various Indian languages before it began to be used by Indians writing in English. The purpose of historicising the genre's progress in India is two-fold: 1. to point out that the novel in our context is not an 'indigenous' but an 'indigenised' form, and 2. to underline that any comment on the state of the Indian novel, in English or otherwise, must take into account developments elsewhere too.

It is for this reason that one feels compelled to discuss the re-emergence of the Indian novel in English in the 1980s—which apparently coincides with the publication of Salman Rushdie's *Midnight's Children*—against the backdrop of the developments within the genre in Europe and elsewhere. In the 1960s and the

1970s, the novel as a genre could be said to have gone through one of its worst ever crises in Europe and America. This was the time when both the theoreticians and the practitioners of the genre across the world had begun to make somewhat loud and magisterial proclamations about the sudden and premature demise of the novel in Europe. While Frank Kermode, an English critic of repute, rather gently hinted at the 'sense of an ending',[6] John Barth, an American novelist, went into an overdrive, with his premonitory pronouncements about the 'proverbial death of the novel',[7] reminiscent of the *fin-de-siècle* pronouncements. Though Barth and several others like him were undoubtedly overstating their case, it is a fact that in the late 1960s and early 1970s, the novel as a genre was dying a slow death in Europe, the land of its origin and early development. No wonder that when *One Hundred Years of Solitude* was published in 1969, Gabriel García Márquez, its Latin American, Columbian author, was hailed as someone who had not only revived a dying form but infused it with unimaginable possibilities rarely ever explored by the European novel earlier, except in the works of the German novelist Günter Grass, especially in his *The Tin Drum* (1959).

A reader may, at this point, ask a question: Why do we need to take this detour into the history of the contemporary novel and place it within the larger framework of the state of the novel in the rest of the world? If we want to understand the impetus behind some of the developments in the Indian novel in English, especially those that followed the arrival of Rushdie on the scene, it is absolutely necessary to understand the state of the genre within this enlarged context. Rushdie and his path-breaking *Midnight's Children* could be seen as closely following the innovations of Günter Grass and Márquez, for they had already experimented with 'magic realism' much before Rushdie took recourse to it. And a host of other writers who came after Rushdie—Amitav Ghosh, Upamanyu Chatterjee, Shashi Tharoor and Arundhati Roy, to name a few—could justifiably be described as the 'midnight's children'. Second-generation novelists who were born in Independent India, they helped spawn an entirely new school of novel writing in Indian context. As Amitav Ghosh, Upamanyu Chatterjee and Shashi Tharoor also happen to be former

Stephanians (alumni of St Stephen's College, New Delhi), Rukun Advani, the well-known critic and publisher and a Stephanian himself, has described them as the practitioners of what he calls the 'Stephanian novel',[8] a term that one may have quarrels with. For one, the label is a little too restrictive, self-limiting and even parochial. Two, it fails to do justice to the cosmopolitan character of these writers and/or their writings. Three, it refuses to recognise the simple fact that these writers inhabit culturally diverse spaces and as such in their writings, the monolithic notions of India, 'Indianness' and 'Indian novel' become keenly contested categories.

Right from Rushdie downwards, the new crop of Indian novelists in English are characterised by their undying commitment to history combined with their constant refusal to internalise the conventional notions of linear, sequential or chronological history. One needs to emphasise that what we see in these novels is not the re-emergence of the old historical novel, à la Walter Scott, but a 'new novel'. They are infused with historical consciousness but they also explore the 'magically' new and strange ways of representing it, à la Günter Grass and Márquez. All of them show a preoccupation with 'subaltern historiography' in one form or the other, and they engage with the problems of exile, cultural displacement, dispossession and emergent plural identities—some of the problems that postcolonial theorists often talk about.

If Rushdie deconstructs historical consciousness by interrogating the history of the nation through foregrounding personal narrative(s) or the history of a minority (as in *Midnight's Children, The Moor's Last Sigh* [1995], *The Ground Beneath Her Feet* [1999], *Shalimar the Clown* [2005], etc.), Amitav Ghosh challenges its limits by penetrating it with local narratives/histories and archaeological materials of an amazing variety (*The Shadow Lines* [1988], *In an Antique Land* [1992], *The Calcutta Chromosome* [1995], *The Hungry Tide* [2005], etc.). If Upamanyu Chatterjee explores the personal histories of individuals/families who occupy the suburban space in contemporary India (*English, August: An Indian Story* [1988], *The Last Burden* [1994], *The Mammaries of the Welfare State* [2000], etc.), Shashi Tharoor (*The Great Indian Novel* [1989], *Show Business* [1992], *Riot* [2001], etc.) fashions new metaphors for mediating the bewildering complexity of the nation. Most of these novelists can safely be described as 'postmodernists', as they often betray a tendency to mediate the notions of self, society, language and culture, from this particular standpoint. However, though the shift to the 'local' narratives or their 'collocations' (which is how Arundhati Roy's Booker-Prize-winning novel *The God of Small Things* [1997] can also be described) is very much in evidence in their works, these writers do not seem to have completely given up the 'pretensions' of 'grand narratives'. Though Salman Rushdie's *Midnight's Children* configures history from the perspective of an anti-hero, Salim Sinai, the novel is certainly much more than a personal or a local narrative. With its sweeping, overarching design, it definitely threatens to grow gratuitously into a powerful narrative-of-the-nation. This tendency to create 'national allegories' to borrow Jameson's phrase, clearly shows that Rushdie and his ilk end up creating grand narratives, even when they possibly intended it otherwise. Much the same could be said about Shashi Tharoor's *The Great Indian Novel* and Upamanyu Chatterjee's *The Mammaries of the Welfare State* too. Ironically, it is in the process of distancing themselves from the totalising effect of the 'realistic', grand narratives that most of our contemporary writers end up creating something they would have otherwise liked to resist.

This second generation of writers is distinguished from the first generation of Indian novelists in English—such as Raja Rao, Mulk Raj Anand and R.K. Narayan—by a high degree of self-consciousness and self-reflexivity that they show in their use of language and grammar and their representation of the relationship of fiction with history. To put it differently, we could say that the novel actually managed to survive through the recognition of its limitations and strengths, facilitating its own reinvention and rebirth in the bargain. No wonder that, after the decline of the genre in Europe, the focus shifted first to the novels written in Latin America and then to the Indian novel in English, as some of our émigré writers began to play a crucial role in this process of rebirth. This explains why, in the 1980s, the global spotlight finally turned upon Indian writers in English, and how they began to command not only 'hefty advances' for themselves, but unprecedented international recognition and readership. To a lesser extent, this has also had a cascading effect on the phenomenal growth of the 'translation industry' in India, which has managed to create a vibrant global market and readership for novels originally written in regional languages.

That the foregoing analysis has not discussed the works of Vikram Seth, a very prominent contemporary writer, may be adversely commented upon. However, in defence, one may argue that Seth cannot be categorised along with the other writers of his generation. He stands apart, not only by virtue of his untiring penchant for experimenting with form and subject matter, but also because of his refusal to fit into any known category or classification. Right from the beginning of his career as a novelist, which took off on a rather formal note with the publication of *The Golden Gate* (a novel in verse) in 1986, Seth has not shown the tendency to return to a particular literary form he had once experimented with. However, it must be noted here that poetry, which is apparently his most favoured form of self-expression, is a happy exception in this regard, as before 1986 he had already published three not very notable collections—*Mappings* (1980), *From Heaven Lake* (1983) and *The Humble Administrator's Garden* (1985). From a novel in verse, he moved on to another two collections of poems—*All You Who Sleep Tonight: Poems* (1990), *Beastly Tales from Here and There* (1992)—and then *A Suitable Boy* (1993), a tome that runs into more than 1400 pages, and is counted among the longest novels ever written in the history of world literature. He also did translations of Chinese poetry—*Three Chinese Poets: Translations of Poems by Wang Wei, Li Bai and Du Fu* (1992)—and published a libretto titled *Arion and the Dolphin* (1994). His latest offering is *Two Lives: A Memoir* (2005), a biographical novel. One may describe Seth as a 'true blue Punjabi' who loves to flaunt whatever he does, especially all the 'firsts' he has to his credit. Though Vikram Chandra, Pankaj Mishra and Raj Kamal Jha have not necessarily followed the same trajectory as that of Seth, their career graphs, too, show a gradual shift from reportage to short story and then to successful or not-so-successful novels. In a manner of speaking, Seth could be said to have spawned a whole new school of 'avant-garde novelists' in contemporary India. Chandra, Mishra and Jha are the true exponents of this particular school. All of them appear to be engaged in a 'modernist quest' (reflected largely in their choice of some variant of a 'realistic novel'), which largely has to do with the search for the ultimate form. But, as evidenced by their works, these efforts often threaten to collapse into abject formlessness. In most of the modernist literature of the early twentieth century, it was the lack of form (or search for a new form) that invariably reinforced the lack of content (or substituted for a new content). In such a situation, avant-gardism was perceived to be a 'controlled experiment' and was, therefore, treated as a virtue, but if it becomes an end in itself, a gratuitous form of self-indulgence, it tends to become anarchic, even self-defeating, as is the case with a host of writers who have ostensibly written under the influence of Vikram Seth.

The last few decades have also seen several women writers making contributions that helped put Indian writing in English on the global map. The most well-known name among them is that of Arundhati Roy, but we simply cannot discount the laudable contributions of several of her predecessors and contemporaries such as Shashi Deshpande, Neelam Saran Gour, Githa Hariharan, Manju Kapur, Jhumpa Lahiri, Kiran Desai, etc. The works of these women novelists are so highly individualistic and keenly distinctive that it is almost impossible to pigeon-hole them into neat categories. To an extent, these women writers do share some of the concerns of their male counterparts, but to a large extent, they have explored hitherto unknown and uncharted territories in their fictional works. While some of them have ended up as fine cartographers of the interiorised spaces and continue to plumb the depths of a woman's psyche, others have ventured into themes and ideas that easily transcend narrow gender concerns or cultural impositions. While Shashi Deshpande, Githa Hariharan and Manju Kapur write with the consciousness of being women, the same cannot be said about Jhumpa Lahiri, Neelam Saran Gour and Kiran Desai. Some of these women novelists, among the latter group more than the former, do transcend the narrow, provincial barriers of gender, class and/or race. But this is not intended to emphasise the perceived 'apolitical nature' of their work—as the feminist maxim has it, 'the personal is always political'—but in the case of the latter group of writers, one does not sense the hardening of ideological positions.

My point in this essay, as I had suggested at the very outset, was not to confine myself to the more restrictive category of Indian English writing, but to find newer spaces and contexts for a much wider category of Indian writing in English. This essay makes no pretentious claim of covering a new ground in this regard, as all it seeks to do is to defamiliarise the familiar. We have so far confined our discussion to the emerging trends in the arena of Indian fiction in English. Within fiction, we have restricted ourselves to some general observations and perhaps, to a general survey of the field as it unfolded itself in the last few decades. This survey is in no sense exhaustive or complete and this discussion, due to its limited scope, has had to leave out many writers of repute. It has also omitted many related trends and developments in the Indian novel in English, but it has tried to re-inscribe the context within which some of these developments could possibly be re-examined.

Notes and References

1. This essay has used the term 'Indian writing in English' (IWE) deliberately, as opposed to 'Indian English writing' (IEW). I find the former much more comprehensive, inclusive and far-reaching in its implications than the latter.
2. This process of reordering our priorities in terms of our M.A. English syllabi and pedagogy started in our context way back in the 1990s. Though this debate was primarily 'academic' in nature initially, later it had a ripple-down effect in terms of de-canonising English studies. In order to get a sense of the debates around the paradigm shifts in M.A. English curricula in Indian colleges and universities, see Swati Joshi, ed., *Re-thinking English: Essays in Literature, Language, History* (New Delhi, Oxford University Press, 1991) and also Rajeshwari Sunderajan, ed., *The Lie of the Land: English Literary Studies in India* (New Delhi: Oxford University Press, 1992).
3. In pre-Independence India, this question was posed with varying results by Mahatma Gandhi, Rabindranath Tagore, Bal Gangadhar Tilak, Sri Aurobindo, Jawaharlal Nehru, K.M. Munshi, D.D. Kosambi, etc.
4. In the post-Independence period, this debate was carried forward, among others, by Sarvepalli Radhakrishnan, Rammanohar Lohia,

Jayaprakash Narayan, V.S. Naipaul, Ved Mehta and others. In recent years, however, this debate has gained a new edge and urgency, especially after India abandoned the path of socialism and embraced liberalisation. In this regard, some of the important works are, Sunil Khilnani, *The Idea of India* (New York: Farrar, Strauss and Giroux Paperbacks, 1999); Pavan K. Varma, *Being Indian* (New Delhi: Penguin, 2005); and Amartya Sen, *The Argumentative Indian: Writings on Indian History, Culture and Identity* (London: Picador, 2006). In recent years, there has literally been a flood of books on this subject. See Ramachandra Guha, *India after Gandhi* (London: Pan Macmillan, 2008); Surendra Kumar and Pradeep K. Kapur, eds., *India of My Dreams* (New Delhi: Academic Foundation, 2008); and Nandan Nilekani, *Imagining India: Ideas for the New Century* (London: Allen Lane, 2009).

5. Sen, *The Argumentative Indian*. In this book, Amartya Sen has passionately and convincingly argued for a 'dialogic culture', which according to him, has been the basis of our 'plural identities' in the contemporary context. Sen rejects the idea of a singular, monolithic identity, and pleads instead for a highly sedimented, multilayered identity.
6. Frank Kermode, *The Sense of an Ending: Studies in the Theory of Fiction* (Oxford: Oxford University Press, 1967).
7. If one has to trace the origin of 'Endism' in critical discourse, one may safely trace it back to the 1960s. In the aftermath of World War II, this sense of 'Endism' was extremely strong, and it was further accentuated by the disillusionment that set in with the beginning of the Cold War. In the 1960s, this was perhaps at an all-time high, when all kinds of pronouncements and prognostications about the 'death' of the novel were extensively made. In the US, it was John Barth who led this campaign with his famous essay, 'The Literature of Exhaustion' (1967), now included in Bran Nicol, ed., *Postmodernism and the Contemporary Novel: A Reader* (Edinburgh: Edinburgh University Press, 2002). With the advent of poststructuralist thought in the late 1960s, this 'Endism' entered an entirely different phase, with the 'end of history', the 'end of progress' and the 'end of grand narrative' proclamations being openly made, and then all this culminated into the 'death of the human subject' and the consequent 'death of the author'.
8. The appellation, 'Stephanian novel' or 'St Stephen's School of Literature', which was jestingly suggested by Rukun Advani, caught the public imagination to such an extent that Aditya Bhattacharjea decided to devote an entire volume to it. See Aditya Bhattacharjea and Lola Chatterjee, eds., *The Fiction of St Stephen's* (New Delhi: Ravi Dayal Publishers, 2000).

CHAPTER THREE

Emerging Trends in Post-Independence Indian English Drama

Before launching into a discussion of the emerging trends and techniques in the domain of Indian English drama in the post-Independence phase, one needs to define the contours of the category under discussion here: Is there a separate category called 'Indian English drama'? Or is it coterminous with Indian drama in Sanskrit and other regional languages? What kind of relationship—filial or otherwise—does Indian English drama share with its counterparts in Sanskrit, regional languages, and folk, rural and urban genres? One may safely assume that it is impossible for us to access, mediate or interrogate Indian English drama in isolation. If it has to be contextualised, that must be done in the broadest sense possible. Indian English drama and its history are complicit with the history of Indian drama in general, and the two cannot be segregated from each other. Our discussion will entail posing and answering some inconvenient questions such as whether Indian English drama enjoys the same popularity, support and patronage from its readers/audience that Indian English poetry and novel often do in our context. If the answer is in the negative, we may have to reflect on some of the factors behind this phenomenon.

It is a well-known fact that India has had a long, established history of theatre and dramatic theory. The origins of Indian theatre can be traced back to ancient works in Sanskrit. Ashwaghosh (first century AD), Bhasa, Kalidasa (fourth century AD), Harsha (seventh century AD), Bhavabhuti (eighth century AD), Bhattanarayana, Murari (between eighth and tenth century AD) and Rajashekhara were some of its prominent practitioners. Bharata's *Natyasastra*, often referred to as the 'fifth veda', written around the second century BC, is one of the extant ancient discourses on drama available in our context. Both the mainstream Sanskrit playwrights and Bharata's treatise, though written for a very different cultural context, continue to guide and influence the course of contemporary drama. Hence, they can be considered inseparable parts of a living tradition of drama in the Indian context. Apart from mainstream drama, we also have had an equally strong and popular tradition of other variants, with regional or local names and characteristics, that have had a symbiotic relationship with two of the most significant epics our culture has produced—the *Ramayana* and the *Mahabharata*. Since as long as we can remember, 'Ramlila' has flourished in various parts of India as much as the dramatic renderings of the anecdotes, episodes and stories from the *Mahabharata* have. These two epics constitute two distinct and almost autonomous living dramatic traditions in themselves. Hence, when it comes to a discussion of Indian drama, we should think of the category in terms of multiple, pluralistic traditions, and not as a unitary or monolithic tradition. In fact, almost all the regions and languages in India have had their own traditions of drama. This cultural diversity and pluralism must be taken into account by anyone who sets out to situate, negotiate or understand some of the new experiments and developments in the realm of Indian drama in general and Indian English drama in particular.

From the standpoint of literary history, both the Indian English novel and poetry have consistently thrown up recognisable traditions and identifiable trends and movements. This helped these genres assert their pre-eminent and hegemonic positions within the literary/cultural space. In comparison, Indian English drama has had a rather uneven growth and development, marked by sporadic, and often frenzied, periods of activity, which have invariably been punctuated by long spells of passivity, or even lassitude. While there has been a slow and steady growth of drama and theatre in regional languages (both in the pre- and the post-Independence phases), Indian English drama does not seem to have thrown up either an overarching movement or dominant or emergent trends or traditions. Significantly, the history of Indian English drama has been a history of absences, silences, ruptures and discontinuities, with its own share of peaks and troughs (where troughs have apparently been more pronounced than peaks). One certainly needs to address the reasons for this: Why has Indian English drama remained a 'poor cousin' of the Indian English novel or poetry, right through its history? Why has it not been able to sustain or consolidate a movement or a tradition? Does it speak of a fundamental sociological or cultural failure or is it merely an expression of some crisis within Indian drama itself? There are also the larger questions of how and in what different ways the notion of 'cultural pluralism' has affected the growth and evolution of Indian English drama or guided its course and direction through history.

Before we set out to address some of these questions, let us take a brief look at the history of Indian English drama. This would help us arrive at some tentative theoretical observations. As noted by Shanta Gokhale in her essay in Arvind Krishna Mehrotra's *The Illustrated History of Indian English Writing*, the earliest play recorded in the history of Indian English drama is *The Persecuted, or Dramatic Scenes Illustrative of the Present State of Hindoo Society in Calcutta* (1831) by Krishna Mohan Banerjea (1813–85).[1] It deals with the conflict between orthodox Hindu customs and the new ideas introduced by Western education. Though Indian English drama had begun to emerge much before the novel or poetry appeared, it somehow failed to keep pace with the other two genres in sustained growth and evolution.

Commenting on the Western influence on the growth and development of Indian drama, Bharat Gupt says that it 'awakened the dormant, critical impulse in the country to bring Indians face-to-face with new forms of life and literature, and to open the way for a fruitful cross-fertilisation of ideas and forms of expression.'[2] We have evidence to suggest that European plays were being staged by touring theatre groups and individuals as early as the 1780s in Bombay (Mumbai) and Calcutta (Kolkata), though these were exclusively performed for the entertainment of British officers. It is believed that a Russian music director, Gerasim Lebedev (1790–1817) produced the first modern Indian play in Calcutta towards the end of the eighteenth century. The fact that this was largely a phenomenon localised in these two imperial centres is also significant, considering that Bombay and Calcutta were to emerge later as the main hubs of theatrical activities through the better part of the nineteenth and twentieth centuries.

The British government in India was compelled to introduce the Dramatic Performances Act (1876) to impose restrictions upon regional theatres, which had already begun to be perceived as potent instruments of protest and dissent.[3] But this Act had no bearing on the Indian English drama of this period. The metropolitan character of Indian English drama, which it has somehow managed to sustain over a hundred years or more (or as some believe, it will not be able to shed ever), largely has to do with this British patronage it received during the early stages. Even within the metropolis, this form of drama appears to have depended exclusively upon the patronage of a miniscule minority of English-educated classes, thus acquiring in the process an 'elitist orientation' of an extreme kind. In other words, all through its history, Indian English drama struggled rather hard to shed its insularity and exclusivity, in an effort to penetrate into the popular and democratic cultural space, without much success, though.

Besides, most of the plays written or produced in Bombay, either in the latter half of the nineteenth century or the early part of the twentieth century, laboured extensively under the influence of the European masters of the genre. It is significant that Indian English drama, in its nascent form, did not draw so much upon the classical though residual tradition of Sanskrit theatre, the dominant form of Parsi theatre, emergent forms within the folk tradition(s) or the other existent Indian theatrical forms, but sought extraterritorial affiliations and allegiances with European forms and styles.[4] No wonder that Shakespeare, Moliere, Henrik Ibsen (Norwegian playwright), Maurice Maeterlinck (Belgian playwright), Eugene O'Neill, Arthur Miller, Samuel Beckett and several others have continued to fascinate, and even haunt, the Indian imagination right through its theatrical history, affecting not only the course of Indian English drama but also the growth and proliferation of regional theatrical forms in certain cases.

One needs to emphasise, as a prelude to a survey of Indian English drama, that unlike fiction and poetry—the two forms which are purely 'literary' in nature—drama is a living, performing and multimedial art form, which draws its sustenance not so much from a passive reading public but from an active, enthusiastic and participatory audience. A play invariably has two lives (or several lives)—as a literary text and as performance(s)—and they must concur, if it has to either survive or succeed. It is for this reason that the 'Is-ness' (as emphasised by Peter Szondi in *The Theory of Modern Drama*) or 'the present tense' of Indian English drama—or for that matter, its engagement with the contemporary audience, patrons and reality—shall always remain one of the main points of discussion and debate.[5]

The aim of this effort to comb through the history of Indian English drama is mainly three-fold: 1. to perceive how and why Indian English drama is positioned somewhat differently from Indian English fiction or poetry, 2. to point out some of the internal contradictions of this particular form, embedded as it is in history, and 3. to identify some of the theoretical challenges its study may throw up. With these assumptions in mind, when one looks back at the history of Indian literature in general, especially in the post-Independence period, one will be compelled to raise several questions: Why has drama not been seen as the preferred mode of self-expression among our writers, when compared to fiction or poetry? Why have we not been able to develop a tradition of 'indigenised' English theatre or drama—not 'indigenous', as we do have a long, uninterrupted tradition of indigenous theatre, both rural and urban—the way we have developed a highly evolved and self-conscious tradition of novel and poetry? Rather than go into these questions directly and answer them purely in sociological or cultural terms (read theoretical), one should look into the practice of Indian English drama over the past forty years or more, so that the answers begin to emerge on their own. Our discussion of Indian English drama here is intended to merely raise certain theoretical issues emerging out of a somewhat wayward, or even discontinuous, history of Indian English drama and explore why this form has suffered the 'historical neglect' that it has. It is not intended to be a completely comprehensive survey.

For this reason, some of the important Indian playwrights such as Asif Currimbhoy (1928–94), Gieve Patel (b. 1946),

Cyrus Mistry (b. 1956), Nissim Ezekiel (1924–2004) and Joseph Mathias Lobo-Prabhu (1906–99) have been excluded despite their significant contribution both to subject and style in Indian drama. There are two reasons for this omission: One needs to guard against turning this essay into a mere catalogue of names, even though it would mean including the writers of importance. Secondly, all these playwrights were seeking to revive in English the dying, if not the defunct, form of Parsi theatre which had been popular right from the 1850s to the 1950s.[6] For this reason, the works of some of the playwrights mentioned above have to be studied in a context which is entirely different from the one we have outlined. It is noteworthy that Parsi theatre, the first-ever commercial form of theatre known in India, developed largely under the patronage of Parsi merchants and traders, who were emerging as a significant economic power in the nineteenth-century Bombay. They were, in turn, deeply influenced by the Western modes of drama/theatre. They desperately wanted to indigenise some of these forms for their own leisure and entertainment or that of the local community. Apart from a very specific urban orientation and local habitation or language, Parsi theatre was known primarily for its European style proscenium stage, elaborate and flamboyant sets, richly painted curtains, lavish and ornate costumes, rhetorical and declamatory style of acting combined with songs and dances popular in nineteenth-century India, etc., and it sought to achieve an overall mesmerising, spectacular and hypnotic effect on the audiences. It is no wonder that, at a later stage, Parsi theatre, with its preoccupation with spectacle, song and dance, became the main source of inspiration for Bollywood cinema. Parsi theatre dealt with wide-ranging ideas and themes, which were often drawn from mythology and history, and experimented with all known forms and styles such as romance, social comedy, tragedy and melodrama. All in all, Parsi theatre was an exotic form of indigenous theatre that did much to inspire a whole range of urban, semi-urban and folk forms of theatre that emerged in India subsequently. For over a century, Parsi theatre continued to facilitate the resurgence of regional, urban theatres, especially in Gujarati, Marathi, Hindi and Urdu, though it had failed to provide the same kind of impetus to Indian English drama, at least, in the pre-Independence phase. This essay does not aim to discuss the impact of Parsi theatre as such a discussion will form a part of a more comprehensive study of post-Independence Indian English drama.[7]

The 1950s was an important period in the history of dramatic culture in our country. If on the one hand, this period saw the resurgence of national consciousness asserting itself in the form of the rapid institutionalisation of 'culture industry' (for all important cultural institutions were set up around this time); on the other, it also saw the revival of Indian English drama. The latter development was largely a privately funded affair, almost completely unaided by government agencies. It is noteworthy that in the 1950s, the central government brought in a specific legislation with the explicit purpose of setting up the prestigious National School of Drama (NSD) in New Delhi. Initially, it was set up as a constituent unit of Sangeet Natak Akademi in 1959. It was converted into an autonomous institution in 1975 and was granted the status of a deemed university in 2005. The 1950s was the time when Pandit Nehru, the then prime minister, was slowly laying the foundation of a modern, progressive and developing Indian nation/economy and NSD, which is how it is now widely known, emerged as an important cultural nucleus for the growth of all living and performing art forms, especially drama and theatre.

Not only did NSD play a significant role in shaping and guiding the future of all cultural activities in our country, but it also helped in nurturing the latent dramatic/theatrical talent there was. It was as though NSD had become the focal point of an extremely significant cultural revolution, spearheaded by Ebrahim Alkazi, the founder-director of NSD, and ably supported by a galaxy of equally well-known alumni such as Bansi Kaul, B.V. Karanth, Habib Tanvir, Ram Gopal Bajaj, Mohan Maharishi, Alam Allana, etc. It is difficult to imagine today what the fate of Indian drama and/or theatre would have been had NSD not come into existence. As NSD was set up with the explicit purpose of offering exclusive patronage to Indian dramatic/theatrical forms/techniques, both in the mainstream and folk traditions, it encouraged the growth and proliferation of regional/folk art forms or what one might call the 'indigenous forms of drama/theatre'. This was the period which produced such towering playwrights as Dharamvir Bharati (1926–97) and Mohan Rakesh (1925–72) in Hindi, Badal Sircar (1925–2011) in Bengali, Vijay Tendulkar (1928–2008) in Marathi and Girish Karnad (b. 1938) in Kannada. Before they appeared on the scene and started giving a decisive direction to the theatre movement in India, drama or theatre had flourished either under the influence of Parsi theatre or owing to that of the progressive movement. In a way, these playwrights scripted the emergence of an 'avant-garde theatre movement' in post-Independence India. No wonder that their works are often characterised by the dialectics of 'tradition and modernity', which, in a way, defined the cultural ethos and sociological milieu of their times.[8]

It is perhaps against this backdrop that we can understand the dynamics of the virtual absence of both the dramatic and theatrical talent in Indian English literature. Over the past forty years or so, Indian English drama has presented a very dismal scenario, with an occasional talent popping up every ten years or so, making its presence felt in limited circles, and then sinking into oblivion. Unlike the Indian novel in English, where we have witnessed the slow emergence of definitive movement(s)—both the currents and the cross-currents—and even their systematic and sustained interrogations, we do not really come across any discernible movements or traditions within Indian English drama. The English theatre in India has, over the years, confined itself largely to metropolitan centres such as Bombay (Mumbai), Calcutta (Kolkata), Madras (Chennai), Bengaluru (Bangalore) and New Delhi and it has flourished, wherever it has, not necessarily because of Indian English playwrights, but in spite of them. Our directors and actors of English theatre have had to rely on the works of European and American playwrights to sustain the movement.

We can trace the trajectory of Indian English drama by focussing our attention on the career graphs of three prominent post-Independence playwrights—Partap Sharma (b. 1939), Gurcharan Das (b. 1943) and Mahesh Dattani (b. 1958). Sharma started writing plays in English as far back as 1956 when his first play, *Brothers under the Skin* was published, and since then, he has been writing plays sporadically, punctuating his theatrical efforts with children's literature, novels and documentaries. Incidentally, his latest offering, *Sammy*, written in 2005 and produced by Lillette Dubey, was doing the rounds of the country until 2008. With the exception of this particular play, which deals with Mahatma Gandhi, Sharma's plays are often not staged in India. One of his plays, *A Touch of Brightness* (1965), which offered a bold portrayal of prostitutes and the red-light district of Mumbai, had created quite a furore when it was first produced there in 1967. The play was banned on the grounds that it 'dealt with subjects which should not be depicted on stage'and was not revived until much later—that too, not in Mumbai but in New York. *A Touch of Brightness* has been taught at various universities abroad, but it could be produced in Mumbai only in 1973, courtesy Indian National Theatre. When it was broadcast over the radio by the BBC Third Programme, Walter Allen, a well-known literary critic, is known to have noted that the play was 'the most imaginatively satisfying' experience.[9]

Sharma's *Zen Katha* (2004) is a historical play about Bodhidharma, an Indian monk and the founder of Zen Buddhism. The monk had been a forgotten figure in his homeland, India, until Sharma resurrected him through the play. *Sammy* portrays Gandhi's journey from a tongue-tied lawyer to a shrewd politician and finally, to the status of the 'Mahatma'. Set against the dramatic background of India's freedom struggle, this play takes the audience by surprise at every turn, bringing to life Gandhi's philosophy and pragmatism with a rare sense of humour and panache. After its European premiere in Brussels in October 2006, the play also travelled to Southeast Asia, UK and the US. *Begum Sumroo* (1997) is, once again, a historical play set in the late eighteenth century. It traces the picaresque adventures of a legendary historical figure who started off as a rebellious courtesan in British India. Known for her political subterfuge and amorous liaisons, Farzana, the peerless courtesan, morphed herself into a powerful ruler. After seducing Walter Reinhardt Sombre, a Swiss-German mercenary, she acquired the kingdom of Sardhana from Emperor Shah Alam and commanded a fierce brigade of 3000 European and Indian soldiers. Like several other plays of Sharma, this one too premiered outside India. Both Sharma and Gurcharan

Das seem to be preoccupied with the colonial phase of Indian history, which they explore with a rare commitment.

It is ironic that most of our playwrights have to first win their plaudits in the West, and then turn to the audiences at home to seek validation and vindication of their efforts. It is doubly ironic because, unlike the novel, theatre is essentially a people's medium and so must thrive and flourish because of their patronage, not in spite of it. One has to address this central issue in any analysis of Indian English drama: How did Indian English drama acquire this elitist orientation and why has it failed to shed it to earn the popularity or patronage of the Indian audiences? Sadly, Indian English drama has never been treated with the kind of seriousness it has always deserved. As a result, all the developments that have taken place in this area are essentially of academic and historical interest, not so much of practical relevance. It also needs to be pointed out that Indian English drama has, over the years, remained bogged down by this heavy baggage of 'academisation'. This, along with its inability to create or fashion the speech rhythms of Indian English or capture the nuances of the spoken word which is so significant for the growth of drama as a popular art form, are among some of the serious limitations of this form. Hence, playwrights like Sharma continue to flirt and experiment with a wide variety of themes and ideas, but they fail to anchor their plays in the 'spoken idiom' in the way in which it deserves to be treated in our context.

Though Gurcharan Das had written his three plays—*Larins Sahib, Mira, 9 Jakhoo Hill*—way back in the late 1960s and early seventies, he dared to publish them only after he had won acclaim as a columnist, novelist and commentator in 2001. *Larins Sahib* (1970) is a romantic tragedy set in the period of extreme political turbulence that ensued after the death of Maharaja Ranjit Singh in 1839. Rather than look at the history or explore its deviations, Das simply uses it as a backdrop to deal with the amorous liaison between a British officer and Maharani Jinda, and also his failed attempt to step into the Maharaja's shoes. *Larins Sahib* has been performed in major Indian cities and at the Edinburgh Festival. *Mira*, 'a rite of Krishna for five actor-dancers', was initially premiered at the La Mama Theatre in New York in 1970. It explores the phenomenon of sainthood through the story of Mirabai, the sixteenth-century Rajput poetess-saint. *The New York Times* described it as 'remarkable in the way it combined Indian legend with the sophistication of Western total theatre … [it] has something of the quality of a dream ritual'.[10] *9 Jakhoo Hill* (written in 1973–74 and staged in 1996) is set in the autumn of 1962, in Shimla. It examines a number of themes—the rise of the new middle class and the changing social order, the incestuous obsessions of an ageing uncle, the hold of Indian mothers over their sons, and the eventual betrayal of sexual love in a typically Indian situation.

Like Sharma before him, Das too had tasted Broadway success much before he found favour with the audience on the home turf. Though he worked tirelessly on his plays and injected into them an element of robust theatricality (for he is known to have worked very closely with the production units of his plays) and even managed to fashion class-specific dialogues (as in *Larins Sahib*), his plays never found many admirers in India. If what Peter Szondi says about the 'Is-ness of drama' is anything to go by, Das does not quite succeed in achieving it. To an extent, the international recognition and popularity of both Sharma and Das is directly proportionate to their efforts at exoticising Indian reality, which in a way prevented them from nativising their dramaturgy in the real sense.

It was not until Mahesh Dattani came on the scene in the late 1980s that Indian English drama found its genuine and authentic voice. Unlike the plays of Sharma and Das which have enjoyed greater success outside India, Dattani's plays have always struck a chord with Indian audiences much before they travelled abroad. One of the reasons why his plays have been so eminently successful both as dramatic texts and as performances is that, like Shakespeare, Dattani creates his plays within the spatial openness of the theatrical space. Hence, his plays are eminently 'stageable' and possess an awesome theatricality, which both surprises and intrigues critics. To a large extent, Dattani has managed to overcome the limitations that had afflicted Indian English drama and succeeded in creating plays which work both as powerful dramatic texts and equally powerful theatrical productions. This has been achieved by reproducing the speech patterns of Indian English, complete with all their inflections, verbosity, exactitude, witticisms and humour, and also by handing drama back to the 'great Indian middle class', to borrow a phrase from Pavan K. Verma. In his effort to fashion an idiom most suited to the Indian tongue, Dattani has taken recourse to common Hindi and filmy expressions, including swear words. As far as Dattani is concerned, it is not purely a matter of semantics or of nomenclature—as was the case earlier, where Jack often became Jagdish, and Jill turned into Jayshree, while Manhattan and Soho became Chowpatty and Connaught Place. Dattani has managed, quite successfully, to reinvent the spoken word that is, at once, indigenous and contemporary, and so his plays instantly strike a chord with his predominantly middle-class, English-speaking, small-town audiences.

In most of his plays, Dattani explores a wide range of contemporary social and political themes in an idiom that is both hybridised and pluralistic, reinforcing our impression that he is self-consciously engaged in the process of decolonising the English language. Though the dysfunctional Indian family remains one of the main areas of his critical scrutiny, Dattani is not merely content with capturing the process of its gradual and inevitable collapse or dissolution. Going far beyond it, he seeks to probe into the larger sociocultural framework, thereby penetrating into the dynamics of how the dissolution of the Indian family now threatens to rupture the very existence of all known forms of relationships, based upon a variety of social, political, religious or community networks.[11] Even in the face of such a dismal scenario, Dattani does not allow himself to indulge in despair. Without sounding simplistic or propagandist, he searches for robust and vital alternatives, even in the midst of apparent ruins.

It is this search for multiple identities in our context—which he attempts in terms as varied as existential, political, religious and gender-driven—that makes Dattani a truly contemporary Indian playwright. Using realism and expressionism, Dattani goes about revealing the cultural crisis of contemporary urban Indian, in a manner that is both amusing and self-assured. He deftly uses stage setting, lighting and music to capture the nuances of a cultural predicament resulting from the ongoing cultural shifts at work in contemporary urban India. Dattani's plays prove that the success of drama as an art form is dependent on its synergic relationship with society. Justifying the trend he ushered in with his *Bravely Fought the Queen* (1991), Dattani says, 'For a class-conscious lot, English used to be spoken as the white man does. There was complicity between them and their limited elitist audience because performing and watching such theatre enhanced the feeling of being a class apart. But all that is changing now.'[12] Alyque Padamsee, the famous director, actor and adman, further corroborates this when he projects Dattani as one of the agents of change in India today. He says, 'Unlike so many of his contemporaries, Dattani is not writing plays that revive old myths and legends. He is one of the few, really the only playwright in English today who writes about modern India and who uses theatre as a forum for airing social and political issues.'[13] Dattani is the first Indian English playwright to gain both popularity and recognition on his home turf, thereby reversing the trend that Sharma and Das had unwittingly set. One discerns a sense of urgency and a passionate commitment to contemporary issues and problems in several works of Dattani such as *Dance Like a Man* (1989), *Where There's a Will* (1986), *Final Solutions* (1993) and *Tara* (1990). It is no wonder that his plays have been such resounding successes everywhere.

Ironically, despite the social relevance of Dattani's themes, Alexander Viets insists that

> Indian-English theatre is still considered a theater of the elite, using a language that is used by only 10 to 12 per cent of Indians. Unlike the scores of successful novels written in English by Indian authors, playwriting is held to a different standard. People speak of Indian-English theatre as self-conscious and unnatural. Indian intellectuals whose mother tongue is English often admit to preferring regional language theatre over an English language play.[14]

This controversy over the reach of Indian English drama shall continue to dog the genre for a long time. But if we wish to resolve it, we can turn to Dattani, who has always been eager to dismiss this 'snobbism': 'English is another Indian language. To most people English theatre means English plays and English accents. If they hear Indian-English, they think, it just doesn't ring true, but that is changing, though ever so slowly.'[15]

One cannot deny the fact that Indian English drama is, today, poised at a critical juncture. Now that it has found its idiom and also its synergy with a wide cross-section of the audiences, it can definitely take a leap towards a more confident, if not an entirely secure, future. That in the last decade or so, Manjula Padmanabhan (b. 1953) has gone on to win the prestigious Onassis Award and also the much sought-after international recognition for her play *Harvest*, the only play she has written so far, is clearly a pointer in that direction. Besides, the fact that some of the younger playwrights such as Anahita Uberoi, Roysten Abel, Sunny Singh, Vikram Kapadia and several others are diligently engaged in fashioning, discovering, and even reinventing both the language and grammar of Indian English drama also augurs well for its future.

Ultimately, if Indian English drama has to secure a niche for itself in the realm of literary history, it has to enter into a dialogue with other Indian languages, and the folk, regional and mainstream traditions flourishing in the broader arena of Indian drama/theatre. In the ultimate analysis, it is this kind of synergy, resulting from an increased flow of ideas across languages, theatre traditions and institutions that shall pave the way for the kind of cultural pluralism that Indian English drama should aim at. It has to find the tangy crispness of its local voice and flavour, its responsiveness to local problems and issues, and above all, command local patronage among the growing English-speaking Indians living in the metropolises as well as the small towns. It is only by shedding all its pretensions to internationalism, and zealously pursuing its local name, habitation, character and patronage that Indian English drama can ever hope to sustain a movement or initiate a sustainable emergent trend. If it does not have to end up as an expression of a saloon culture, somewhere it may even have to fight a rather long-drawn-out battle with the other popular cultural forms such as television, Internet and cinema, whose growing penetration and popularity has been a constant threat to the very existence of all forms of theatre—local, folk, regional and national. Here again, history comes to our rescue, and our dramatists can easily take a leaf out of what Bertolt Brecht did in the 1930s to fight the overwhelming assault of cinema on theatre. He simply went ahead and incorporated cinematic techniques into theatre, thus not only reinventing European theatre, but also releasing newer possibilities for its future, which not many thought really existed then, and still fewer could anticipate.[16]

Notes and References

1. The factual and historical information on the major developments in Indian English drama of the nineteenth century has been derived largely from Mehrotra's volume. See Arvind Krishna Mehrotra, ed., *An Illustrated History of Indian Literature in English* (New Delhi: Permanent Black, 2003).
2. Bharat Gupt, *Dramatic Concepts: Greek and Indian – A Study of Poetics and Nāṭyaśāstra* (New Delhi: D.K. Printword, 1994), 86.
3. Shanta Gokhale, 'The Dramatists', in *An Illustrated History of Indian Literature in English*, ed. Arvind K. Mehrotra (New Delhi: Permanent Black, 2003), 331–50.
4. As far back as in 1784, English plays were being staged by European/ English travelling theatre groups that visited British India. Calcutta and Bombay were their preferred destinations as these two metropolitan centres, owing to certain strategic reasons, had the largest British military presence. In most of the cases, these performances were staged for the exclusive viewing of the British army and naval officers. Somewhere, this made Indian English drama acquire its elitist orientation rather early on in the process of its evolution.
5. Peter Szondi, *The Theory of Modern Drama* (Minnesota: The University of Minnesota Press, 1987).
6. This fact has been recorded by Nilufer Bharucha in 'Retreating into Tribal Mansions: Race and Religion in the Plays of Gieve Patel and Cyrus Mistry', in *Modern Indian Theatre: A Reader*, ed. Nandi Bhatia (New Delhi: Oxford University Press, 2011). She emphasises this particularly in the case of Gieve Patel and Cyrus Mistry whose work, she claims, is deeply embedded in the question of Parsi identity.
7. The influence of Parsi theatre upon the growth and development of regional theatres across north-west India is a well-known historical fact documented in several sources. See Somanatha Gupta and Kathryn Hansen, *The Parsi Theatre: Its Origin and Development* (Calcutta: Seagull Books, 2004); Stuart H. Blackburn and Vasudha Dalmia, eds., *Indian*

Literary History: Essays on the Nineteenth Century (Hyderabad: Orient Blackswan, 2004). However, its influence upon Indian English drama has not yet been assessed or evaluated. It is a matter that deserves to be investigated, both in the pre- and post-Independence phases.

8. One of the popular ways of reading or conceptualising the dilemmas and conflicts of post-Independence trends in literature and drama has been to read it in terms of the dialectics of 'tradition and modernity'. This was the time when India was breaking away from traditions and taking its first hesitant steps towards modernisation. This social and cultural situation, to a significant extent, found echoes in literature as well. For a sociological explanation of this phenomenon, see T.N. Madan, *Dialectic of Tradition and Modernity in the Sociology of D.P. Mukerji* (New Delhi: Manohar Books, 1978).

9. As quoted on the back cover of Partap Sharma, *A Touch of Brightness* (New York: Grove Press, 1978).

10. As quoted on the back cover of Gurcharan Das, *Three English Plays: Larins Sahib, Mira, 9 Jakhoo Hill* (New Delhi: Oxford University Press, 2003).

11. To see what the critics have to say on Dattani's plays, see Asha Kuthari Chaudhuri, *Mahesh Dattani: An Introduction* (New Delhi: Foundation Books, 2005); Bijoy K. Das, *Form and Meaning in Mahesh Dattani's Plays* (New Delhi: Atlantic Publishers and Distributors, 2008); Neeru Tandon, ed., *Perspectives and Challenges in Indian English Drama* (New Delhi: Atlantic Publishers and Distributors, 2006); Santosh Gupta, Urmil Talwar and Bandana Chakrabarty, *Contemporary Indian Drama: Astride Two Traditions* (Jaipur: Rawat Publishers, 2005); Shubha Tiwari, ed., *Contemporary Indian Dramatists* (New Delhi: Atlantic Publishers and Distributors, 2007).

12. As quoted by Atanu Saha in 'English Theatre: New Directions', *The Tribune*, June 29, 2001, www.tribuneindia.com/29/06/01.

13. As quoted by Alexandra Viets in 'A Stark Look at Modern India', *The New York Times*, Global Edition, July 27, 1994. www.nytimes.com/27/07/94.

14. Alexandra Viets, 'A Stark Look at Modern India'.

15. As quoted by Alexandra Viets in 'A Stark Look at Modern India'.

16. The influence of Bertolt Brecht (1898–1956), the German poet, playwright, and theatre director, on the growth and development of European drama, especially the political theatre in the twentieth century, has been phenomenal. In the early 1930s, he broke away from the Aristotelian dramaturgy almost completely and introduced an entirely radical, revolutionary idea of 'Epic Theatre', which sought to breathe

fresh lease of life into the jaded theatrical traditions all over Europe. A less-known fact about him is that he brought about this revolution in theatre at a time when theatre in Europe was fast losing out to cinema, an emergent multi-medial cultural form that sought to displace theatre from its pre-eminent hegemonic position. It is a well-known fact that Brecht did not reject cinema altogether but instead incorporated some of its techniques and strategies to re-energise and revitalise theatre itself.

SECTION TWO

Punjabi Literature: Some Contexts and Texts

CHAPTER FOUR

Punjabi Literature through the Prism of History

The beginnings of Punjabi language lie in the hoary past, going as far back as the tenth century. Its emergence in the Indo-Gangetic plain, strangely enough, coincided with the growth and development of the English language in a far-off island inhabited by the Anglo-Saxons. It is another matter that English has confidently marched on ahead, spreading across several continents, while Punjabi has had to stay confined rather diffidently to the plains of Punjab, the place of its birth. It is only in the past fifty years or so that the Punjabi people and their language have started making their presence felt across the globe. Despite their vast geographical, historical differences in terms of reach and spread, the common lineage of both English and Punjabi can obviously be traced back to the Indo-European family.

Much in the manner of other world literatures, Punjabi literature too had its beginnings in poetry. A Sufi strain was very much in evidence in the compositions of Baba Farid, a twelfth-century saint who is widely recognised as one of the early practitioners of Punjabi poetry. Though Baba Farid was not a very prolific poet—only 122 of his *shlokas* have survived—his poetry influenced not only the poetic traditions of *qissa-kavya*,[1] but also the narrative traditions of *varaans* (heroic legends) initially, and then the other forms of popular narratives such as storytelling, and long and short novels. Interestingly, the early or medieval Punjabi literature does not make any divisions among the poetic, the narrative and the dramatic traditions—the divisions that were prevalent in the West. People perceived Baba Farid's poetry as 'otherworldly', soaked as it is in mysticism and spirituality, inimical to social and material realities that gave birth to it. The lines that follow are, however, quite instructive: '*Kandhi wehan naa dhaye / toh bhi lekha dehna*' (O River! Don't rush headlong to corrode your banks / For you too shall have to answer someone, somewhere). A rich and evocative expression of the Punjabi mindset, these lines carry a warning for those who choose to disregard human values altogether, emphasising that, 'You too shall have to answer, one day.'

It needs to be emphasised that apart from being a Sufi, Farid was also an inveterate social dissenter, who raised a banner of revolt against established clergy, orthodox religious practices and the ruling establishment. This anti-hegemonic strain has been present in Punjabi literary tradition right from the times of Guru Gorakh Nath, who was responsible for starting the cult of Nāth *jogis* (Gorakhpanthis)[2] way back in the ninth century. The importance of these *jogis* to the religious and social life of their times, is evident from the verses of Charpat Nath, one of the *jogis* and known for his caustic denunciation of selfishness and hypocrisy:

> The limbs of the body have become feeble,
> The knotted hair on his head have become grey,
> And no teeth are left in his mouth.
> Taking the help of a stick, the old man walks,
> But even then, the hope (to live forever) hasn't left his body (*Charpat Shataka*, 33).

If there is a single, most dominant strain that runs through the gamut of Punjabi literary/cultural tradition, it is, undoubtedly, the element of social dissent and non-conformism. This surfaces, again and again—be it in the satirical verses of Nāth *jogis* or the Sufi poetry of Farid or other Sufis such as Bulleh Shah (1680–1757) or Waris Shah (1722–98).

Farid was conscious that only those who had already been liberated from the oppressive social or historical reality could possibly hope to develop or forge an equation with the *Murshed* or the Divine. No wonder that he strongly advocated a more personalised relationship between the devotee and the guru, the acolyte and the master, an ordinary, servile subject and the royal, sovereign 'sahib'. Both in its conception and its praxis, Farid's understanding of this dialectics is quite similar to the dynamics of *bhaktiyoga*. The *bani* (compositions) of Farid has an eternal, immutable quality about it, and it continues to resonate, in different ways, not only within the marginalised Sufi tradition but also in the dominant Sikh tradition.

For almost three hundred years after Farid, until the advent of Guru Nanak Devji (1469–1539) on the scene, Punjab went through an extended, nightmarish phase of foreign invasions, bringing its literary/cultural march to a sudden, temporary halt. Whenever violence strikes or people are faced with unstable social and political conditions, instinct for survival asserts itself rather vigorously. Such conditions do not allow creative activity to either flourish or come to fruition. Whatever little was written or produced around this time was destroyed and mutilated in the course of these innumerable foreign invasions. In the context of Punjabi literary history, this period is euphemistically known as an 'epoch of silence'. However, this does not mean that no significant body of literature was produced or written in this period. But the literature of this period does not, in any way, compare favourably with either what had preceded them or was to follow. In other words, this period was not dominated so much by individual literary efforts as it was by the community-based efforts such as *varaans* (heroic poetry).

As these *varaans* were essentially meant to celebrate the collective spirit of the people, they did little to advance or foreground the cause of the individual writers/poets. It is significant that the emergence of this genre of heroic poetry coincided with one of the most turbulent phases in the history of Punjab. In fact, *varaans* were not only steeped in the local colours and folk history but also offered a strange mix of the poetic and the narrative. Though this form had actually begun to emerge in the time of Nāth *jogis*, it began to proliferate only in this particular period. Some of the well-known *varaans* are *Var of Dulla Bhatti and Jaimal Fatta*, *Tunde Asraj di Var*, *Kahn Bhagwan di Var, Asa di Var*, etc. Sung by professional singers (*mirassis*) to entertain royalty and commoners alike, these *varaans* were more like the ballads of European literature. These songs were centred around subjects as varied as the occasions on which they were sung, ranging from the protest of a young girl refusing to adorn herself for the unsuitable man her father had chosen for her, to the travails of a people constantly under siege of invading armies. Often dealing with wars and conflicts, these *varaans* continued to surface in Punjabi literature up until the middle of the nineteenth century. In a way, Shah Mohammed's (1780–1862) *Jungnaama* (c.1846), which presents a record of the first Anglo-Sikh war (1845–6), can be seen as one of the last surviving documents of this particular genre. Apart from sensitising people about historical developments and the need to offer resistance to invaders and marauders, these *varaans* also served as significant efforts at chronicling the people's view of history.

However, this literary/cultural inertia did not last very long. There is a certain doggedness about the Punjabi character that constantly pushes itself forward, always seeking and creating newer spaces for assertion and articulation. The birth of the great poet Guru Nanak Dev in 1469 caused the flush of a new dawn, heralding a new chapter in the cultural history of Punjab. His poetic effusions do not find very many parallels in the history of the Bhakti movement, either. Spiritualism may have been the main force of his poetic content, but it always drew its ideological strength from a certain view of social reality. Perhaps, only a Punjabi sensibility could have thought of love for *Brahman* in the way Nanak essentially did: '*Jau tau prem khelan ka chau / Sir dhar tali gali mori aao*' (page 441, line 6). [Whenever you wish to play the game of divine love, come to my street, balancing your head upon your palms.]

This image of love fused with violence could not have struck roots in any soil other than that of Punjab. When the invading armies of Babar reached Punjab, Nanak commented: '*Paap ki janj lai Kabolahu dhai-i / Jori mangai dan ve Lalo*' (page 722, line 17). [Bhai Lalo! This Babar has come from Kabul, accompanied by a sinful *baraat*—his army—and is now coercing us into the act of *kanyadaan* (the act of giving away one's daughter in marriage).] As the atrocities of Babar became severe and brutal, Nanak's protest too became more strident and vociferous: '*Jin sir sohan pati-a mangi pa-e sindhoor /se sir kaati munni-anh gal wich avai dhoor*' (page 417, line 2). [This one has kicked all heads into dust, even the ones that were flower-bedecked and *sindhoor*-laden.] And when Babar's savagery became virtually intolerable, he raised his voice against it, saying, '*Je rat lage kaprai jama hoye paleet / Jo rat peeveh mansa tin keyon nirmal cheet*' (page 140, line 10). [If a piece of cloth loses its purity the moment it is stained by blood, how can all those people, who suck other people's blood, hope to retain their piety.]

This defiance in the face of tyranny and oppression is not merely a hallmark of Guru Nanak's sensitivity, it is also a cultural marker of Punjabi resilience and courage. Rejecting ritualism and superstition, Nanak emphasised social equality and brotherhood as the essence of true religion. However, once the Guru's *bani* had begun to resonate through the fields of Punjab, soaking up and fertilising its large tracts, there was no looking back. Being both philosophical and mystical in its thematic content, this *bani* ultimately found its rightful place in the Sikh scripture, the *Guru Granth Sahib*, a rare combination of the spiritual and the secular heritage of Punjab. Guru Angad (1504–52), the second of the ten Sikh gurus, contributed a great deal towards the growth and evolution of Punjabi language, as he was the one who actively promoted the Gurmukhi script by extensively using it for his teachings.

However, the ambitious project of compiling the *banis* of the Sikh gurus in the form of the holy *Guru Granth Sahib* was initiated by none other than Guru Arjan Dev (1563–1606), the fifth guru, a process completed by Guru Gobind Singh (1666–1708), the tenth guru. The *Guru Granth Sahib* is truly a repository of the collective wisdom of the Sikh gurus, a confluence of all faiths—Sikhism, Hinduism and Islam. Composed in thirty-one different *ragas*, the hymns of the *Guru Granth Sahib* correspond to different moods, times and seasons. Apart from the verses and teachings of the Sikh gurus, *Guru Granth Sahib* gives a fair representation to the hymns and thoughts of Kabir (1440–1518), Namdev (1270–1350), Ravidas (fifteenth century AD), Sheikh Farid and several others. In the context of Punjabi literature, *Guru Granth Sahib* occupies the same pre-eminent, canonical position that is often conceded to the *Bible* in the realm of English literature. Undoubtedly, it is one of the greatest works of poetry and/or literature in the history of Punjabi culture and tradition.

Apart from poetry, the other literary forms that are often associated with Guru Nanak Dev are called the *Janam Sakhis* or the life stories of Guru Nanak. Believed to have been written between 1620 and 1640, these *Sakhis* are, in fact, hagiographies, concatenation of anecdotes about Nanak's life gathered from oral sources, primarily with a view to establish his divinity. Almost every anecdote either reveals his teachings or emphasises his divinity by projecting him as a miracle man. The language of these *Sakhis* is either a combination of two dialects or the Multani or the central dialect, and all of them bear a strong influence of *Braj Bhasha* (a dialect of Hindi predominantly spoken in central India). The syntax is often simple, and the imagery homespun and domestic. Hence, the *Janam Sakhis* instantly appeal to the popular mind.

If on the one hand, medieval Punjabi literature was dominated by Sikh thought and philosophy, on the other, it was ceaselessly nurtured by the uninterrupted flow of Sufi poetry, in forms as varied as *qissa* (a narrative in verse), *kaafi* (a poetic form) and *masnavi* (another form of poetic expression). Though Sassi-Pannu, Sohni-Mahiwal, Mirza-Sahiban, and Heer-Ranjha are some of the prominent tragic love legends of Punjab, it is Heer-Ranjha that has had a perennial fascination for the Punjabi mind and occupied a privileged, archetypal position in the cultural mindscape of the Punjabis down the ages. No wonder that various poets—from Damodar Gulati to Ahmed Yar, Muqbal and Waris Shah—have worked on this eternal legend, in the process producing its different versions. However, it is Waris Shah's *Heer* that has acquired a legendary status in the folk history/culture of Punjab, as it continues to live in the minds and hearts of the common people who often recite it during formal village assemblies or informal poetic gatherings. Written in 1766, Shah's *Heer* is a significant social and historical document as it chronicles a particular period in the history of Punjab, the period when the Mughal Empire was in decline, the British East India Company was spreading its tentacles across India and the pernicious invasions of Nadir Shah and Ahmad Shah Abdali were ruining Punjabi folk life and culture. The other prominent Sufi poets of the medieval period are Shah Hussein (1539–93), Sultan Bahu (1631–91), Bulleh Shah, Hashim Shah (1753–1823), Amam Baksh (1778–1863), Kadir Yar (1805–65), etc. Later, in the modern period, this strain of Sufi poetry reincarnated itself in the poetry of Bhai Mohan Singh Vaid (1881–1936), Shiv Kumar Batalvi (1936–73), Surjit Patar (b. 1944) and several others.

The emergence of modern Punjabi literature, ironically, coincided with the beginnings of the British rule in the region in the early 1850s. This was followed by a number of developments that helped the emergence of modernism in Punjabi literature and culture. A Christian mission had been established in Ludhiana in 1835. A printing press using the Gurmukhi script was installed here, and the first work on Punjabi grammar was printed at this press in 1838. The year 1854 saw the publication of a Punjabi dictionary by Reverend J. Newton. The Singh Sabha Movement of the 1860s—opposed to the proselytising efforts of Hindus and Christians—also facilitated this ripple-down. The term 'modernism', as used in this discussion, is an umbrella term that covers a whole range of developments in Punjabi literary culture—starting with the break from traditions or the past to a commitment to progressive ideology, from the experimental nature of the avant-garde to the newness of forward-looking movements.

Bhai Veer Singh (1872–1957) is often seen as the harbinger of this modernism in the realms of Punjabi poetry and novel. Starting off as a pamphleteer, Singh soon evolved into a major literary figure of his times. He contributed a large body of trailblazing literary works. If Singh retrieved Punjabi poetry from the excesses of its Persian counterpart, he also energised its narrative traditions by shaping the Western form of the novel to suit indigenous expressions and ideologies. Though his poetry, with its dominant mystical strain, can easily be categorised as part of the Sikh philosophical tradition and thought, his efforts at creating historical romances such as *Sundari* (1898), *Satwant Kaur* (published in two parts, in 1900 and 1927, respectively) and *Baba Naudh Singh* (serialised in 1907 and published in book form in 1921) largely remain imitative of Walter Scott and his ilk.

Breaking away from such imitative efforts and under the reformist influence of the Singh Sabha Movement, Nanak Singh (1897–1971) successfully rooted the Punjabi novel in the very soil and substance of Punjab. Turning to the indigenous modes of storytelling such as *qissa*, which were popular in the medieval period, Singh gave the Punjabi novel a distinctive local character and habitation. It was through his efforts that the novel managed to reclaim not only its vital link with the oral tradition, but also its soft, delicate formless texture. In his novels, fluidity of sentimentalism goes hand in hand with the ideological concerns of a social reformer, something that Sohan Singh Seetal (1909–2006) and Jaswant Singh Kanwal (b. 1919), who were to come later, also tried to emulate.

Interestingly, the genre of *anchalik upanyas* (the regional novel, whose beginnings literary historians often trace back to Phaneshwar Nath Renu's Hindi novel *Maila Anchal*) made its first appearance in Punjabi litearture. Kartar Singh Duggal's (b. 1917) *Andraan* (The Entrails, 1949)—a novel written in the *Pothoari* dialect and steeped in the local culture of the same region and its geography, economy, ecology, customs and conventions—was published as far back as 1948. In a way, emergence of this particular form of novel did help in foregrounding hard-core social realism in Punjabi novel, which was to acquire its ideological underpinnings from a curious blend of Marxist thought and Gandhian socialism. Sant Singh Sekhon (1908–97), Surinder Singh Narula (1917–2000), Amrita Pritam (1919–2005) and Narinder Pal Singh (b. 1923), among several others, made consistent and significant contributions towards this paradigm shift. By enabling fiction to shed its obsessive, maudlin sentimentality and its quasi-romantic character, these luminaries slowly but surely paved the way for the advent of a truly modernist novel in Punjabi, with a distinctive psychological and sociological thrust.

Until the times of Gurdial Singh (b. 1933), two diametrically opposed ideologies—a brand of naïve romanticism and an indigenous form of realism—had continued to exert pressures and counter-pressures upon the content and/or form of the Punjabi novel. Apart from these ideological tensions, which helped shape the aesthetic concerns as well as their articulation, Punjabi fiction had continued to shift back and forth between the rural and the urban, the past and the present, and the poetic and the realistic. The historical importance of Singh's fiction lies in the fact that it sought to encapsulate the dialectics of tradition and modernity, even tried to attain a rare synthesis of the two, wherever possible—something that had eluded Punjabi fiction until then. If Singh radicalised the Punjabi novel by infusing into it a new consciousness about the oppressed/underprivileged, Ajit Cour (b. 1934) and Daleep Kaur Tiwana (b. 1935) opened up newer possibilities by interrogating the marginalised status/position of Punjabi women in a heavily accented, feudal and patriarchal societal regime. Niranjan Tasneem, Mohan Kahlon, Surjit Sethi and several others, in their distinctive ways, have continued to push the frontiers of Punjabi fiction.

Apart from Bhai Veer Singh, Dhani Ram 'Chatrik' (1876–1954), Puran Singh (1881–1931), Mohan Singh (1905–78) and Amrita Pritam are among the prominent poets of the first generation, who sought to re-inscribe the ideology and aesthetics of Punjabi poetry in the modern context. Though in some form or the other, their poetry bore the scars of the trauma of Partition, each one had her/his own idiom and distinct voice. Steeped in the Indian tradition of romance and conforming to the classical rigour, Chatrik used poetry to celebrate varied moods of nature or, occasionally, to evoke an undying sense of patriotism through his nationalist verses. Brought up on a heavy dose of English and American poetry, Puran Singh was definitely more liberal and direct than most of his predecessors, and his poetic expression always bristled with naked sensuousness and primal celebration of the human body. Most explicitly Freudian, he openly proclaims in one of his poems, 'I want to be an animal again.' Mohan Singh could be described as a 'progressive modern' for it was he who liberated Punjabi poetry from the constraints of mysticism and/or revivalism. His range was simply astounding as he moved imperceptibly from the romantic felicities of *Saave Pattar* to the political consciousness of *Adhvate*, from the Freudian flights of *Kasumbhara* to the socialist fancies of *Vadda Vela*. If there is anything that defines Amrita Pritam's poetry, it is the boldness of her expression, pungency of her social criticism and the relentless critique of defunct morality that often works to the detriment of women. In a poem entitled *Kumwari* (The Virgin) in her collection *Kagaz Te Canvas*, which won her the prestigious Jnanpith, she tells the story of a young girl in her characteristic sardonic tone:

When I moved into your bed
I was not alone there – there were two of us
A married woman and a virgin
To sleep with you
I had to offer the virgin in me
I did so

This slaughter is permitted in law
Not the indignity of it . . . .

In the 1950s, when Mohan Singh and Amrita Pritam had already won great accolades and the future of Punjabi poetry did not appear to be very encouraging, it was the soul-stirring lyricism of Shiv Batalvi (1936–73) and the thought-content of Harbhajan Singh (1920–2002) that infused new possibilities into it. Attuning himself to the raw, jagged rhythms of his work-a-day, earthy life, Shiv Batalvi created such haunting melodies of pain and suffering that they continue to resound in our hearts even today. A skilful craftsman of words, he had this rare ability to make even a fleeting, ordinary moment pulsate with eternal possibilities. To this day, his poetic drama *Luna*, in which he reinterpreted the popular legend of Puran Bhagat from a woman's standpoint, remains one of the best works ever produced in contemporary Punjabi literature. Harbhajan Singh's breadth of experience and range of sympathies are simply unnerving, as he responds to the bombing of Hiroshima and Nagasaki with the same inwardness with which he portrays the exploitation of an underdog in his own society. Often his aestheticism becomes a challenge to the critical and militant mood of the progressives, as in these lines:

Whenever I enter into a dialogue with you
My breath sends out notes of a flute
....Or if you cannot trust yourself with the flute
You may ply your sword on the flute and go.

Among the second generation of poets, we may mention Pritam Singh 'Safeer', Santokh Singh Dheer (1920–2010), Prabhjot Kaur and Jaswant Singh Neki (b. 1927). They, through their varied contributions, enriched the ever-growing corpus of modern Punjabi poetry.

In the 1960s, Punjab suddenly found itself in the vortex of the Naxalite movement, like in the case of many other states where the failure to implement land reforms had backfired. So extensive was the influence of this movement that it threatened to swallow up all the benefits that had accrued on account of the Green Revolution. These conditions led the progressive movement into its militant phase, with Bawa Balwant (1915–72), Paash (1950–88), Ravinder Ravi (b. 1937), Ajaib Kamal (b. 1932), Harbhajan Halwarwi, Amarjit Chandan (b. 1946) and several others emerging as its major votaries. While others, fearing persecution, migrated to foreign lands, Paash, Bawa Balwant and Halwarwi continued to spearhead the movement, even when it was on the decline. Later, when the high tide of terrorism swept through Punjab, Paash and Ravinder Ravi fell to assassins' bullets. But while they lived, Paash and his friends were swept off by the ideology of Ernesto 'Che' Guevara and Fidel Castro, and charmed by the poetic practices of Pablo Neruda and Octavio Paz. They have left behind a rich corpus of poetry that sizzles with political radicalism and revolutionary fervour, and articulates a transnational commitment to the solidarity of the oppressed.

Though this phase did not last very long, it seems to have left a lasting impact on the growth of contemporary Punjabi poetry. Surjit Pattar and Dr Jagtar were among those who came riding the crest of militancy. They have, over the years, softened a great deal, and now integrate their lyrical aestheticism with social criticism. In one of his verses, written during the heydays of militancy, Pattar agonises over the tragedy, saying,

> This Punjab spanning two rivers and a half
> Perhaps belongs to a political leader
> I'm not a leader
> My Punjab was done to death
> A long time ago.

A gentle, persuasive irony runs through the whole gamut of his poetry, though sometimes, he does allow the mellifluousness of his Sufi-like voice dominate, especially in his *ghazals*, through which he has helped redefine and expand the frontiers of Punjabi poetry in recent times. Among others, some of the younger poets who have left an indelible impact on the contemporary scene are Mohanjit, Jaswant Deed, Swrajbir, Joga Singh, Sati Kumar and Dev.

Another feature of modern Punjabi poetry is the presence of an overwhelmingly large number of women poets, who have impressed their readers not only by virtue of their prolific output but also the quality of their contributions. Manjit Tiwana, Pal Kaur, Surjit Kalsi,

Nirupama Dutt, Gagan Gill, Amar Jyoti and Vineeta are some of the younger women poets who, through their sustained interrogation of patriarchy, have charted new paths in the Punjabi poetic tradition. Not only are they more liberal and less inhibited in their portrayal of man–woman relationships, but also more aggressively innovative in fashioning the contours of an entirely new 'female aesthetics'. Unlike their predecessors, who thought women were incomplete without men; these poets emphasised the emotional and intellectual autonomy of women, thus bringing significant questions of gender identity and difference to the fore. One of the collections of Amar Jyoti is significantly titled as *Mainun Sita Naa Kaho* (Don't You Call Me Sita!). Confronted with the maniacal frenzy of terrorism, Manjit Tiwana is forced to ask: 'What times are these / Sitting on its threshold / We ask the whereabouts of our home.'

It is an established historical fact that the short story, in its archival, primeval form, is essentially Indian in its origin and character, and that its beginnings can safely be traced back to its mythological/archetypal sources such as the *Mahabharata*, *Pauranik* tales, *Panchtantra, Kathasaritsagara* and *Jatak* tales. It is also a fact that, owing to a large number of factors, the short story slowly lost out its pre-eminent position in our literary culture and did not regain it up until the end of the nineteenth or the beginning of the twentieth century. When it finally did resurface in several Indian languages, including Punjabi, it carried a definitive ideological and aesthetic imprint of the realistic form that Balzac, Flaubert, Maupassant, Chekhov and other European masters had helped to develop.

Charan Singh Shaheed (1891–1935), Joshua Fazal Deen, Heera Singh Dard (1889–1965) and Nanak Singh (1897–1971) were among the early practitioners of the short story in Punjabi. Proliferation of printing presses across Punjab, mushrooming of literary magazines, journals and newspapers, and the spread of literary education helped in popularising this form in its early days. In its initial stages, at least, the Punjabi short story was subversively used as a tool for propagating Sikh ideology and thought, as most of the storytellers also happened to be strong votaries of the Singh Sabha Movement.

With the emergence of Gurbaksh Singh Preetlari, Sant Singh Sekhon, Kulwant Singh Virk (1921–87), Kartar Singh Duggal and Sujan Singh, the Punjabi short story anchored itself firmly into progressive, Marxist ideology. This was also the time when attempts were made to harmonise the conflicting claims of ideology and aesthetics. More than others, it was Virk who understood and responded rather well to the multiple challenges that the short story, as a modern form, often poses. Along with his irresistible penchant for the dramatic mode, his stories reveal his remarkable sense of control over his material and expression. Virk knew the art of counterbalancing economy of style with forceful and profound understanding of human psychology. Most of Virk's successors—especially Mohan Bhandari, Gurbachan Bhullar, Prem Parkash and Gulzar Sandhu—owe their broad sense of 'new humanism' and 'catholicism', and their understanding of the art and craft of story writing, to him. This tradition is being ably supported and enriched through the efforts of some of the promising storytellers on the scene today, among whom we could easily count people like Chandan Negi, Jasbir Bhullar, Prem Gorky, Waryam Sandhu, Swaran Chandan, Harjit Atwal and Veena Verma. It would not be preposterous to claim that contemporary Punjabi short story, being an extremely vibrant and innovative form, has a fairly bright future, and even the potential to compete with the best anywhere in the world.

Unlike the short story, drama as a form in Punjabi has not had a very eventful or a consistent track record of growth and evolution. Interestingly, the beginnings of the Punjabi drama/theatre are often traced back to the fortuitous efforts of Norah Richards (1876–1971), the Irish wife of a Unitarian minister preaching in Punjab. An amateur actor, she had also been associated with the Irish National Theatre in Dublin. Around 1913–14, Richards started drama competitions among her students at Dyal Singh College, Lahore, where she was a teacher. It was in one of these competitions that Ishwar Nanda, then a student and now widely recognised as one of the pioneers of Punjabi drama, discovered his talent for playwriting. His one-act play *Suhag* (1913) was adjudged the best and that marked the beginning of the indigenous theatre movement in Punjabi. Nanda went on to write over twenty one-act plays, all of which show a definite influence of Ibsen, fired as he was by an unsparing zeal for social reform and change.

Among others, this tradition of playwriting found able and worthy legatees in Sant Singh Sekhon, Gurdial Singh Phul and Harcharan Singh, who not only strengthened but also nurtured the dramatic tradition founded by Nanda. From time to time, Kartar Singh Duggal, Surjit Sethi, Harsharan Singh and Balwant Gargi contributed significantly towards the incremental growth of this tradition. Of course, Gursharan Singh (1929–2001) stands apart by virtue of his formidable contribution to the popularity and growth of street theatre in the far off villages of Punjab. Over a period of time, Punjabi drama has not only acquired a distinctive identity of its own, but also managed to get overwhelming support from the public as well as the much needed official recognition. That for two successive years, Sahitya Akademi has chosen to confer its prestigious literary award upon two eminent playwrights in Punjabi, Charan Das Sidhu and Ajmer Aulakh, is ample proof of the kind of popularity Punjabi drama is beginning to enjoy.

Atamjit Singh, who invariably writes and directs his own plays, and whose talent and genius has, at long last, been recognised by the Sahitya Akademi very recently, is no less competent than any of his contemporaries. Atamjit has, in fact, crossed the narrow, geographical barriers of Punjab and staged his plays in Canada as well as the US. Neelam Man Singh Chaudhury is another person who is responsible for giving international exposure to Punjabi theatre, though she is primarily a director, not a playwright. Fusing elements of Punjabi folk and classical forms such as the *dhadhi* (a form of recital), *kavishar* (an ad-lib performance) and *gatha* (martial arts), she has, under the banner of her production house, The Company, staged plays in France, England, Germany, Japan, the US and elsewhere.

One could also go into the growth of Punjabi prose and criticism, but as there are constraints of space, we will have to leave it out of the scope of the present essay. Also, we have not been able to take up the literature produced by the Punjabi diaspora as a separate category. Despite that, this essay has tried to offer a comprehensive view of Punjabi literature and/or its history. In the ultimate analysis, all surveys only succeed in offering a bird's-eye view of the subject, and howsoever hard one may try, often remain partial and even prejudiced. Though we have not been able to cover all the major trends, movements and developments that have swept through Punjabi literature and/or its literary forms in the course of its long march over a thousand years or so, we have certainly tried to map out some of the major ones.

Notes

1. *Qissa-kavya*: The word '*qissa*' is of Arabic origin and found its early expression in this very language, especially through the efforts of writers in West Asia. Some of the early *qissas* were based on the love story of Yusuf and Zuleikha inscribed in the Holy Quran. Usually, a love story constitutes the core component of a *qissa*, but it also extrapolates both the secular and the sacred meanings of 'love'. Human love in *qissas* is treated as an expression of divine love and vice versa. Essentially a poetic form of narration, *qissa*, like other medieval literary forms, is also allegorical in nature. Written in the local dialect, preferably in the dialogue form, interlaced with sights, sounds and flavours of the local community, geographical terrain or region, *qissa* often transcends the local and the personal to acquire universal signification. It is in order to emphasise the poetic character of *qissa* that the term *kavya* is sometimes suffixed to it. Some of the popular *qissa-kavyas* in Punjabi language are those of Mirza–Sahiban, Heer–Ranjha, Sassi–Punnu, Shirin–Farhaad, Sohni–Mahival, etc. The later Sufi poets in Punjabi such as Waris Shah, Ahmed Yar and Kadir Yar used *qissa* as an instrument of social criticism. Through this poetic form, they articulated their denunciation and disapproval of the existing social/cultural conventions and practices.
2. The Sanskrit word '*nāthā*' is the proper name of a Hindu initiatory tradition and the word itself literally means 'lord', 'protector' or 'refuge'. The related Sanskrit term *Adi Natha* means the first or original Lord, and is therefore a synonym for Shiva, Mahadeva or Maheshvara, and beyond these supramental concepts, the Supreme Absolute Reality, as the basis supporting all aspects and manifestations of consciousness. The *nath* tradition is a heterodox *siddha* tradition containing many subsects. It was founded by Matsyendranath and further developed by Gorakshanath. These two individuals are also revered in Tibetan Buddhism as *Mahasiddhas* (great adepts) and are credited with great powers and

perfected spiritual attainment. The *Nath* is known to lead the followers like a mother. Gorakhnath (often called Goraksha, Gorakshanath, or simply Gorakh) is an elusive figure historically. He is many things to many people. Gorakhnath is traditionally said to be the originator of Hatha Yoga, the yogic system of *asanas* (physical postures) that are part of the Tantric alchemical process of physical perfection and energetic awakening. He is one the semi-divine siddhas and is considered to be the founder of the *nath siddha* lineages, the supreme guru of the Gorakhnathi *Jogis*. For some, Gorakhnath is no less than an incarnation of Shiva himself. Gorakhnath is also a bearer of the Buddhist *Tantra* lineage in Tibet. Gorakhnath is said to be the author of the *Goraksha Paddhati* (Track of Goraksha, also called the *Goraksha Samhita*, a foundational treatise on esoteric Hatha Yoga, translated into Georg Fuerstein's excellent book *The Yoga Tradition*), *Goraksha Shataka* (Goraksha's 100 Verses), and several other works.

References

Banerjee, Tarasankar. 1987. *Historiography and Modern Indian Languages 1800–1947*. Calcutta: Naya Prakashan.

Brown, Kerry. 1997. *Sikh Art and Literature*. London: Routledge.

Diwana, Mohan Singh. 1972. *History of Punjabi Literature*. Patiala: Publications Bureau.

Kohli, Surinder Singh. 1993. *History of Punjabi Literature*. New Delhi: National Book Shop.

Majumdar, Ramesh Chander. 1969. *The History and Culture of the Indian People*. Vol. 7. London: G. Allen and Unwin.

Nabha, Bhai Kahan Singh. 2006. *Encyclopedia of Sikh Literature*. Vol. I. Patiala: Publications Bureau.

Narang, C.L. 1997. *History of Punjabi Literature 850–1850 AD*. New Delhi: South Asia Books.

Ray, Niharranjan. 1975. *The Sikh Gurus and the Sikh Society*. New Delhi: Munshiram Manoharlal.

Sekhon, Sant Singh, and Kartar Singh Duggal. 1992. *A History of Punjabi Literature*. New Delhi: Sahitya Akademi.

Serebriakev, Igor Dmitrievich. 1975. *Punjabi Literature: An Outline*. Moscow: Progressive Books.

Shackle, Christopher, Arvind-pal Singh Mandair, and Gurharpal Singh. 2001. *Sikh Religion, Culture and Ethnicity*. London: Routledge.

Uberoi, Mohan Singh. 1971. *A History of Punjabi Literature* (1100–1932). New Delhi: Sadasiva Prakashan.

CHAPTER FIVE

The Novel as a Site of Cultural Memory: Gurdial Singh's *Parsa*

Plato's famous dictum about writers and artists can well be a fitting prelude to a discussion on Gurdial Singh's (b. 1933) *Parsa* (1991). In his *Republic*, Plato stated that he looked upon a carpenter as a far better, far superior artist than the poet or the painter.[1] For Plato, the carpenter embodied the image of a complete artist, or rather that of a complete human being. After all, he was the one who imbued the formless with a sense of form and structure, infusing the rugged material reality with untold creative possibilities.

By all counts, Gurdial Singh answers the Platonic description of a complete artist rather well. Born to a carpenter father who insisted that his young son should step into his shoes, Singh chose to become a carpenter of words, a sculptor of human forms and a painter of life in all its myriad hues. When he was refused funding by his parents for an education beyond Matric, he decided to be his own mentor, slowly toiling his way up from the position of a JBT (Junior Basic Training) teacher to a school lecturer, from there to a college lecturer and ultimately, a professor at the Regional Centre of Punjabi University. This is a saga of courage, a profile in patience and gritty determination, which reads more like a work of fiction in progress. As one of the most illustrious exponents of Punjabi language and culture, he has served its cause for well over four decades now.

While reading the classics, Singh developed a strong, irrepressible desire to emulate the literary masters. Life had taught him quite early on that the social milieu, locale and specific problems varied according to the cultural context, and he worked hard to first discover and then hone his own distinctive literary voice. His own life and personal convictions born out of his experiences motivated him to identify with the poor and the marginalised. It was this 'authentic' presentation of a slice of life that gave him his early success. In 1957, he published his first ever story, 'Bhaganwale' (Chosen by Destiny), in *Panj Darya*, a magazine then edited by Mohan Singh, the well-known Punjabi poet. Most of his stories were published in *Preetlari*, edited by the redoubtable Gurbaksh Singh, the eminent Punjabi novelist and short story writer. Singh tasted success as a novelist when he published his first major, path-breaking work *Marhi Da Deeva* (Memorial Lamp) in 1964. Translated into English as *The Last Flicker* (brought out by Sahitya Akademi in 1991), it was hailed as a modern classic soon after it appeared in print. This early success was followed up with equally powerful and significant works of long fiction such as *Unhoye* (The Survivors, 1966), *Kuwela* (The Inauspicious Hour, 1968), *Addh Chanini Raat* (Night of the Half-moon, 1972), *Anhe Ghore Da Daan* (Alms in the Name of a Blind Horse, 1976), *Parsa* (1991) and *Aahan* (The Locusts, 2007).

Despite his immense success and popularity as a pioneering novelist in Punjabi, Singh continues to nurture his first love for short fiction. It is no wonder that he has managed to produce as many as eight collections of short stories so far, the more notable among them being *Saggi Phul* (The Ornaments, 1962), *Kutta Te Aadmi* (The Dog and the Man, 1971), *Begana Pindh* (An Alien Village, 1985) and *Kareer Di Dhingri* (The Kareer Branch, 1991). Apart from the ten novels, all of which have been widely read and acclaimed, he has authored three plays, two prose works and no less than nine books for children. Besides, he has translated several of his own works into Hindi and those of the other reputed Indian and non-Indian writers into Punjabi. In addition to *Marhi Da Deeva*, three other novels of his—*Addh Chanini Raat* (*Night of the Half-moon*, 1996), *Parsa* (2000) and *Unhoye* (*The Survivors*, 2005)—are available in English translations.

Gurdial Singh's Fiction in Perspective

To assess the importance and merits of Singh's literary output, one needs to read his works in the wider linguistic, historical and cultural frame of Punjabi literature—both the past and the contemporary. As we have discussed in the preceding chapter, the

Punjabi novel began to emerge in the latter half of the nineteenth century. The early novels in the language, such as the works of Bhai Veer Singh, were clearly influenced by the European models.[2] The Punjabi novel found its first nativist effort in the works of Nanak Singh (1897–1971) who strove to find a local idiom for the genre, drawing upon traditional modes of storytelling. Nanak Singh had worthy successors in writers like Sohan Singh Seetal and Jaswant Singh Kanwal. A related development was the emergence of the *anchalik upanyas* ('regional' novel), with its stark social realism, in Punjabi literature. The social and political consciousness that comes through the works of writers such as Sant Singh Sekhon, Surinder Singh Narula, Amrita Pritam or Narinder Pal Singh ushered the Punjabi novel into a truly modernist phase.

Singh's early works appeared in a context where two diametrically opposite ideologies—a brand of naïve romanticism and an indigenous form of realism—had continued to influence the Punjabi novel. Punjabi fiction had long been shifting back and forth between the rural and the urban, the past and the present, the poetic and the realistic. Against this background, Singh's fiction attained a rare synthesis of tradition and modernity. Conscious of his role in reconstituting the novelistic discourse, he ruptured the tradition of the Punjabi novel from within, while continuing to nurture it from without. By pulling the genre out of the morass of bourgeois morality into which it had largely sunk in its post-Independence phase, he opened up possibilities that would have otherwise remained unrealised.

Though not strictly a proponent of the *anchalik upanyas*, Singh could be seen as an exponent of the regional novel in the sense in which Thomas Hardy and R.K. Narayan essentially were. In novel after novel, he has assiduously recreated the insulated, self-enclosed and provincial world of the Malwa region, comprising parts of Punjab and Haryana between the Sutlej and the Yamuna rivers. He has lived all his life in the region and he understands and empathises with its dreams and desires, its folklore and culture. Most of his novels seek to capture the distinctive flavour of the regional (*Malwai*) dialect and its linguistic angularities. Malwa comes alive in his novels both as a place in history and as a cultural metaphor. Its stubborn and unyielding land, sandy soil and prickly air, low-roofed mud houses and vast open fields mingle and overlap with stifling caste prejudices and intriguing questions of land ownership. They come together to create a befitting backdrop to his incomparable sagas of human courage, resilience and sacrifice. However, the self-limiting nature of the Malwa region does not in any way prevent Singh from giving the readers an artistically wholesome expression of the complexities of life he has set out to explore.

Singh's works have radicalised the Punjabi novel and re-inscribed its ideological and/or aesthetic space by infusing into it a new consciousness about the underprivileged and the oppressed. Commenting on *Marhi Da Deeva*, Namwar Singh, an eminent Hindi critic, once said, 'When the novel was a dying art form in Europe in the middle of the nineteenth century, it was Tolstoy's *War and Peace* that resurrected the faith in novel as a form. In a similar fashion, when in the Indian languages, novel was going through its worst ever crisis, Gurdial Singh's *Marhi Da Deeva* revitalised this form as only he could.'[3] Through *Marhi Da Deeva*, for the first time ever in the history of Punjabi fiction, a social and economic outcast leapt out of his shadowy terrain into the centre stage of the 'fictionscape'. However, while projecting the sufferings of the hopelessly marginalised individuals and social classes/castes in a rather involved manner, Singh has never lost sight of the imaginative/creative demands of his own vocation as a novelist. Often seen as a proponent of hard-core social realism, he is equally at ease with the poetic and the symbolic modes of expression.

Even his sternest critics unhesitatingly concede that Singh has ploughed fresh ground by turning the genre of the novel in Punjabi into a trenchant critique of dominant social discourses without in any way compromising on its poetic resonances. Steeped in history without being explicitly 'historical', his fiction mediates its way through myriad, and often disparate, cross-currents of mainstream as well as folk traditions of storytelling, latent in both 'orature' and 'ecriture'. Though he did radicalise the Punjabi novel by infusing it with greater ideological strength and vitality, at the level of the form, he is neither an exhibitionist nor a maverick experimentalist. Convinced that the form must ultimately follow the dictates of the content, Singh describes himself, after the Hungarian Marxist philosopher Georg Lukacs' well-known phrase, as a 'critical realist'. As Lukacs defined it, devoid of the bourgeois obsession with formalist experiments, 'critical realism' is the preferred mode of artistic expression for a socially conscious writer. Though there are 'organic' links among all his fictional works, Singh has never returned to the same subject or style ever again. An inveterate progressive, he subscribes to the Darwinian notion of continuous, uninterrupted struggle with the environment/circumstances, and also to the positivism of the evolutionary principle, while rejecting their ruthless competitiveness, as much as his characters often do.

Gurdial Singh's Fiction: A Brief Overview

In *Parsa*, a lower-caste *siri* (servant), Tindi, requests his benevolent master to tell him an 'interesting story'. On being asked what really makes for such a story, Tindi first hesitates and then shoots off a counter-question: 'Why are the stories always about kings and princes?'[4] More than a mere rhetorical question, it is the very raison d'être of Singh's counter-narratives. He has consistently and tirelessly tried to put the dispossessed, the dislocated and the underprivileged in the centre of his fiction. From a poor, illiterate farmhand, a small-time labourer or a peasant, to an overburdened rickshaw-puller or a low-caste carpenter—it is always the primal rawness of human life that strikes a sympathetic chord with Singh.

Conceived as victims of social/historical tyranny, most of Singh's characters fight back even in the face of imminent defeat. He strongly believes that a human being's ultimate dharma is to fight the tyranny and the oppression built into his/her own situation. This means that his characters and even his novels are imbued with a definite sense of tragic inevitability. This is certainly much more pronounced in his early novels, such as *Marhi Da Deeva* and *Kuwela*, than in his later works. While Jagseer in *Marhi Da Deeva* falls an easy prey to the machinations of a beguiling feudal power play, Heera Dei in *Kuwela* stands firm, refusing to cringe before a taboo-ridden society. However, the heroic or revolutionary potential of his characters began to surface with the creation of Bishna in *Unhoye* and Moddan in *Addh Chanini Raat*. Unlike Jagseer, both Bishna and Moddan not only refuse steadfastly to become accomplices in the process of their own marginalisation but also make untiring efforts to rise in revolt against this process. They even go so far as to interrogate the dehumanising social/legal practices working against them, but they stop short of overturning them. It is their lack of self-awareness that ultimately makes failed revolutionaries out of them. With *Parsa*, a novel named after the central character, a Jat-Brahmin, the dialectics turns inwards. Parsa's consciousness becomes the ultimate battleground where social tensions and conflicts wage their most fierce and intense battle. Parsa seeks to overcome the tyranny of caste and class divisions not through exclusion or rejection, but assimilation and inclusion. All forms of contradictions find a happy resolution in his person. It is in recognition of this fact that *Parsa* has widely been acclaimed as an important cultural text, a real triumph of Singh's lifelong commitment to the art of fiction. It is quite rare for any writer to make an attempt to reclaim the diverse and complex strands of his cultural memory within the scope of a single work of fiction, and that too with some measure of success. In this respect, *Parsa* remains a rare instance in contemporary Punjabi literature.

There is both a touch of authenticity and self-absorption about Singh's ability to fashion a wide range of characters. But he does not ever allow his interest in or sympathy for his character(s) to either overwhelm or undermine his primary commitment to social concerns. For him, each and every one of his characters is essentially a social and historical being. As a natural corollary, his characters remain intermediate agents—individualised, yet typical concretisations of the context in which they live and operate.

All his novels are set amid the shifting contours of the Malwa region whose economic backwardness sometimes obscures its cultural richness. It is significant that despite his emphasis on its local colours, sounds and smells, Malwa manages to become, in his fiction, a microcosm of the world within which the larger drama of human existence plays itself out. Working within this framework, Singh has managed to convey richly evocative vignettes of rural life, complete with the region's distinctive codes, customs and conventions. He is always alive to its throbbing pulse and rhythm. He sees a village not as static but as an ever-changing, dynamic unit. Often, the trauma of change is chronicled with an unnerving sense of verisimilitude. It is this dialectics of tradition and modernity that gives an overarching expression to his insistent social concern.

Marhi Da Deeva relocates the twin questions of ownership and dispossession within the ambit of the Green Revolution and redefines them. *Kuwela* probes into the problem of widow remarriage in an orthodox Hindu society. *Rete di ik Muthi* is a sensitive portrayal of how the blind pursuit of materialism leads to slow erosion of human values such as love and fidelity. *Anhe Ghore Da Daan* bemoans the loss of kinship culture, casting an oblique look at the issue of shrinking land-holding and attendant problems of forced migration, unemployment and destitution. Set in pre-Independence India, *Unhoye* records the impact of the nation's early forays into industrialisation with a rare precision, and shows how dehumanisation creeps in, in the process, almost imperceptibly. Unlike his other works, *Parsa* is not so tangibly located in a time–space continuum. As the main focus of the novel is on reclaiming the rich literary/cultural history of Punjab, social reality is just marginally touched upon. It is almost as if, after having created several narratives of oppression and marginalisation, and failed rebellions, Singh has broken free through *Parsa*, moving rather self-assuredly towards a 'narrative of emancipation'. For those readers who have walked with him through the fire and brimstone of the inferno that Jagseer, Moddan or Bishna lived through, *Parsa* brings the ultimate, much-awaited 'Dantesque' vision of the Paradise.

Even when he portrays social realities in all their searing passion, as he does in his earlier novels, Singh takes care not to allow the narratives to become either morbid or squeamish. He retains the poetic nature of his narratives and this helps him smooth out the jagged edges of social realities. His novels function the way poetic metaphors do. Loaded with rich cultural signification, the titles that he chooses for his fictional narratives—*Marhi Da Deeva, Rete di ik Muthi, Addh Chanini Raat*, etc.—acquire a suggestive power far beyond their immediate contexts. His poetic vision offers a transcendental edge to everything he portrays.

Singh's creative imagination is imbued with a rare gift of synthesis. Like a true artist, he understands the dilemmas and conflicts of both art and life exceedingly well. It is no wonder that his poetic effusions go so very well with a restrained expression and an economy of detail. He is a minimalist in the true sense of the word, as he manages to make it not just an expression of his style; rather, the very texture of his vision and thought. He is able to strike a fine balance between the narrative and the dramatic, the personal and the historical, the political and the artistic. Nowhere does this become more conspicuous than in his all-encompassing view of life. As he once told this writer, 'Had I not taken to writing, I would have probably exploded. So, my view of life is nothing if not tragic.'[5] For him, tragedy is not a by-product of a fortuitous set of circumstances or an ingrained personal failing. It is immanent in the very condition of being human or rather becoming so—the result of a constant dialectical struggle between the two. It is an expression, even a triumphant assertion of man's unending search for honour, dignity and self-respect. Such a view of life confers no heroism; it cannot even induce despair or defeatism.

In novel after novel, Singh succeeds in renewing our faith in the irrepressible spirit of human nature and the undying power of human endurance. On being asked how he felt after receiving the Jnanpith, the most coveted literary prize in the country (which he shared with the stalwart Hindi writer Nirmal Verma in 2000), Singh said, 'It's the recognition for those who live in my pages.'[6] Singh's works can amply justify such a claim. In his case, the award is not just a personal triumph. The credit goes to all those who are still fighting for the honour and dignity that history has denied them through the ages.

Parsa: An Overview

Now before we get into the finer nuances of exegesis, it is important to recount the story-line of the novel, at least in a skeletal form. The novel *Parsa* is built around its central character or consciousness, Parsa, a Jat-Brahmin, who derives his name from *Parashurama*, one of the avatars of Vishnu. It is the same *Parashurama* who was known for his furious temper and who had taken a deadly vow to exterminate all *kshatriyas* from this earth, once he learnt of how some of them had subjected his mother to utter disgrace and humiliation. Though not a direct descendent of *Parashurama*, Parsa has inherited some of the *Brahmanical* traits from him such as his phenomenal elephantine memory, severity of temper, unforgiving nature and an unfailing instinct for learning and knowledge. But unlike other Brahmins, who are often engaged in the business of disseminating knowledge, he works on the land for his sustenance and survival. As this relationship with land, too, goes back several generations, he has instinctively developed a mindset of a Punjabi Jat too. He is a Brahmin by birth and a Jat by vocation. This gives Gurdial Singh an opportunity to create a character that transcends the narrow confines of caste politics; someone who lives and functions in a space that easily synthesises the Hindu–Sikh dichotomy, as much as it resolves the dualities and/or contradictions of religion and politics. No wonder, he comes across as a true inheritor of the mystic, Sufi tradition that has dominated the cultural landscape of Punjab over the centuries. He sings *shabads* from *Gurbani* with the same ease and abandon that he shows while singing *kafian* of Bulleh Shah or other Sufi poets.

When the novel opens, Parsa is waylaid by a group of hooligans, whom he manages to fend off with the same alacrity and courage that his father had once displayed in a similar situation. Apart from this, another pattern that runs through the family is that women do not survive for long and men, in all such cases, have to bring up the children, single-handed. Parsa's wife, too, dies in the prime of her youth, leaving him with three sons, whom he brings up with a touching sense of dedication and devotion. Though he spares no effort in giving his three sons a dignified and healthy environment to grow in, they grow up in three different directions, away from him. None of them inherits the sincerity, integrity and authenticity of Parsa, a fact that continues to rattle him all through their growing years, and even later. Though he had nourished their hair with milk and curd, the elder ones just go ahead and cut their hair, without a thought for their father's sentiments. What really upsets him is that they lead unreflective lives and take unreflective decisions. He is not much perturbed when one of his sons decides to leave the country and settle abroad, or when the other one joins the police force, but he is furious when he learns that his sons have taken these decisions as peremptorily as some other decisions affecting their lives.

Parsa is a true *karamyogi* and for him, consistency of actions and thoughts is the only hallmark of personal integrity in life. Though his youngest son stays back home, tends to the cattle, tills the land and develops an abiding relationship with his environment, he lacks the sensitivity and spiritual insight that his father possessed. At some point, this youngest son is seduced by the ideology of the Naxalite movement. He joins their ranks, and is arrested and tortured before being killed in a police encounter. Parsa lives through all this with an amazing degree of stoic acceptance, and not even for a moment does he flinch over his personal loss or grief. With his faith in life intact, he goes through the rituals and ceremonies connected with his son's death. To perform these rituals, he goes to Haridwar, where he comes in contact with a *sadhu*, who is impressed with his worldly detachment and native wisdom. At Haridwar, Parsa also comes in contact with a middle-aged woman, Mukhtiar Kaur, who had accompanied her impotent and ailing husband there, in search of health, vigour and spiritual peace for him as well as herself.

Ironically, Haridwar witnesses the beginning of yet another cycle in Parsa's life, when he is drawn into a physical relationship with Mukhtiar Kaur—an act that has been a subject of raging controversy among the critics. What most people fail to understand is that Parsa does not subscribe to the societal norms and/or conventions, which he, in any case, finds dubiously immoral and decadent. Instead, he sets up his own moral imperatives and lives by them. He defines his own concept of *dharma*, which does not bind him to society, morality or religion, but liberates him from all such crippling belief systems that often shackle the soul of an individual. Towards the end of the novel, we are left with a towering image of a man who lives on the borderland of time–space and timelessness, moving back and forth with ease, often transcending both. Ultimately, he manages to attain a rare balance between individual and social responsibilities when he brings home the child born to Mukhtiar Kaur, and before that, on the death of his youngest son he accepts Tindi, a low-caste farm hand, as his surrogate son. For Parsa, life is not a way of seeking personal gratification or happiness, but a mode of fulfilling a larger, divine purpose inherent in each human life. The final image of *Parsa* is that of a man who has made peace with life, and is now living out the divine dispensation in grace and humility.

Cultural Memory as an Alterity

Although Gurdial Singh belongs to the mainstream tradition of the Punjabi novel, Singh's novels have synergised this tradition from below. Rather than function within the restrictive framework of the dominant tradition, he has constantly interrogated and even subverted and deconstructed it from the perspective of folk traditions within the popular consciousness. Rejecting the conventional notion of official, monumental historiography, he has strongly advocated and subscribed to the notion of the worm's-eye view of history. Often, the representations of cultural history or the folk representations within the dominant tradition are seen in terms of 'alterity' (or otherness, as being separate and different when seen from within the dominant cultural framework), which challenges the conventional notions of chronological, linear, and dominant history or the discourse constituted by it. Not only does Singh locate his narratives within the larger space of cultural history, but he also posits 'cultural memory'[7]—an alterity within the framework of cultural history—as the basic trope for constructing his novels. In several of his novels, including *Parsa*, cultural memory functions as the basic structuring device for constituting a discourse that runs counter to the dominant discourse(s).

The notion of 'cultural memory' emerged in the social sciences in the wake of World War II, and the horrors of Nazism and the untold sufferings of the Jews in Germany.[8] It is only when the fragmented or fragmentary accounts of the holocaust began to emerge out of the persecuted minority of Jews who survived its horrors, that 'cultural memory' became a worthwhile area of investigation for social scientists. To this extent, it would not be wrong to say that the notion of 'cultural memory' is implicated in a definitive sense of historical consciousness. Often seen as a reaction against systematic, wilful attempts of official, monumental historiography to suppress historical memories, especially of a very brutal, inhuman nature, cultural memory takes on the form of a dialectics of 'remembering and forgetting', as has been emphasised by Jens Brockmeier.[9] He goes on to suggest that 'in this discourse, narrative practices are of central importance because they combine various cultural symbol systems, integrating them within one symbolic space'. According to him, three narrative orders—'the linguistic, semiotic and performative or discursive of any artwork'—are examined as these 'constitute a mnemonic system, a symbolic space of remembering and forgetting in which the time orders of past and present are continuously recombined'.[10] For this reason, cultural memory operates in all those cultures and communities where people have either been oppressed and subjected to the process of wilful suppression, or where the complex processes of hegemonic control and subsequent 'cultural repression' or 'amnesia' have taken place. If seen from this perspective, cultural memory can be perceived as an attempt to come to terms with the repressed content and/or processes of history. It is necessitated by the reclamation of subjectivity, which is threatened with extinction, especially in the face of multiple historical oppressions.

Considering the extent to which 'cultural memory' plays a decisive role in the restitution or reclamation of subjectivity, one can say that it is crucial to the process of identity formation or identity construction.[11] However, this process of identity formation is recapitulated through a notion of history which is not only unconventional but also presupposes a non-linear, discontinuous, non-chronological and anti-authoritarian representation. It is precisely this notion that Michel Foucault supports when he refers to the discontinuous processes of history and the presence of significant gaps, silences and fissures in our reading of history.[12] To put it somewhat differently, cultural memory resides in those fissures, gaps and silences or in the residual elements where history deconstructs itself. For this reason, its reclamation is possible only through such non-hierarchical, cultural sources as folk stories, songs or 'little narratives' of the people, as opposed to grand, universalising narratives. In other words, the ideology behind this process of reclaiming cultural memory is definitely anti-authoritarian, anti-capitalistic, anti-imperialistic and anti-hegemonic. Cultural memory constitutes a counter-hegemonic discourse, and tends to interrogate and subvert the assumptions of cultural dominance and hegemony operating within a culture.

It also needs to be pointed out that despite all its individualistic articulations, cultural memory is as intensely personal as it is representatively communal or collective.[13] It posits a situation where the distinction between the individual memory and the collective memory ceases to exist, as the individual is seen only as a carrier of the cultural codes of collective memories. Not only do the cultural memories reside inside an individual, but they also manifest themselves in and through the life of an individual. As the novel often deals with the fate and fortunes of individual characters, it has the potential to turn into an extremely fascinating site for the reclamation of cultural memory. It is as though the past becomes a living reality or entity, with its 'present-ness' becoming a 'pre-text' for both what is 'remembered' as much as what is conveniently 'forgotten'. It is in this sense that a novel often becomes an instrument of subverting the dominant discourse, or a mode of discovering hidden as well as revealed knowledge about the past or its continued, everlasting presence.

The 'spillover effect' of memory is another fact that needs to be stressed in relation to the fictional representation of cultural memory. Not only do the memories tend to constantly elide, and go through the process of slippage (also called 'forgetting'), but they often display an equally strong tendency to simply run through the butter fingers, to use a metaphor. This is precisely why it becomes imperative for a fictional work dealing with cultural memories to take recourse to a framing device to structure the events, situations and anecdotes. They can be perceived or read only when they are effectively framed. The framing device marks off the boundaries between memories, provides space for the diversified and rich material, and also provides the 'archival traces' through which memories become recognisable, identifiable, and even decipherable. Hence, such narratives are often termed the 'narratives of recovery',[14] as Marita Sturken suggests.

Parsa: A Significant Cultural Text

In the context of the preceding discussion, we now look at how *Parsa* can be perceived as an effective site for the cultural memory of the people of Malwa, and their poetry, language and history. First and foremost, it is important to see how *Parsa* is completely different from the other novels of Singh, and why it must be looked upon as a significant cultural text.

Unlike Singh's other novels, *Parsa* operates simultaneously within a dual frame of time and space—the narrative time–space and the comic/eternal/epic time–space. Parsa, the main protagonist, lives at two different levels at the same time, moving freely from one end of the spectrum to another without much ado. In other words, if the other novels bear the burden of history and its multiple oppressions, *Parsa* seeks to create its own logic of emancipation or liberation. If in his other novels, Singh's main purpose is to create 'narratives of oppression', in *Parsa*, he is certainly far more transgressive as he manages to create a 'narrative of liberation'. This fact has certainly been lost on a number of Punjabi critics who have consistently failed to see this significant paradigm shift in Singh's novelistic discourse. They continue to insist upon reading *Parsa* as an extension of many of his earlier novels. Their readings fail to respond to the cultural specificities of *Parsa* as much as they fail to take cognisance of the novel's epical scale and the vast, panoramic view it offers of Punjabi cultural history. Though there are basic stylistic, formal, artistic and ideological differences between the two novels, *Parsa* can be read as a cultural text in the same sense in which Gabriel García Márquez's *One Hundred Years of Solitude* is a cultural text. Both the novelists recreate their cultural contexts within a definitive historical/cultural framework. In this kind of fiction, the novelist's concern is not so much with a specific period in history as it is with the cultural history of a specific culture. The extent to which the authorised versions of history representing the dominant, hegemonic discourse, are often systematically challenged and interrogated within the space of such fictional works, fiction does allow for an indirect mediation of history.

Parsa: A Site of Cultural Memory

The cultural frame of *Parsa* begins to define itself the moment we start exploring the rich signification of its deceptively innocuous title. The title reminds us of the mythological character Parashurama, a Brahmin who declared himself the sworn enemy of the Kshatriyas and vowed to eliminate all Kshatriyas from the face of this earth.[15] Why did Singh extend the cultural frame of his novel beyond history, into the realm of mythology and folklore? To put it simply, he sets up a frame within which cultural history becomes not just an alterity, but perhaps, the only discourse available within the novel. Moreover, it has definite implications for his characterisation of Parsa. Parsa has been conceived as a complex figure, a product of both mythology and history, a Brahmin by birth and a land-owning Jat by profession. In fact, it is by invoking this context that Singh reconstructs a specific notion of the cultural history of Punjab, within which transgression of caste divisions is as real as the transgression of the boundaries between discourses. Singh needs such a framing device to situate or locate his vision of the syncretism of Punjabi traditions where the Hindu, Muslim and Sikh identities are not constituted separately, but are caught up in a melee of time and history, constantly shaping and reshaping one another.[16]

Cultural Memory and Individual Identity

Singh presents Parsa, the main protagonist, as both a witness to the processes of history and as an active participant in them, both as a worthy inheritor of the cultural memory and tradition, and also its worst denouncer and critic. This dichotomy is built into the very conception of Parsa's character, and is evident in the way in which he is located. Singh locates him not in the actual physical, social or moral space but instead, within the plural, folk and amoral cultural space where rigid caste boundaries are as irrelevant as the material and historical contingencies of his situation. He manages to establish the fact that cultural history neither supports nor legitimises caste divisions, which in any case, have become irrelevant and unsustainable. The sociology of such caste distinctions in our contemporary society, he suggests, is far more complex.[17] As the division of labour and the principle of specialisation have now long ceased to be the determining factors, there is much greater intra-mobility among and across different caste formations (both in Indian and Punjabi situations), though this fact is not widely accepted. This redefinition of caste boundaries allows Singh to combine in Parsa's character the proverbial Brahminical memory—which is traditionally regarded as the result of the long-established practice of memorising the *Vedas*, but in Parsa's case, the result of his inheritance of the eclectic folk tradition of Sufism—and the rebelliousness, non-conformism, and the intransigent, self-willed rigidity inherent in Jat identity. If Parsa refuses to live by any code other than the one he defines, it is because he posits himself outside the framework of conventional social morality. His refusal to accept or honour any social, moral or religious code testifies to his status as an archetypal rebel, an eternal outsider who lives his life purely on his own terms.

The influence of folk cultures is another aspect of Parsa's character that deserves a closer scrutiny. He has had no formal or informal education, but the entire folk tradition not only lives inside him but is also readily available to him. In his moments of intense pain or joy, Parsa often breaks into snatches of poetry—verses that he has neither heard nor read. A closer scrutiny reveals that the lines he recites are the eternal words of Farid, Guru Nanak, Bulleh Shah or Waris Shah, sung in a highly inflected, or even conflated, style. Significantly, his attempts at reclaiming cultural memory are intensely personal as he often improvises on the Sufi songs, the most precious collective heritage of Punjabis even today. If there is any creed that Parsa either believes in or subscribes to, it is the all-embracing mysticism propounded by the Sufis who look upon both life and death with unconcern, indifference and detachment. When his wife passes away, Parsa performs her cremation without any fuss and blatantly refuses to go through rituals or ceremonies, none of which he personally believes in.

Though he brings up his three sons single-handedly, he neither has great expectations of them nor does he try to control or run their lives in any way. When his elder sons leave him one by one, he simply acquiesces and does not even protest. When his youngest son,

Basanta, joins the Naxalite movement and leaves home, he makes no effort whatsoever to either wean him away or dissuade him. He remains impassive when he gets the news of Basanta's death in police custody and goes through all the formalities as if it were someone else's tragedy. This is not to suggest that in Parsa, Singh has created an emotionally vapid or an atrophied character, someone who is reminiscent of Meursault, the indifferent and emotionally detached central character of Albert Camus' *The Outsider* (or *The Stranger*). In contrast, Singh has bestowed this character with a rich array of emotions. Parsa believes in their worthwhile 'investment' and refuses to squander them away. That he is both capable of emotional plenitude and its rich investment is evident from the way in which he takes moral responsibility, initially for Mukhtiar Kaur and then their young son, though he could have easily discarded them both. His decision to start his life all over again with Savitri and the son he had with Mukhtiar Kaur is a testimony to his personal philosophy—that human beings too must seek renewal and reconstruction almost as naturally as does the nature. He sees no contradiction between the human and the natural worlds, and his acceptance of life as well as destiny essentially springs from this understanding.

Cultural Memory and State Repression

Punjab has had a long and established history of state repression, the earliest recorded memories of which easily go back to the Mughals who invaded this territory in the sixteenth century, and continue well into the later phases when the British managed to occupy this terrain in 1849.[18] Some historians of the region claim that state repression continued well into the post-Independence phase. Many even argue that the process became much worse and even more subversive after India attained freedom, and that it was now perpetuated by our own people. Regardless of whether we go along with this view of history, the fact remains that in the post-Independence phase, Punjab has witnessed a number of ideologically charged movements—such as the Naxalite movement of the 1960s which was supported by hard-core Marxist ideologues, the movement for the creation of a Punjabi Subha, again supported by a political outfit called the Akali

Dal, and a more militant movement of the 1980s, supported by the hardline factions among Sikh nationalist organisations. One way or the other, this long history of state repression—and the often violent reaction from the masses—has led to the suppression of the region's history and its fissured contents.

Though Singh has deliberately not located his novel in a specific time–space continuum or historical context, he has imbued his narrative with a non-linear and non-chronological sense of historical consciousness, which becomes, inter alia, a form of folk cultural history. While no specific references have been made to the Naxalite movement of the 1960s, the entire context is poetically evoked through Basanta's involvement and complicity with it. Young boys and girls, especially from rural backgrounds, were attracted to the movement and faced police atrocities and custodial deaths, before the movement began to die down and lost its ideological impetus and credibility. *Parsa* captures this chequered history of the Naxal movement with sure, almost deft, strokes. However, it is not too difficult to see where the personal sympathies of the novelist essentially belong, provided we understand the intense attention to details with which he has created the character of 'Master', the main ideologue. Singh does understand that though this movement may have largely failed to realise its socioeconomic objectives and the desire to achieve social justice and a more equitable redistribution of land among the landless, it certainly did leave behind a rich legacy and a poetic discourse that can hardly be ignored. To an extent, *Parsa*'s poetic inheritance spreads as far back as Farid and Guru Nanak on the one hand, and Shiv Batalvi, Surjit Pattar and Paash, on the other. In other words, in his attempts to recover the cultural memory, Singh abolishes the facetious distinction between the poetic and the political, which, in any case, does not seem to exist in popular consciousness.

Cultural Memory and Fictive Time/Space Consciousness

The time–space frame of *Parsa* is carefully crafted and structured. Unlike the other novels of Singh, *Parsa* is strategically set within a dual time frame, with Parsa moving freely between these two disparate, unrelated time zones. He also serves as an important link between the two time zones. One needs to emphasise that this notion of double time frame is not used here in the sense in which it has been used by Christian Metz, but essentially in the sense in which T.S. Eliot has used it in his famous play *Murder in the Cathedral*.[19] Christian Metz says, 'Narrative is a ... doubly temporal sequence ... There is the time of the thing told and the time of the narrative (the time of the signified and the time of the signifier). This duality not only renders possible all the temporal distortions that are commonplace in narratives ... More basically, it invites us to consider that one of the functions of a narrative is to invent one time scheme in terms of another time scheme.'[20] However, T.S. Eliot reconceptualises this in terms of 'temporality' and 'timelessness'. On the one hand, Singh is concerned about the notion of temporality and so, Parsa is made to function within the specificities of time, place and action. On the other, he is also aware of another, and perhaps more significant, trans-human, trans-historical, cosmic dimension of 'time'. It is this recognition of time scales that gives the novel a transcendental character and sweep, transforming it from just another folk narrative into a significant cultural text. As far as the conception of the novelistic space is concerned, it has been conceived in real, sociological/cultural terms as well as poetic, psychological terms. While the sociological dimension of space is reflected in the way in which linearity of the narrative is emphasised, its psychological dimension is reflected in the way this linearity is disrupted, giving it a transcendental sweep of space and history. Parsa lives at the conjunction of these two distinctive time–space conceptions. In this sense, his consciousness becomes the ultimate battleground for mediating the eternal dilemmas of human beings in relation to one another, time, history and also timelessness. The entire game of cultural memory, polarised by the two extremes of 'remembering and forgetting', and 'amnesia and recovery', is played out here. As memory fails to follow the predictable patterns of linearity, the narrative refuses to organise itself in accordance with the principle of linearity.

This might create a wrong impression that the narrative is 'focalised' in Parsa's consciousness. Though Singh has primarily used the technique of third-person narration throughout the novel, he has refused to privilege a particular viewpoint, a definitive perspective or a dominant ideology. This is achieved in a variety of ways. First, he uses a number of framing devices which lend a definite degree of clinical objectivity to the narrative. Besides, we do not always view incidents through the eyes of Parsa. Not only do the strands of 'focalisation' keep shifting in the narrative, but the vulnerability of Parsa's point of view is constantly exposed through the dogged refusal of his sons, Jetha and Pohla, to fall in line with him or through Basanta's decision to lead a life his father would not have ever approved of. Moreover, both Basanta and Tindi become not just the commentators, but virtually the surrogate protagonists of this story. Tindi's relationship with Parsa is vaguely reminiscent of Lear's relationship with the fool in *King Lear*. It is through the mediation of Tindi—who represents the fascinating world of folk stories, folk songs and folk wisdom (which is what Parsa often shares with him)—that Singh deconstructs both history and the dominant ideology.[21] Going far beyond the expectations, Tindi proves to be much more than a son to Parsa, something he had never imagined. His acceptance of Tindi towards the end of the novel marks an important stage in the ultimate integration of his individual/collective psyche. This is how he manages to synthesise the residual, vestigial elements of 'lowliness' into his supposedly 'high and mighty' Brahminical self.

A number of Punjabi critics have denounced *Parsa* on the grounds that, in this novel, Singh has abandoned his critical concern for the dispossessed and the marginalised. They allege that he has trapped himself in abstractions such as '*karma*', '*dharma*' and/or man's relationship with nature.[22] Singh had built his reputation by churning out 'narratives of oppression', and by doing so, succeeded in exorcising his impinging sense of socioeconomic oppression that had rattled him through his years of struggle. In *Parsa*, he has created a novel that transcends the narrow boundaries of caste and class, the dominant and the marginalised, and the high and the low. The novel moves towards a more integrated vision of human consciousness where dualities of all kinds simply cease to exist. It is important to stress here that Singh's vision is not located so much in the exclusionary or dominant Hindu view of life or Adi Sankara's philosophy of monism (*advaita vedanta*), as much as it is within the eclectic and egalitarian notion of Sufi mysticism, popular in folk consciousness.

Cultural Memory and Narrative Framing

Cultural memory necessarily needs the mediation of a framing device, if the 'spillover' is to be avoided and its encryption into a narrative is to be successfully realised. Conscious of this fact, Singh has used a framing device for structuring a variety of incidents and situations. For instance, there is a kind of pattern that runs through Parsa's life, as is evident from the way in which an incident involving his father Sarupa is narrated right in the beginning. To an extent, this is primarily to suggest that Parsa is the inheritor of his '*karmic* destiny' as much as he is a victim of a curse his family is afflicted with. Like his father, Parsa too gets embroiled in a physical fight and emerges triumphant, and like so many of his ancestors, he too is condemned to become a widower at a relatively young age and bring up his children single-handedly. It goes to the credit of Singh that he manages to create a narrative that does not simply legitimise this pattern of life but breaches it, thus creating unimaginable possibilities for Parsa's vertical growth in the process.

Another framing device used effectively in the novel is the 'story-within-a-story' frame, essentially a carryover from the *Mahabharata* and the *Panchatantra* tales. It is no coincidence that the novel opens with a *Pauranik* tale about Hiranyakashipu, the legendary demon-king and the father of Prahlad who was killed by Narasimha, one of the incarnations of Vishnu.[23] By thus framing the narrative with a mythological story, Singh not only manages to extend the context of his novel beyond history, but invokes a shared cultural context within which the moral problems confronting the characters must be examined. In the immediate context, it offers a moral twist to the fight that first Sarupa and then Parsa puts up for the vindication of personal valour and honour, and later, it becomes a metonymic frame for the moral choices other characters such as Jetha, Pohla and Basanta make from time to time. If Singh has created any specific moral frame for judging or evaluating the actions or deeds of his characters, it is defined only in terms of various tales, mythological or folk, that he insinuates into the narrative. For instance, much before Parsa comes into contact with Mukhtiar Kaur and enters into a physical relationship with her, Singh presents a folk tale framing the entire incident and guiding the readers' moral perceptions. It is the tale of a physically strong young man who refuses to gratify the carnal needs of a married woman, simply on the grounds that she belongs to another man. What he fails to realise is that her husband, being mentally challenged, is unable to fulfil her needs. Going beyond the commonsensical, sociological view of morality, Singh explores its trans-human, cosmic dimensions, by suggesting that a seeker in one situation could also be a giver in another. This is what the folk tale essentially demonstrates when the same young man has to beg that very woman for the sweat of her palms to get his skin rash healed. It is obvious that Singh would not like us to judge the Parsa–Mukhtiar Kaur episode from the standpoint of conventional or commonsensical view of morality. Nothing that Parsa ever does actually fits into the frame of ordinary logic. It is only by defying this logic of conventionality that he manages to liberate himself from the constraints of ordinariness that often chain us down to our own small dreams, desires and fears. It is no wonder that despite being a householder, he is shown miles ahead of a *sadhu* he meets in Haridwar. If Parsa is able to acquire a larger-than-life stature towards the end of the novel, towering far above the level of the ordinary mortals and dwarfing virtually every other character in the novel, it is only because he shows innate strength and courage in defying all the given frames, and displays an existential doggedness in accepting the consequences of his own actions and choices.

Singh's purpose in using the device of a framed tale is two-fold: to provide a frame within which a vast repertoire of cultural memories can be contained and to create a character who ultimately transgresses all such frames and grows beyond them. In the person of Parsa, he has certainly created such a character. And by using the stories—drawn mostly from the folk tradition—for framing the incidents and situations, Singh allows the reader the freedom to interpret the novel without the mediation of the narrator or the 'author'. It is in this double sense that *Parsa*—and also its central character—tends to become a 'narrative of liberation or emancipation'.

To conclude, one may say that in *Parsa*, Singh has managed to create a narrative space within which cultural memories/history and/or caste hierarchies can effectively be subjected to a process of re-negotiation. Here, the term 'narrative' is *not* used in its more specialised sense, the sense in which it is often used in narratology, but in its most generalised sense where it is considered almost coterminous with the novel. Though the novel has traditionally been seen as a sociological tract, there has been a definitive change, over the years, in our perception of its role and function. The genre is no longer seen only as a form of representation in the modernist or the premodernist sense, but is increasingly perceived as a self-reflexive genre, with a specific archaeological function of digging into the past. However, this archaeological function is somewhat different from its engagement with history—which gave rise to the historical novel per se—as it liberates it from the well-defined, structured notions of reality and representation, and fixed notion of identity. Now that the structured notions of reality and narrative representation have collapsed, the 'fictive space' has re-negotiated its internal structure and its modes of representation. In fact, it has now ceased to be a 'space' and has instead become a 'site', both for the inscription and the excavation of personal/cultural memory and/or history. To an extent, this is what has now made the novel as a genre into a 'site' for the contestation of multiple ideologies, which is what *Parsa* too tends to become, should we now say, fairly successfully.

Notes and References

1. Plato, *The Republic*, trans. A.D. Linday (London: The David Campbell Publishers Ltd., 1992), 282–6. Though Plato introduces this comparison between the painter/poet and the carpenter in these specific pages of Book X, it constitutes a part of his much larger discussion on the 'Theory of Forms', which he develops through *The Republic*.

2. This discussion derives itself from my reading of several histories of Punjabi literature. However, the section on Gurdial Singh is based upon my reading of his works. For a more comprehensive analysis, see Kartar

Singh Duggal and Sant Singh Sekhon, *A History of Punjabi Literature* (New Delhi: Sahitya Akademi, 1992).

3. As quoted in the postscript to Gurdial Singh's *Marhi Da Deeva* (Chandigarh: Lokgeet Prakashan, 1964), 167. Though the original quotation was in Hindi, it has been reproduced in the book in Punjabi. The English translation in this case, as in several other similar cases, is mine.

4. Gurdial Singh, *Parsa*, trans. Rana Nayar (New Delhi: National Book Trust, 2000), 242.

5. As quoted to the author in an interview published in Rana Nayar, *The Tribune Sunday Reading*, June 16, 1996, 5.

6. As quoted to the author in an unpublished, personal interview.

7. The concept of 'cultural memory' was introduced to the archaeological disciplines by Jan Assmann, a German Egyptologist, who defined it 'as the outer dimension of human memory embracing two different concepts: "memory culture" (*Erinnerungskultur*) and "reference to the past" (*Vergangenheitsberzug*). Memory culture is the process by which a society ensures cultural continuity, by preserving, with the help of cultural mnemonics, its collective knowledge from one generation to the next, rendering it possible for later generations to *reconstruct* their cultural identity. When we speak about cultural memory, we are including in this definition two distinct characteristics: 1. the survival of a historically, politically and socially marginalized group of people, and 2. the role of spirituality as a form of resistance.' (1). As Jan Assmann's writings are mostly in German and are not available directly, I have accessed his ideas through the work of Jeanette Rodríguez and Ted Fortier. For detailed exposition of the concept, see Jeanette Rodríguez and Ted Fortier, *Cultural Memory: Resistance, Faith and Identity* (Austin: University of Texas Press, 2007). For the relationship between the individual and the social memory, see Paul Connerton *How Societies Remember* (Cambridge: Cambridge University Press, 1989). For the relationship between cultural memory, narrative framing and identity, see Lewis P. Hinchman and Sandra K. Hinchman, eds., *Memory, Identity, Community: The Idea of Narrative in the Human Sciences* (New York: State University of New York Press, 2001), and the Introduction by Mieke Bal in Mieke Bal, Jonathan V. Crewe and Leo Spitzer, eds., *Acts of Memory: Cultural Recall in the Present* (Hanover: Dartmouth College Press, 1999).

8. This fact has been stated by Jeanette Rodriguez and Ted Terrier in their Preface (ix–x) to *Cultural Memory*, and has also been corroborated by Michael Stewart in 'Remembering without Commemoration: The Mnemonics and Politics of Holocaust Memories among European Roma', *Journal of Royal Anthropological Institute* 10, no. 3 (2004).

9. 'Memory and forgetting' are the twin processes that Jens Brockmeier associates with 'cultural memory'. My understanding of this concept is borrowed from a secondary source as Brockmeier's essays are, once again, available only in German. So I have reproduced Brockmeier as he was quoted by Stewart in 'Remembering without Commemoration', 561–82.

10. Stewart, 'Remembering without Commemoration', 568.

11. In their book, Dan Ben-Amos and Liliane Weissberg have sought to explore this relationship between cultural memory and identity formation. See Dan Ben-Amos and Liliane Weissberg, ed., *Cultural Memory and the Construction of Identity* (Michigan: Wayne State University, 1999).

12. Though Foucault was not a professional historian, he did alter our perception of both history and historiography. Challenging the conventional notions of history as a chronological sequencing of events, he emphasised, in the manner of a true poststructuralist, discontinuous, fragmented, fissured and subterranean notions of history. It is this kind of history that he excavated in most of his works. In a way, all his works were explorations of the counter-hegemonic discourse of history, attempts to create alternative histories, be it of sexuality, social practices, legal systems or madness. For detailed discussion, see Michel Foucault *The Archaeology of Knowledge* (London: Routledge, 2002).

13. For cultural memory being, at once, an expression of collective as well as individual articulation, see Connerton, *How Societies Remember*.

14. Marita Sturken, 'Narratives of Recovery: Repressed Memory as Cultural Memory', in *Acts of Memory: Cultural Recall in the Present*, ed. Mieke Bal, Jonathan V. Crewe and Leo Spitzer (Hanover: Dartmouth College Press, 1999).

15. Several accounts of Parashurama's legend are found in the *Mahabharata* and the *Bhagavat Purana*. According to some stories available in Punjabi folklore, when Guru Gobind Singh baptised the Sikhs, he was reviving the tradition of Parashurama. It is for this reason that Gurdial Singh has returned to this story in his novel *Parsa* and used it to look at the dissolution of caste divisions and the emergence of Brahmin-Jat (Hindu-Sikh) hybridity in Punjabi culture.

16. The history of Punjab has so far been reconstructed in two ways: as a separatist discourse and as a shared, syncretic discourse. Over the years, attempts have been made—either by the Sikh historians or the sectarian historians—to construct a 'Sikh history' of Punjab or a 'community-oriented history' of Punjab. Such attempts seek to appropriate history

to build or project either the majoritarian or a minoritarian discourse. These historical constructions have fuelled communal passions and created divisions and fissures within the communities living in Punjab or even outside the region. Of late, there have been attempts, endorsed, of course, by the Cambridge School of historians, to project the region's history as that of the Jats living in Punjab. All such exercises in historical constructions are exclusionary in nature and are not only hegemonic but also politically motivated and even biased. On the other hand, a small band of historians continue to emphasise the spirit of '*Punjabiyat*' in their constructions, and have managed to resurrect the spirit of commonality, mutuality and multiple identities that are so important for the preservation of our common heritage and principles. Official, hegemonic historical constructions can be challenged by reconstructing or resurrecting narratives of cultural history and/or cultural memory, for which there is no better form available to us than fiction. This explains Singh's emphasis on cultural memory.

17. The caste divisions enunciated by the *Manusmriti*, which were blindly superimposed on the Indian society for centuries, have been invalidated by historical experiences. People no longer follow the profession assigned to their caste. One may hear of a Brahmin who has taken up the profession of a farmer (Jat), as is the case in this particular novel, or a Kshatriya who is into teaching, traditionally considered to be a Brahminical vocation. The rigid caste boundaries have collapsed and consequently, a new sociology of Punjabi culture has emerged. Over a period of time, this new sociology, which draws its strength from the collapse of traditional/conservative caste divisions, has thrown up a renewed consciousness of caste structures. Though there is a growing recognition of the fact that caste distinctions are no longer either possible or sustainable, efforts are being made to articulate them in social and political discourses. It is this kind of sociology that lies at the heart of Punjabi life and culture and Gurdial Singh has merely represented its many configurations in his several works of fiction.

18. For an extended discussion, see J. S. Grewal, *The Sikhs of the Punjab* (Cambridge: Cambridge University Press, 1990).

19. In *Murder in the Cathedral*, T.S. Eliot used a dual time scheme to present his dramatic action. The play functions both in the temporal (material) and the timeless (spiritual) worlds at the same time, as Thomas Beckett, the protagonist, moves freely in and out of these two worlds.

20. Christian Metz, *Film Language: A Semiotics of Cinema*, trans. Michael Taylor (New York, 1974), 18.

21. Parsa is not a hero in the conventional sense, as he consistently refuses to fit into all our known constructions of a hero. If at all he can be regarded

as a hero, he can be regarded as a folk hero who inhabits a 'timeless cultural space', moves freely across the two regions—the material and the spiritual—and has this uncanny advantage (which no other character in Singh's oeuvre seems to enjoy) of being able to observe this world from below as well as above. He feels the anguish of the common man and yet can look at his mundane activities with a degree of transcendental detachment. By positioning his narrative within this cultural space of folklores and traditions, Singh manages to critique the social, political and cultural distortions of his times. This also enables him to deconstruct all possible hegemonic constructions and dominant ideologies operating within Punjabi society and culture.

22. On the publication of *Parsa*, a good number of Punjabi critics were extremely unhappy and even disillusioned with Gurdial Singh. They felt that, in this particular work, he had abandoned his Marxist perspective and was sliding into the insidious trap of abstractions like '*karma*' and '*dharma*' (most of which not only constitutes the main ideological bulwark of the novel, but also the central theme of the multiple discussions Parsa and Pala *Raagi* engage in) that he had scrupulously eschewed all his life. They even saw a negation of his own Marxist philosophy and ideology in the way he had conceived the character of Parsa. They were equally resentful of the fact that he had chosen to present a Brahmin and not a Shudra as his main protagonist. What is often not understood by these critics is that Parsa has been conceived on an epic scale as someone who inheres in his person the entire cultural history—the shared and not the separatist one—of Punjab. They also fail to see that the dialogue between Parsa and Pala *Raagi* is more in the nature of an internal dialogue—a dialogue between the lower and the higher selves, a dialogue between a Brahmin and a Sikh peasant, a dialogue between the two discourses they represent. In the person of Parsa, both the aspects of Punjabi culture—knowledge and action, material and spiritual—find their articulation. The novel deals as much with human beings' relationship with social, economic and political environment as it does with their relationship with forces like faith, destiny, nature and spirituality.

23. Just as Singh uses the legend of Parashurama in the title of his novel, he starts off his narrative by referring to the story of Hiranyakashipu. According to a story from *Bhāgavata Purāna*, the four Kumaras—Sanaka, Sanandana, Sanatana, and Sanatkumara who were the *manasaputras* of Brahma (sons born from the mind or thought power of Brahma)—visited Vaikuntha, the abode of Vishnu. Due to the strength of their *tapasya* (penance), the four Kumaras appeared to be mere children, though they were of great age. Jaya and Vijaya, the gatekeepers of Vaikuntha intercepted the Kumaras at the gate, thinking them to be children. They also told the Kumaras that Vishnu was resting and that

they could not allow the Kumaras to disturb him. The enraged Kumaras replied that Vishnu is available for his devotees any time, and cursed both the gatekeepers that they would have to give up their divinity, be born on Earth, and live like normal human beings. Vishnu appeared before them and the gatekeepers requested Vishnu to lift the curse. Vishnu replied that the curse could not be lifted. Instead, he gave Jaya and Vijaya two options. The first option was to take seven births on Earth as devotees of Vishnu, while the second was to take three births as his enemies. After serving either of these sentences, they could reattain their stature at Vaikuntha. Jaya and Vijaya could not bear the thought of staying away from Vishnu for seven lives. As a result, they choose to be born thrice as enemies of Vishnu. In the first life they were born as Hiranyakashipu and Hiranyaksha. Vishnu took the avatar of Varaha to kill Hiranyaksha and the Narasimha avatar killed Hiranyakashipu. In the second life, they were born as Ravana and Kumbhakarna and were defeated, during the Tretayuga, by Rama as depicted in the great Hindu epic *Ramayana*. Finally, in their third life, they were born as Sishupala and Dantavakra during the time of Krishna (as narrated in the *Mahabharata*), during the Dwaparayuga.

Hiranyakashipu and Hiranyaksha were born to Diti (daughter of Daksha Prajapathi) and Sage Kashyapa. It is said that the *asuras* were born to them as a result of their union at the time of sunset, said to be an inauspicious time for such a deed. After his brother's death at the hands of the Varaha avatar of Vishnu, Hiranyakashipu started to abhor Lord Vishnu. He decided to kill Vishnu by gaining mystical powers, which he believed Brahma, the chief among the *devas*, would give him if he underwent many years of great austerity and penance. Pleased by Hiranyakashipu's austerities, Brahma appeared before him and offered him a boon of his choice. Hiranyakashipu asked for immortality. However, Brahma refused. Hiranyakashipu then requested the following:

'O my lord, O best of the givers of benediction, grant me that I not die within any residence or outside any residence, during the daytime or at night, nor on the ground nor in the sky. Grant me that my death not be brought by any being other than those created by you, nor by any weapon, nor by any human being or animal. Grant me that I not meet death from any entity, living or nonliving. Grant me, further, that I not be killed by any demigod or demon or by any great snake from the lower planets. Since no one can kill you in the battlefield, you have no competitor. Therefore, grant me the benediction that I too may have no rival. Give me sole lordship over all the living entities and presiding deities, and give me all the glories obtained by that position. Furthermore, give me all the mystic powers attained by long austerities and the practice of yoga, for these cannot be lost at any time.'

It is this aspect of the boon that Singh has recapitulated in the opening section of the novel. In the opening section, Singh has used the story of Hiranyakashipu as a framing device. This helps him invest his narrative with multiple possibilities, while allowing him to scrupulously stay away from becoming a controlling, intrusive presence within the narrative. Singh never becomes a narrator/commentator within his narratives as he scrupulously allows his dramatic narration to speak for itself, a quality that sets him apart from his other contemporaries and even his predecessors.

Chapter Six

Atamjit Singh's *Kamloops Dian Macchian*: Polyphonic Discourse and Dramatic Art

When Martin Buber, the Jewish existentialist philosopher, made an apparently simple suggestion that 'all art is from its origin essentially of the nature of dialogue,'[1] he was not simply trying to underscore the obvious fact that the basic function of all art is communication. In fact, it was a way of demonstrating his article of faith, which emphasised the relational nature of all beings and art forms. Being an existentialist thinker whose view of philosophy lay rooted in the logic of 'I–Thou' dialogism, Buber was always eager to emphasise connectivity, intersubjectivity and dialogical modes of relatedness. Buber's assertion about art applies as much to the representational forms of art as it does to the non-representational forms. Be it a symbolic painting, a cubic or a realistic one, the basic purpose behind its creation is always to initiate a dialogue at different levels of discourse. This dialogue can operate at a purely aesthetic level, as an interplay of various formal elements within the 'creation' (or a work of art/literature) or at a more functional level as an act of communication between the creator/author and the audience/reader. In other words, there are two levels at which discourses constitute themselves—internal/private and external/public. And all great art can often be said to hover between two extreme possibilities—one that strives towards the reconciliation of these two levels and the other that thrives on the dynamic tension between them.

When judged from this standpoint, Atamjit Singh's Punjabi play *Kamloops Dian Macchian* (The Fish of Kamloops, 1998) certainly does qualify as an excellent work of dramatic art. As a playwright, Singh has always sought to initiate dialogues at multiple levels of discourse—ranging from the dialogue with the self and the society, and beyond that, with the cultural forces that define both self and society. Singh started his career as a hard-hitting, propaganda playwright in the best traditions of monologic agitprop (left-wing propaganda communicated through art). However, over the years, he has slowly internalised the process of dialogism. The fact that he has sobered down his shrill, almost strident, pedantic messages into an ever-growing, though gently persuasive, concern for his society is proof enough for his growing preoccupation with matters of aesthetics. Already an established name in the world of Punjabi and Indian drama, Singh has made his mark on the international scene with *Kamloops Dian Macchian*.

The play derives its title from the city of Kamloops in south-central British Columbia, located at the confluence of the two branches of the Thompson River and near Kamloops Lake. Every year, a strange and rather bizarre phenomenon is witnessed here. Thousands of fish born in this part of the river return to this very point of confluence to die. This particular idea that fish always return to the same spot where they were initially born to die became for Singh, an evocative metaphor for all migrants, who also nurture a similar dream. This is what triggered the play and so the title. *Kamloops Dian Macchian*, a play about four generations of Punjabi settlers in Canada, began to seed in Singh's mind during his first ever visit to North America in 1994. This visit gave him a rare opportunity to understand the 'double lives' which most Punjabi immigrants lead in Toronto, Vancouver and other parts of Canada. By the time he returned to Canada in 1996, Singh was ready to produce the play among the people whose lives had inspired the play in the first place. Spread over three months, starting from November/December 1996 to January 1997, *Kamloops Dian Macchian* was staged as many as seven times. The play travelled to places as far removed as Calgary, Toronto, Edmonton and Vancouver. All these performances were produced under the guidance of the writer (who believes in directing his own plays), with the liberal support of the Indian Workers Association, Calgary. Each production turned out to be a resounding theatrical success, going far beyond the expectations of the playwright and the producers. Commenting on the theatrical success of the play, Surinder Dhanjal, a poet–critic and a resident of Kamloops, said, 'Like a genuine well-wisher, Atamjit has knocked at our doors, offering an apt metaphor for a series of problems confronting the Punjabi immigrant community. While some of us have bolted our doors from inside to feel safer, others have thrown their doors wide open, welcoming him with a smile . . . By virtue of the dialogue it has helped generate, the play has become a reference point for all the ideas it deals with, and shall continue to be so for a long time to come.'[2]

How did this play, based as it was on the lives of an immigrant community, capture the imagination of the community it intended to portray? How did Singh manage to synergise this dialogue between the native perception and the diasporic tensions, conflicts and dilemmas of the Punjabi community at one level and between different members of this community at another? Much before these questions are answered, it is important to point out here that Singh was certainly not the first playwright in Punjabi to focus his/her attention upon the Punjabi immigrants and their multiple trials and tribulations. If one were to look through the recent history of modern Punjabi drama, several other plays with similar themes would readily come to mind. In this respect, special mention ought to be made of the efforts of Ravinder Ravi, Ajaib Kamal, Jagtar Dhah, Harbhajan Singh Birk, Ajmer Rode and Tarsem Nilgiri. In his plays—*Bimaar Sadi* (The Ailing Century) and *Dar Darwaaza* (The Threshold and the Door)—Ravinder Ravi offers poetic and realistic portrayals of the problems faced by Punjabi immigrants. As he was primarily a poet, Ravi's 'verse dramas' offer some delectable poetry but they fail to create the necessary theatrical impact. Much the same can be said about Ajaib Kamal's collection, *Langhra Asmaan* (The Lame Sky). In *Ik Supna Machali Da* (A Dream of a Fish), Jagtar Dhah comes quite close to offering a realistic portrayal of how traditional communitarian bonds wilt under the weight of market forces. But he, too, is unable to resist the excesses of poetic exuberance, in the process cramping his own theatrical powers.

Harbhajan Singh Birk's *Mitthi Jail* (A Sweet Prison) does manage to capture the conflicts within the immigrant community with some degree of credibility, but his vision somehow fails to acquire a sense of inwardness. Despite the fact that he is an immigrant himself, Birk's understanding of the community remains woefully inadequate, and even partial and alien in a somewhat bizarre way. Throwing a backward glance at history, Ajmer Rode's *Kama Gata Maru* reconstructs a well-known phase in the history of Punjabi settlers with both gusto and power. But he chooses not to look at the contemporary problems afflicting the lives of the immigrant community. However, in most of these cases, the plays were either not staged in England or Canada, or if at all they were, they did not get a warm and encouraging response from the audience.

Kamloops Dian Macchian has to be read against this background of recent efforts in Punjabi literature to portray diasporic communities. For all practical purposes, Singh owes his success largely to two factors. His ability to achieve a rare synthesis of the poetic and realistic modes enables him to score over his contemporaries. And Singh's writing exhibits a certain inwardness with which he approaches both the individual/collective psyche of the Punjabi community and the sociology that rarefies or refracts it. Whether it is *Rishtiyan Da Ki Rakhiye Naa* (What Name Do We Give to Relationships!), one of his early plays written in 1982, or his most recent production, *Main Taan Ik Sarangi Haan* (I'm Only a Sarangi, 2002) it is always the complex web of personal/social/artistic relationships that constitutes the very stuff and material of his dramatic content and structure. If in the first play, he explores the sociology of fragmented relationships in the post-Partition scenario, in the other, he casts a hard, angular look at the process of dehumanisation and debasement that a woman often has to undergo in a male-dominated, feudalistic and patriarchal society such as ours. In other words, Singh has always been passionately engaged in exploring those subliminal, psychological depths of human behaviour that often define as well as defy the limits of human understanding. He has always been interested in penetrating those less luminous areas of the collective and/or individual psyche of the diasporic Punjabi community, areas that even the well-trained psychoanalyst would sometimes fear to tread.

Singh's treatment of the problems of the immigrant Punjabi community is characterised by this rarefied understanding of human impulses, his sharpness of focus and intensity of feeling. Though he could, at best, be perceived as a practitioner of what the Norwegian master Henrik Ibsen calls the 'drama of ideas', Singh's plays certainly possess the 'poeticity' that characterised the works of some of the genre's best practitioners—Ibsen himself, August Strindberg and Anton Chekhov. One could argue that the substratum of Singh's plays essentially rests upon the binary tension between the realistic and the poetic modes. It is this structural tension that acts as the main propelling source of the dramatic synergy. Like several other plays of his, *Kamloops Dian Macchian* too is structured on this principle of binary opposition. While the play is essentially poetic in its conception, the treatment of the dramatic action is largely realistic. Built around a rich, poetic metaphor, the play is realistic in terms of its setting, ambience, delineation of characters, presentation of theme(s) and its overarching vision. With the exception of Scene 5, which brings to the fore a 'fantasy'—played out in the form of a surrealistic dialogue between an old *bhaaiya* confined to the basement and an eight-month-old *kaka* hobbling on the stage in a walker—all other scenes are cast in the realistic mould. Introduced at a strategic point in the dramatic action, this scene, despite being a fantasy, 'has been designed to help capture the inner reality of the characters', as unambiguously pointed out by the playwright in his stage directions.[3] Penetrating the self-imposed, claustrophobic layers of realism, which often tend to border on the sordid and the grotesque, this scene provides the much-needed dramatic relief and leaves room for the playwright's imagination to soar beyond the immediate. Apart from peeling off the complex layers of falsehood, self-deception and hypocrisy within which the lives of characters like Harry, Barjinder and Kuljit lie cloaked, this fantasy helps us mediate the playwright's liberatory message in terms of the dialogue across generations. This 'fantasy dialogue' is Singh's way of underlining both the woeful absence of, and an imperative need for, a dialogue among several members of the immigrant Punjabi community, as also among the members of a single family around whom the play is constructed.

Almost with a Chekhovian wry humour, the playwright points out the discrepancy between the outward show of bonhomie and camaraderie among Harry, Barjinder, Surjit, Jagg and Kelly and their inward struggle with loneliness. It is interesting to see how in most of the situations—especially in scenes 1 and 4 where conscious efforts are made by this particular group of friends to whip up a state of frenzied excitement and even a sort of saturnalia—dialogues often degenerate into a series of monologues. It is as though each of his characters is trapped within a self-enclosed loneliness and is making a desperate, and rather futile, effort to make contact with one another. It is no wonder that their moments of facile celebrations, through the Sophoclean mode of dramatic irony, often turn into moments of intense sorrow and grief, especially when the characters either turn confessional or are forced to confront their naked selves.

Appearing in the middle of the play, this fantasy dialogue neatly divides the dramatic action in terms of two distinct structural movements. Starting in Scene 1, the first movement attempts to create a yawning gulf between the past and the present, the inner and the outer, and the Punjabi psyche and the Canadian social ambience. The second one, which starts only in Scene 5, moves either towards the resolution of the tension thus generated or its hapless, almost passive acceptance. Harry's poignant realisation towards the end about the immigrants being no different from the fish of Kamloops (who must die at the same place where they were born) is as significant as Jagg's total surrender to his mean, vulgar, inferior self, reflected in his facile rationalisation of why he rejected his long-forgotten Indian wife. At one level, rejection of his Indian wife is a symbolic gesture on Jagg's part, through which he cuts himself off from his cultural bearings, discarding the baggage of his cultural past in totality. Undeterred by the emotional loss he may thus have to suffer, Jagg is eager to surrender his cultural identity. He is more than willing to succumb to the pressures of assimilative multiculturalism. Indifferent to the egregious demands of identity politics, he snatches every opportunity to sing hosannas to North America. By presenting Jagg more as a 'poetaster' or a 'versifier' than a 'poet', the playwright ultimately manages to denounce the over-glorification and romanticisation of the adopted culture and warns us against the total rejection of the mother culture. While Jagg's awareness about the extent of his own degeneration and/or debasement does redeem him somewhat in the eyes of the audience, it fails to humanise him completely.

The counter-point to this element of pastiche in the poetic conception of Jagg's character and/or situation is set up by the real issues afflicting the lives of the immigrant community. The play traces, with a rare sense of sensitivity and empathic involvement, the slow, painful process through which 'men' are reduced to 'a pair of hands' and describes how, in time, 'a pair of hands' are turned into 'convenient, expendable tools'. Commenting on the changes that the adopted culture has wrought in them, Jagg says, 'What has this country made out of us? We couldn't be what we wanted to be, and what we are, we certainly can't accept' (82). Apparently, Jagg is speaking here not only for himself, but also as the playwright's voice, representing the collective sentiments of the entire community to which he belongs.

Interestingly, no single character in the play has been accorded the privileged position of being 'the central consciousness' through whose eyes the entire dramatic action is either perceived or evaluated. In other words, no character has been permitted to speak exclusively on behalf of the playwright. The play essentially deals with shifting viewpoints and multiple perspectives, thus enabling the playwright to choose different spokespersons for different situations and thematic concerns. If it is Jagg in one situation, it is Kelly in the other and Micky in yet another. While Jagg gives expression to the predicaments and conflicts faced by every immigrant, Kelly debunks the false notion of piety and religiosity most immigrants pretend to live by. Commenting upon how divisive politics has virtually ruined the entire fabric of the collective religious life of the immigrants, Kelly says, 'Surjit Singha, not that I'm really piqued by your suggestion of setting up another Gurdwara. Far from it, Gurdwara has served several common ends here. Initially, the Gurdwaras belonged to the common heritage of all the Indians, everyone's social and cultural centres. And now, you know where things really stand. What bothers me is that now we've a Gurdwara for every denomination; a Jat Gurdwara, a Ramgarhia Gurdwara; if this one belongs to the *bhapas*, that one to the *adharamis* . . .' (60). Micky's tirade against Ravi has a touch of déjà vu. Her condemnation of Ravi is a disguised form of self-condemnation, rather like a self-flagellation that is as much personal as it is collective. Lashing out at him, she says, 'It was my illusion that you wanted to protect yourself against the garbage of the West. In fact, you hide the garbage of the entire earth inside you. You're the leftover of an Indian male and the grime of the Western values, too. *You're no more than shit*' (53). Behind her acerbic words is hidden the condemnation of a 'no-where generation' to which she herself belongs, a generation that has lost its way in the 'jungle of values', one that is simply muddling along reeling under the ghastly impact of de-culturation. In the manner of a true humanist, Singh has portrayed the most abominable of characters with a degree of sympathy and compassion. If on the one hand, this creates an alternating rhythm of sympathy within the play, on the other, it also imparts a rare sense of objectivity and fair play to his treatment of characters and situations. Despite wielding a strong authorial and directorial control over the action, Singh adroitly manages to wriggle out of the need to own up either his own statements or those of his characters.

However, the characters of *Kamloops Dian Macchian* are not defined only in terms of the shrillness of their voice or the stridency of their views and ideas. They come alive through the distinguishing features of Singh's characterisation—the angularities of his characters' speech rhythms, their mode of articulation or their preference for one register or the other. Singh's plays are often characterised by their plurality of dialects and heterogeneity of styles. They create the much-needed space for polyphonic discourse. Commenting on the importance of such a discourse in fiction, Mikhail Bakhtin said, 'Incorporated into the "novel" are a multiplicity of "language" and verbal–ideological belief systems—generic, professional, class-and-interest-group . . . but these languages are, it is true, kept primarily within the limits of the literary written and conversational language; at the same time, these languages are not, in most cases, consolidated into fixed persons.'[4] Though Bakhtin essentially developed his theory of 'heteroglossia' in relation to the novel, it has relevance and significance for other genres. He was emphatic that the novelist must always strive to use 'different voices' and never 'different dialects of the same language' in order to create the effect of 'heteroglossia'. However, as a playwright, Singh does often take the liberty to use different dialects of the same language as much as he creates different voices. His understanding of the linguistic features of each dialect is reflected in the adroitness with which he converts 'speech' into 'dialogue'. In this respect, it is important to take note of what the Hungarian comparitist Peter Szondi has to say about the way in which the European drama has changed since Renaissance. Theorising about the nature of modern drama, he says, 'The whole world of the Drama is dialectical in origin . . . It exists because of the always achieved, and from that point, once again disrupted sublation of the interpersonal dialectic, which manifests itself as speech in the dialogue . . . The Drama is possible only when dialogue is possible.'[5] As opposed to Bakhtin's use of the term 'dialect', which essentially draws attention towards the linguistic aspects of the language, Szondi's understanding of the term 'dialectical' is necessarily Hegelian in nature. Hegel talks of this in triadic terms as something consisting of thesis, anti-thesis and synthesis. Engaged as he is in the search for the 'possibilities of art', Singh shows a definite preference for the 'dialect' and/or the 'register' of his characters, which often depends upon his themes, his characters, their class, educational background and their location.

As most of the characters in *Kamloops Dian Macchian* are Jats from the Doaba region (areas surrounded by the rivers Beas and Sutlej), with varying educational backgrounds, and Canada being their common location, their language does become a significant lexical marker of their cultural identity or the lack of it. This is how Singh manages to set up the 'interpersonal dialectics' between and across different 'dialects'. Harry's language carries the burden of his lack of formal education and social background. His opening dialogues in the play carry the weight of this burden: '*Barjinder Sian, sara samaan katha ho gaya bire*?' (25) [Barjinder Sian, is everything ready, *Bire*?], and '. . . *Bire badaam kaju tann peanuttan tan main rakh tian*' (25). [... *Bire*, I've already kept the almonds, cashew nuts and peanuts.] His highly inflected speech rhythms and his preference for the distorted form of the hybridised language are markers of his confused mind and his inability to reconcile the duality of his position as an immigrant. While he prefers an anglicised version of his real name, Harjinder Singh, he stubbornly opposes the idea of providing the benefit of Western education to all immigrant children, saying,

'*Parh ke ehni kerian purian pa denian, appan ki khateya niane paraah ke. Lonian tan ant nu shiftan ee aa*' (32). [How is education going to help them, anyway. What did we get out of educating our children? After all, they're only going to work in the shifts.] Refusing to treat the immigrant children as anything more than just 'a pair of hands', he fails to realise that unless they partake of the Western system of education, they would certainly be left behind in the process of upward social mobility. It is this verbal–ideological confusion about adopting a system of beliefs that makes him complicate the lives of his own children. It is no wonder that his son Ravi has turned into an incorrigible Casanova who, as his father admits, 'changes women with the same ease with which one changes clothes' (36).

At one level, Kelly's (alias Karnail Singh) roots in Majha (a region in Punjab comprising the modern districts of Amritsar, Gurdaspur, Tarn Taran, etc.) makes him distinct from his other 'unlettered friends' from Doaba. It is reflected in his use of the *Majhi* dialect as much as in the 'register' of his characters, which invariably carries the imprint of his education and social class. At another level, he is a man of few words and speaks with poise, grace and ease rarely ever found in any of his friends. For instance, when Surjit slips into his characteristic hyperbole—'Oh, there's going to be a deluge, a real deluge'—Kelly offers the much-needed reassurance, saying, 'Friends, there's really no need to be down in the dumps. After all, problems have their solutions, too' (36). His words are carefully cadenced and measured, and his tone, often reflective, is serious. His is a voice of sanity and reason, which constantly undercuts, and in turn is also undercut by, the falsity and inconsistency of his friends' viewpoints. Sometimes he is even forced to suffer the ignominy of either being pooh-poohed or dismissed summarily by his pleasure-seeking, irrational friends. Barjinder openly jeers at him for supporting the cause of education, saying, 'Kelly Sian, don't be angry, but you own only one car and that too, is almost twelve years old. We have three lined up outside our house, that too, all new ones. Your house is still on mortgage and our basements are also fetching rents' (36–7). As opposed to the 'cultivation of mind and spirit', it is really the 'cultivation of the material body' that appears to fascinate the Punjabi immigrants' imagination. By thus bringing two divergent, oppositional ideological systems into dialectical tension, Singh has succeeded in initiating a dialogue between different members of a group that is homogeneous only in its appearance and is essentially heterogeneous in its character.

If at one level, *Kamloops Dian Macchian* is about the failure of first-generation immigrants to make sensible and right choices, at another, it is also about the way in which this failure could ultimately wreck the lives of successive generations. If the first generation is still trapped within its orthodox belief systems, its caste affiliations and caste prejudices, and its feudal and patriarchal mindset, the second generation is into ceaseless exploration and blind experimentation, with the unlimited freedom that the West offers. Without allowing the play to slip into a seemingly simplistic East–West encounter, Singh retains the complexity of his characters and the dramatic urgency of his thematic concerns by constantly altering and shifting his perspectives and modulating his sympathies. Not only does he sympathise with each and every viewpoint and character without becoming egregiously moralistic, but he creates the necessary dramatic space within which audience's sympathies could also be effectively monitored and even manipulated.

It is in this respect that the play ultimately succeeds in setting up a dialogue between the playwright and the reader, the actors and the audience, the characters and the actors, the theme and the structure, the poetic and the realistic, the dramatic and the narrative, and the past and the present. The dualities of *Kamloops Dian Macchian* provide the necessary wherewithal for a dialectical mode of articulation and also, the dramatic tension necessary for its sustenance. If the final resolution eludes the audience, it is only because Singh's intent is to initiate the debate, not to conclude it.

Notes and References

1. Martin Buber, *I and Thou*, tr. Ronald Gregor Smith (New York: Charles Scribner's Sons, 1958). Buber contends that the '*I–Thou* relation between the individual and God is a universal relation which is the foundation for all other relations. If the individual has a real *I–Thou* relation with God, then the individual must have a real *I–Thou* relation with the world. If the individual has a real *I–Thou* relation with God, then the individual's

action in the world must be guided by that *I–Thou* relation.' According to him, human beings may adopt two attitudes toward the world: *I–Thou* or *I–It*. *I–Thou* is a relation of a subject to another subject and *I–It* is a relation of a subject to an object. In *I–Thou* relationship, human beings are aware of each other as having a unity of being. In *I–Thou* relationship, human beings do not perceive each other as consisting of specific, isolated qualities but engage in a dialogue involving each other's whole being. In the *I–It* relationship, on the other hand, human beings perceive each other as consisting of specific, isolated qualities, and view themselves as a part of a world which consists of things. *I–Thou* is a relationship of mutuality and reciprocity, while *I–It* is a relationship of separateness and detachment (26).

2. Suirinder Dhanjal, as quoted in *Kamloops Dian Macchian: A Play by Atamjit* (Chandigarh: Balraj Sahni Yaadgar Prakashan, 1998), 110.

3. Atamjit Singh, *Kamloops Dian Macchian* (Chandigarh: Lokgeet Prakashan, 2001), 65. All subsequent textual quotations are cited from this edition and relevant page numbers are placed within parenthesis. As the original text is in Punjabi, all translations are mine.

4. Mikhail Bakhtin, *The Dialogic Imagination*, trans. Michael Holoquist (Texas: University of Texas Press, 1981), 311.

5. Peter Szondi, *Theory of the Modern Drama*, trans. and ed. Michael Hays (Cambridge: Polity Press, 1987), 10.

CHAPTER SEVEN

Narratives of Dispersal: Reading Raghbir Dhand's Stories

Among all the first-generation diasporic Punjabi writers, no short story writer can be said to command the kind of awe and respect that Raghbir Dhand (1934–90) often does. If he had the advantage of being a pioneer of sorts, Dhand complemented it with a rare artistic control, fine understanding of his craft, economy of style and expression, fusion of character and incident, and a deep commitment to basic human values. Described by one of the Indian writers as 'Saraswati's favourite son',[1] Dhand had become a legend in his own lifetime. He inspired a whole generation of young Punjabi writers settled in England. His acolytes, who are now established writers in their own right, recall how he loved to quote Goethe's immortal words of advice to young artists: 'Don't orate, artist, create!'[2] Such was the power of his vision and the dynamism of his conviction and character.

Born on 1 November 1934 at Jandiali Kalan in Sangrur district, Dhand lost his mother at the age of seven, a loss that haunted him throughout his life. As a child, he was fond of listening to the stories narrated by village elders, which helped him develop an early interest in the art of storytelling. His formative years were spent at Ahmedgarh where he received most of his formal education. He was barely thirteen when Partition struck, and though he was never a direct victim of this tragedy or the violence that followed, it did scar him for life, leaving indelible impressions on his young, sensitive mind. After completing his Gyani from Panjab University, Dhand started working as a schoolteacher at Majitha, near Amritsar. While teaching, he first did his BA as a private student and then earned a BT (Bachelor of Training) degree from the local Khalsa College. He was a bright student with a keen, perceptive mind and an insatiable thirst for knowledge. He later went on to do his MA in History from Panjab University, Chandigarh, in 1959. He had begun to familiarise himself with the writings of Karl Marx, Gorky, Chekhov, Lenin, Premchand, Faiz Ahmed Faiz, etc., rather early on in his student life. He admired and read the works of such great minds as Balzac, Graham Greene, Dostoyevsky, John Steinbeck and many others.

Dhand had already served as a schoolteacher for a couple of years in various parts of Punjab before he chose to migrate to England in 1965. Initially, he worked in various factories and offices for a couple of years, and after earning a degree in teacher-training from the University of Leeds, Dhand started teaching in local schools. Teaching was for him a way of improving his own mind, and in keeping with the best traditions of scholasticism, he continued to nourish this right through his life. Neither the lure of a comfortable life nor his debilitating bouts of asthma could deter him from pursuing a PhD degree, which he received from the Kim-U-Sung University, Pyongyang, North Korea, in 1979. Dhand's experiences propelled him towards the Marxist ideals of social justice, equality and change, which incidentally constitute his *weltanschauung*, too. Never a mere armchair intellectual, Dhand was an inveterate activist who not only helped found the Progressive Writers Association of Great Britain in 1969, but also remained its most vociferous exponent until his death in 1990.[3]

Although Dhand started publishing short stories in magazines and journals as far back as 1956, his literary career did not get off to a formal start until 1972, at which point he published his first ever collection, *Boli Dharti* (The Deaf Earth). Set largely against the background of rural Punjab, most of the stories in this collection give a very intimate and authentic account of the social life, captured in all its hues by a cultural insider. The ethos is rural and so are the characters, but the sensibility that enlivens the stories is fairly catholic, and even cosmopolitan. Published in 1975, *Us Paar* (Across the Shores) offers a medley of images, both of rural Punjab and of cosmopolitan England, seen from the double perspective of a cultural outsider. Products of the transitional phase (when Dhand was trying to strike roots in the English soil), these are the stories of 'in-betweenness', combining the vestiges of nostalgia for the homeland with an equally strong, irresistible fascination for the host land. Of course, the crucial questions of identity—both personal and cultural—do leap into focus here.

Dhand's third collection, *Kaya Kalp* (The Metamorphosis, 1980), is set in the darkest period of contemporary Indian history—the Emergency. The narrator of these stories, as also that of his fourth collection *Kursi* (The Chair, 1988), is not a 'lost immigrant' but a 'self-assured settler' who has developed this rare ability to perceive his homeland from outside, without compromising on his empathy. These stories can be read as an extended lament on the slow erosion of the social/moral fabric of Indian society and the collapse of a collective dream. *Shan-e-Punjab* (The Pride of Punjab, 1990), the last collection Dhand published in his lifetime, only accentuates this sense of disillusionment and despair. In some of these stories, the insider/outsider watches helplessly as Punjab slides into the vortex of terrorism. Though saddened and shocked at the loss of 'Punjabiat' and its language and culture, Dhand never gives up hope. Reasserting his humanism, Dhand locates it within the larger space of cultural pluralism and ethnic multiculturalism that define the British society he had migrated to.

Dispersal: Etymology and Signification

It would help us to explore the etymology and the multiple significations of the term 'dispersal', before we locate it in Dhand's works. If we go along with the dictionary meaning, 'dispersal' signifies a movement *away* from the centre—a kind of scattering and distribution of seeds, human beings, etc. away from the parent organism/formation—a movement which is often regarded as a necessary and sufficient condition for the growth, evolution and perpetuation of the species.[4] In order to locate the originary meanings of the term, we need to turn first to biology and then to military sciences. In these two discourses, the notion of 'dispersal' acquires a more specialised meaning and signification. In biological sciences, dispersal essentially has to do with the scattering of seeds through air, water or other mechanical means, so that the species of a particular plant can perpetuate itself away from the parent plant. Biological dispersal is based on the Darwinian notion of the survival of the fittest and so has largely to do with the principles of adaptability and procreation. Apart from the notion of biological dispersal, we also come across the term 'force dispersal', which comes to us from the military sciences. In this sense, dispersal signifies a military strategy or a significant formation in military operations, guerilla warfare or counter-insurgency operations whose ultimate aim is to minimise the collateral damage during emergency operations. In other words, it is a form of defense mechanism that soldiers are expected to deploy in somewhat unusual or extraordinary circumstances, wherein they are scattered away from the centre in such a way that the damage to both men and material is considerably mitigated. Now, whether we look at 'dispersal' as a biological process or as a man-made military formation, in both the cases, the twin notions of 'adaptability' and 'survival' are intrinsically bound up with the term. To put it differently, dispersal could either be understood as a natural phenomenon or as a human-made artifice or construction, an invention, or quite simply, both. However, this discussion uses the term 'dispersal' in its most extended form, complete with all its elliptical significations.

Postcolonial discourses and narratives use a variety of terms—for instance, 'diaspora', 'migration', 'displacement', 'exile', etc.—to convey this sense of scattering and distribution. Though the term 'dispersal' has been as much a part of the postcolonial lexicon as any other term, its importance has not been overemphasised as much as it should be.[5] Unlike 'diaspora', which almost takes a fixed and centralised notion of 'homeland' for granted (for diasporas cannot exist without the prior existence of a homeland), 'dispersal' emphasises a constant and endless process of decentring, thus ruling out the possibility of any central organising principle in our understanding of the immigrant experience. It points out quite clearly that centre–margin relations in this case cannot be negotiated very easily, as the contours of what constitutes the 'centre' are constantly defined and redefined. Moreover, unlike 'diaspora', where the centrality of the homeland and also the possibility of an actual, physical or a mythic psychological return to it are often perceived as inescapable conditions, 'dispersal' imposes no such preconditions. It essentially emphasises the provisionality and tentativeness of the immigrant experience, thus nullifying both the centrality of the homeland and its emotional and/or psychological burden. This emancipatory aspect of 'dispersal' offers the term a definite theoretical edge over other related terms such as 'diaspora', 'migration', 'displacement' and 'exile'. It may be noted here that the Greek meaning of the term 'displacement' incorporates the term 'dispersal' and does not exclude it. Besides, the idea of 'exile', as has been pointed out by Edward Said, resonates with a permanent, unrecoverable sense of loss, which is not the sense in which it could effectively be used in relation to Punjabi migrant experience and/ or the Punjabi psyche. Implicated in the ideology of postcolonial, transnational, transcultural and 'multi-locational identities',[6] the concept of 'dispersal' offers a distinct advantage over other related terms.

The term 'dispersal' also helps to bring out a deeper understanding of Punjabi society, history and culture and the complex negotiations they enter into with one another. Dispersal is a phenomenon that is rooted in the collective consciousness of Punjabis and their history and culture. Much before they territorialised this mass of land known as Punjab, they were essentially wandering nomads who travelled from one village to another, from one region to another, and also from one geographical terrain to another. If seen from this perspective, the idea of 'dispersal' is almost innate to the Punjabi psyche and culture, and it also pre-dates the notion of the Punjabi settlement and/or nativisation. So deeply ingrained is this idea of 'dispersal' in the collective psyche of the people of Punjab that it continued to assert itself even after they had begun to assert their 'homing in' instincts (the instinct to return home). It is in this sense that our emphasis on the notion of 'dispersal' becomes a kind of historical gesture, a pretext for mediating, within a relatively larger cultural framework, the dynamics of mass migrations from Punjab to other parts of the world over the past two centuries or so.

Our emphasis on the notion of 'dispersal' also draws attention to the fact that, owing to this constant tendency to 'disperse', Punjabis have developed an equally strong and irrepressible sense of attachment to land—not necessarily the land of their birth or origin. One may even go so far as to suggest that it is because of this tendency that Punjabis have been able to strike roots wherever they have settled and even purchase land, exhibiting this strange dialectics of finding 'roots' through 'routes', always pushing the limits of the frontier in the process. This is often reminiscent of the true spirit of the American frontiersman. If we are able to respond to this dynamics of 'dispersal' operating in the Punjabi psyche, we may also be able to understand to some extent, the psycho-dynamics of an equally strong, irrepressible sense of 'sub-nationalism' or 'nationalism' operating among them. And this brand of nationalism, I argue, often acquires aggressive and militant postures, especially when the Punjabis are located away from the land of their birth or origin.

Dilemmas of Dispersal: Perspectives of Popular History

To understand the dynamics of some of the major dilemmas of dispersal, we need to once again turn to history, especially the history of colonialism in Punjab. The dilemmas of dispersal are essentially rooted in the cultural history of Punjab. They are externalised through complex processes that show both collaboration with and subversion of, the English language, its literary formations, people, race and culture. If we look at the history of colonial Punjab, we come across this strange schism where the rootedness to the land which manifested itself in the form of resistance to the English and their language and/or religion (Punjab was one of the last outposts of India to fall under the British dominion/rule), coexisted with an equally strong tendency to collaborate with the dominant imperialist ideology, especially in the context of its educational, literary, political and cultural formations. The process of resistance also had a cultural politics of a very different kind: it was largely the result of the combined influence of a variety of factors such as 'injured sense of Punjabi merit and pride', 'inherent sense of Punjabi rebelliousness', 'non-conformism' and its 'strong anti-authoritarian and/or anti-hegemonic impulses'.[7]

One needs to emphasise that while the resistance to the British hegemony (or before that, to the Mughals) worked largely on the ground—the level at which the popular, folk consciousness operates—the complicity and collaboration functioned purely at the level of politics and culture. It is no wonder that historically, one of the eternal dilemmas of the Punjabi people has to be seen in terms of their undying love for the land/language and their equally irrepressible tendency to disperse away from the land.

It is customary to speak of the Punjabis' legendary love for the land. Punjabi literature—both folk and canonical—is replete with tales of how a Punjabi values *his* land (the ownership of land being defined as a purely male domain). A popular saying in Punjabi underlines this rather well. It says, 'A Punjabi is prepared to give up almost anything for the sake of three things, *jar*, *joroo* and *jameen*.' Undoubtedly, in popular Punjabi consciousness, personal honour, dignity and self-respect are inextricably bound up with land and women. Given this fabled status that land occupies in popular Punjabi imagination, it is indeed strange and incongruous that Punjabis have displayed a strong instinct for travel and migration. Ordinarily, an average Punjabi undergoes a minimum of two migrations, both inter- and intra-state, in a lifetime or within a generation—a fair testimony to her/his high spiritedness and undying nomadic instinct.

Though the contours of the Punjabi diaspora have only begun to emerge in the past fifty years or so, the process of the dispersal of Punjabi population is as old as the history of Punjab itself. It would not be wrong to say that the propensity for dispersal and/or migration is as indigenous to the Punjabi psyche/character as is the sense of rootedness and/or belonging. As a result, 'rootedness vs dispersal' is one of the emergent, if not the dominant, themes in much of the Punjabi literature created within the Punjabi diaspora. If, in the pre-Partition phase, overseas migration from Punjab was a mere trickle, it turned into a veritable deluge in the post-Independence period. Favourable immigration laws in the West, widespread displacements caused by Partition, shrinking land holdings within Punjab and expanding economic opportunities outside were mainly instrumental in this exponential growth of Punjabi migration. In the United Kingdom alone, Punjabis constitute almost one-fifth of the total migrant Asian population and almost one-twentieth of the total population of the country.

Of the nearly five hundred thousand Punjabis living in the United Kingdom, only a few hundreds have, over the years, turned to writing and only a score of them, or perhaps even less, have made their mark as writers. Lauded for their indomitable courage and conviction, and their sense of initiative and enterprise, the Punjabis in England are better known for their pop music and *bhangra*, and spicy curries and pickles. In short, their legendary business enterprises, rather than their literary acumen, have defined them as a community. Despite the considerable volume of their literary output, the Punjabis have failed to make a strong impact on the literary scene of England. We can cite several reasons for it.

Most of the writers of the Punjabi diaspora are from among the first-generation immigrants who chose to make England their home in the late 1950s or early 1960s. As they were primarily motivated by the idea of seeking greener economic pastures abroad, migration was more of a personal or situational necessity for them, and not really a matter of free choice. Unable to procure white-collar jobs, they had to settle for low-paid, menial jobs. Under these circumstances, some of the more fortunate ones turned to writing as an escape route, as the only possible means of connecting with the soil and as a way of reclaiming and reasserting their bonds with their own language and culture.

Interestingly, when they chose Punjabi as their preferred mode of creative self-expression, they knew that such a decision could actually fly right in their faces. In the early 1960s, when some of these writers were struggling to establish their literary credentials, the odds were loaded rather heavily against them. The Punjabi immigrant population in England was not organised enough to offer either the benefits of readership or the monetary support on a more sustainable basis. The network of Punjabi literary societies was virtually nonexistent, and the local publishers were not keen on backing their literary efforts for obvious reasons. Moreover, the local libraries in England, at that point in time, were a little too conservative in their approach to allow the literary productions of the UK-based Punjabi writers to be either showcased or actively promoted. Significantly, today, these writers have managed to turn the tide by creating a substantial and recognisable body of writings which has found its readership. These writers now have a definite presence in the school curriculum for Punjabi language/literature at A-levels in the UK as much as in the Punjabi literary canon taught in various Indian universities.

Narratives of Dispersal and Raghbir Dhand

As Dhand was among one of the pioneering writers within the Punjabi diaspora, his stories often carry the historical burden of some of the dilemmas of dispersal. The location of most of his stories, as this essay will discuss, is not India but England, where he spent close to twenty-five years of his productive life. During this period, he undoubtedly returned to India for short intervals, but in the ultimate analysis, he had made England his home, and had also come to terms with the fact of being a permanent settler, not just an uncertain immigrant. Both as an individual and a writer, Dhand constantly sought to negotiate the complex, ghettoised, feudal Punjabi identity through the mish-mash of racism and the politics of exclusion/identity/language/culture.

Although a good number of Dhand's stories deal with a strong, irrepressible sense of nostalgia for the 'lost homeland', this essay will foreground only those stories that deal exclusively with the dilemmas arising out of the process of dispersal. In a way, the problem of dual cultural identity emerges as one of the subsidiary themes in these stories. To an extent, this essay attempts to provide an against-the-grain reading of Dhand's works, as most of the Punjabi critics tend to celebrate only those stories that deal with 'nostalgia' and ignore in the process, much of his important works that show his complex negotiations with the English language, society, race and culture.

Though most of Dhand's contemporaries have chosen to focus on the question of how the Punjabis living in the UK have sometimes been at the receiving end of racial discrimination, Dhand, in his story 'Bondage', looks at the notion of racial discrimination in reverse.[8] A multi-layered narrative structured around the principles of 'inverted racism' and 'social hierarchy', 'Bondage' is a story of a young Englishman called Peter. He works as an assistant in a store owned by Urvashi, the narrator's sister-in-law. Retained at a salary of twenty-five pounds a week, he is literally slave-driven by Urvashi. She knows that owing to his desperate financial condition, Peter is not likely to leave her. Her approach is based on a mix of semi-feudal, semi-paternalistic code characteristic of Punjabi community (which she has incidentally internalised, and of which, Dhand would have us believe, she herself is a victim of sorts), catering to his basic needs, and also humouring, indulging and mothering him occasionally. All through the story, we get the impression that it is Peter who is in a state of bondage, but only towards the end do we realise that Urvashi too is hopelessly dependent on him. When the ironic significance of the term 'bondage' is revealed to us, the situation literally turns upon its head, blurring the facetious distinction between the 'victim' and the 'victimiser'.

Dhand's point is loud and clear: in a paternalistic, capitalistic, money-oriented culture, there are no masters, only slaves. This culture has reduced all human equations and relationships to mere convenience, commodifying them in the process. Strangely enough, it is in this commodified space that both Peter and Urvashi tend to construct a new sense of community, away from their respective cultural identities. Dhand seems to be suggesting that it is the power of money that is ultimately responsible for causing the 'dispersal' away from the community to which one belongs, forging a new sense of community or symbiosis or both. Interestingly, the narrator situates himself literally in the middle of these two distinct cultural identities, which gives him the advantage of observing the Punjabi culture from outside and also the English culture from below. As an 'observing consciousness', he not only offers a trenchant critique of capitalism, but also suggests a humanistic solution, which is, of course, rejected by Urvashi. Pained at the fact that Peter has to suffer so much of personal humiliation, when he suggests that Peter should set up his own store, Urvashi virtually admonishes her brother-in-law saying, 'Look, you shouldn't give such ideas to Peter. He's a straightforward, honest chap; you could even trust him with gold . . . If he were to start picking up such dangerous ideas, he'd stop working for us . . .' (32). Dhand appears to be suggesting that 'bondage' is a condition of mind, not necessarily a state of being—economic or otherwise. Though the liberal, enlightened approach of the narrator/observer falls flat on its face, he does succeed in calling into question the value-system practised by his sister-in-law. By ripping off the complex layers of every known form of human bondage, Dhand compels us to reflect on the condition of our own lives.

The 'observing consciousness' of the narrator in 'Bondage' becomes a 'translating consciousness' in 'Dustbin', bringing to the fore the question of 'cultural translation'. Unnerved by the sudden hospitalisation of his wife and his own inability to manage the household and/or the children, the narrator turns first to his young, adolescent daughter and then to other members of his own community for help. His daughter, who has been born and brought up in England and has never visited India, ends up rolling out *chapattis* that remind the narrator of the map of India. Quite literally, his daughter ends up creating a perfect metaphor for the cartography of dispersal, as the map of India appears to be subliminally encoded in her psyche. If, on the one hand, the narrator, positioned in the proverbial 'third space', translates his own culture to his England-born daughter (for he is the one who points out to her that the *chapattis* she is rolling out resemble the map of India), on the other, he translates her inability to comprehend the surreal, exotic Indian reality into a local proverb, saying, 'Oh listen Camel! Every limb in your body is crooked . . . ' (34). Going beyond, the narrator also translates the apathy, indifference and the refusal of the other members of his community to extend any possible help in times of crisis as a loss of the sense of community and solidarity, caused by a state of cultural anomie. When he approaches three women, his wife's acquaintances, for help, they refuse to lend a helping hand, citing one flimsy reason or the other. At a more serious level, it is this slow breakdown and gradual dispersal of the sense of community that Dhand seems to be bemoaning in the story, though his wry humour and ironic postures do tend to suggest otherwise.

In 'Dustbin', Dhand has very effectively offered a self-critical narrative of the diasporic Punjabi community which appears to be on the verge of a collapse, threatened as it is by the pressures of facile individualism and false gestures of acculturation. 'Dustbin' captures the 'double vision' of a 'translating narrator'. The narrator is desperately searching for effective cultural metaphors so that he may be able to synergise his own creative resources and also attain, if possible, a measure of self-expression. Exploring the comic possibilities latent in the situation, Dhand manages to create a self-reflexive narrative of dispersal, which foregrounds the failure of the narrator's cultural imagination along with his equally pathetic attempts to reclaim his 'writerly' self. Dhand tries to reinforce the idea that the 'translating consciousness' has to locate its linguistic resources, metaphorically, within the frame of the host culture, if it has to become an effective instrument of 'writerly consciousness'. Written in a characteristic self-deprecatory style, the story is as much a translator's delight as it is a creative artist's envy.

In the story 'Eye of a Serpent', once again, Dhand casts an angular look at how the conventional markers of Punjabi identity such as kinship culture, strong sense of community and interdependence are imperceptibly being replaced by the wayward and somewhat false notions of individual freedom and independence, often wrongly attributed to the West. Unable to understand the complex matrix of individualism, Tara ends up making false, hypocritical gestures towards modernisation and Westernisation. For him, making love to a white woman, regardless of whether one is married or not, is not only a sign of an over-exuberant Punjabi masculinity, but also an expression of individual freedom that the West supports as well as promotes. Though a village lad himself, Tara is extremely unhappy with his illiterate wife Bacchni, whom he hates with his whole heart. He holds her responsible for driving away Jean, his white girlfriend. In order to overcome the trauma of separation, he takes to drinking heavily. One day, while walking back home in a state of drunken stupor, it suddenly dawns on him that he cannot meet his own growing financial needs and also those of his parents back in India, without Bacchni's income supplementing his own. It is this realisation that ultimately pushes Tara, a ghettoised Punjabi mind, into reordering his perceptions and priorities. In the process, he succumbs to the 'serpent-sting' of the materialistic, commodified culture. Significantly, through Tara's morally self-defeating gesture, Dhand also points out his inability to negotiate the complexities of the 'dual cultural space'. He hints that the failure of negotiation, at some deeper, subliminal level, results directly from the failure of human imagination.

Going beyond the narrow confines of Punjabi identity/culture, 'No Exit' focusses on the problem of dual identity in relation to a Jamaican youth, Trevor, who shuttles relentlessly between and across cultures, unable to find his moorings. His only reasons for staying back in England, where he has been living for over twenty-five years now, is that here, 'he's assured of dole, allowance for children, free education and medical care' (176). But England is also the place where his house has been burnt down by his white neighbours, his five-year-old child has been scarred for life and where he was refused business even after he bought his own vehicle. Though Trevor is not a narrator—he is only a 'narratee' (to whom the story is narrated)—the roles of narrator and narratee are shuffled around in such a way that his story becomes, by implication, an objectified version of the narrator's story as well. By thus shuffling the roles around, Dhand forges a new definition of human identity based on the solidarity of the oppressed. Rather than celebrate the idea of victimhood, the story leaves us with a hauntingly evocative image of Trevor's car moving 'neither forwards nor backwards,' with its wheels 'half-sunk into slush' (181). It is this image that sums up the essential predicament of all those who are forever caught between the conflicting claims of rootedness and dispersal.

Conceived in the form of an interior monologue, 'Fault Lines', with its astounding range and vast canvas, is perhaps the best tribute to Dhand's cosmopolitanism and liberal humanism. As he babysits his six-months-old granddaughter, wondering what to write against a column in her admission form that demands to know her religion, the narrator's thoughts wander across the vast amphitheatre of human history. He is reminded of the inevitable relationship between religion and violence that history often legitimises and he shudders at the thought of the world his granddaughter is likely to grow up in. As he reflects on her loss of innocence, sordid and painful memories of the Partition come leaping forth. During the Partition of the subcontinent violence had ceased to be an abstraction and it had instead acquired a savage and a brutal face. However, the narrator's indictment of violence is not based on mere random reflections, but is grounded upon an incisive understanding of history. With his granddaughter Snowber acting as a mute witness, the narrator first retrieves and then interrogates all known notions of history, and also the wayward manner in which it has progressed over the centuries. In this particular story, the notion of dispersal acquires very different connotations as the narrative, structured around the archetypal polarities of love and violence, disperses itself between the two extremities of intensely personal reflections and consciousness of historical determinism.

In 'Snowbound in London', Dhand again takes recourse to the interior monologue, though this time round he reflects upon the changing relations between the 'self' and the 'other'. Travelling in a bus late one evening, Channo, the protagonist, is besieged by the fears of 'otherness' and 'exclusion'. As she looks around fearfully, the memories of how her husband was mauled by some English goons for no fault of his, return to haunt her. She cannot even understand why, how and when exactly her '*bapu*' became a 'daddy' for her. All she knows is that this kind of superficial change has not in any way facilitated the process of integration or assimilation, either for her or her husband. And if they ever think of packing up and going back to their village, either his parents or her brothers demand more money. As a result, she feels that both of them are condemned to live like prisoners of their situation, unable to make their own free choices. Using the visual language with the deftness of an artist, Dhand communicates ideas of cultural isolation, individual alienation and dual estrangement very effectively. Though the situation has the inherent potential to turn somewhat maudlin, Dhand saves it by allowing Channo to step out of her obsessive fears and express concern for her daughter. Dhand suggests that in this process of dispersal, the only way one can possibly salvage one's humanity is by shedding one's self-obsessed and self-focussed tunnel vision. By weaving a complex web of characters, situations and settings, this story easily foregrounds its own powers of suggestiveness.

Nowhere is the double potential of Dhand, the satirist and the humorist, tapped so brilliantly as in 'Ode to Donkeys'. Looking over his shoulders, the self-deprecatory narrator of this story casts a nostalgic look at his land, recounting with a rare fervour his childhood obsession with donkeys. As the story progresses, the narrator's desire to catch a glimpse of his 'childhood obsession' gets more and more intense, even desperate. Ultimately, the much-desired and longed-for 'encounter' does take place, though in a manner the narrator had least expected. His chance meeting with four young Punjabi visitors from India makes him realise that donkeys can sometimes appear in a different garb. Though all of them have lived all their lives in Punjab, they have little respect for the Punjabi language and very little knowledge of the region. Despite the predominance of the comic/satirical mode, the story goes on to raise some serious questions about the conventional notions of 'rootedness' and 'dispersal', and also the interrelationship of the two. Practically turning these ideas upon their head, Dhand points out that 'rootedness' may sometimes trigger off a process of 'dispersal' that one may find rather hard to imagine.

'Meeting Point' provides an interesting critique of the British brand of multiculturalism, bringing to the fore some of its inherent contradictions. Set inside a hospital, the story positions members of the diasporic Asian community as the patients and white British men and women as the doctors and nurses attending to them. The story becomes an imaginative exploration of the operational aspects of multiculturalism, provided the implications of the 'symbolic order' are fully realised. In the over-sanitised and somewhat impersonal environs of a London hospital, the narrator, like so many other patients in the general ward, longs for a sense of personal warmth and contact. Of course, this longing sometimes takes on bizarre forms, especially when the patients either start ogling at the white nurses bustling in and out of the wards, or make passes at them in languages they do not seem to understand. Apart from being a marker of cultural identity, language is also seen here as a barrier or an obstacle in the way of building the proverbial multicultural bridges. The metaphor of hospital, as a miniature version of English society, works fairly well. It is through this metaphor that Dhand first exposes the multiple afflictions of multiculturalism and then goes on to explore its therapeutic or redemptive possibilities.

Going beyond the self-limiting postures of identity politics, 'Matching Horoscopes' brings home to us the need for forging intensely personal bonds based on class (and not affiliations based on race). On being fired from his job as a school teacher by a headmaster who makes no secret of his racist ideology, Lok Nath seeks help from Jagatjeet, a local political heavyweight. But he receives no help. In the middle of this depressing scenario, Lok Nath's only reassurance is the friendship he shares with Jenny, who is willing to testify against the headmaster, regardless of the consequences. Apparently, sometimes the horoscopes do match, not necessarily within the community but across the races.

Departing from his self-professed Marxist position, in 'The Canker', Dhand captures the fervour of religious fanaticism with the empathy of an insider. Set in the post-Operation Blue Star period, this story maps out the slow, almost imperceptible conversion of a liberal secularist into a hard-core fanatic. In this particular story, Dhand emphasises that the notion of dispersal has definite implications for individual as well as collective identities, especially when the search for the 'imaginary homeland' is constantly thwarted.

Etymologically, the term 'diaspora' signifies displacement and dispersal, and so, rupture, discontinuity and fragmentation are built into the very nature of these stories. In a manner of speaking, each story is a 'situational narrative of dispersal' and so, each is equally unstructured and open-ended. In these stories, Dhand refuses to conform to the notions of continuity, coherence and/or a unified subjectivity. In these stories, the notion of subjectivity is often constituted in 'the third time-space', though it is never constituted fully or conclusively. As a result, the notion of identity is never stable or fixed, but it constantly elides, and therefore, remains fluid, tentative and provisional. For most of the characters of Dhand, 'diasporic consciousness' is constituted both positively and negatively. Reified memories often define the shifting planes of their fragmented consciousness. Searching for a toehold, some of them return to the 'reality' or the 'myth' of the memory-locked, imaginary homeland; while others struggle desperately to understand the rationale behind the collapsing affiliative structures; whereas still others, simply race on ahead to embrace whatever shreds of fragmented reality the host land may have left them with. In the ultimate analysis, one may conclude that Dhand not only recognises dispersal as an essential pre-requisite for cross-pollination and/or cross-cultural contact, but also as one of the basic requirements for the construction of a multi-locational, de-centred identity and/or subjectivity.

Notes and References

1. From the 'Introduction' to *Raghbir Dhand Dian Chaunviyan Kahanian,* ed. Kesar Singh Kesar (Ludhiana: Chetna Prakashan), 1.
2. *Raghbir Dhand Dian Chaunviyan Kahanian*, 3.
3. The section where I have discussed the biographical details of Raghbir Dhand is based on two sources: Kesar Singh Kesar, ed, 'Introduction', in *Raghbir Dhand Dian Chaunviyan Kahanian* (Chandigarh: Lokgeet Prakashan), and my unpublished personal interviews with Mrs Dhand and Rajiv Dhand, his son.
4. Dictionary.com, 'Dispersal', htpp//:dictionary.reference.com/browse/dispersal/ (accessed October 11, 2010).
5. Robin Cohen is perhaps the only theorist who has privileged the term 'dispersal' in his discourse. Identifying some nine characteristics of diasporic experience, he considers 'dispersal' to be the most important one. See, Robin Cohen, 'Diasporas and the State: From Victim to Challengers', *International Affairs* 72 (1996): 507–20.
6. 'Multi-locational identities' is a term that Avtar Brah has used in Avtar Brah, *Cartographies of Diaspora* (London: Routledge, 1996).
7. This argument has been developed extensively in the chapter 'Punjabi and English: Mediating the History of Language, Literature and Translation'.
8. The translated version of this story and those of the other stories discussed in this chapter are from Raghbir Dhand's collection which I translated along with an expository introduction, some years ago. See, Raghbir Dhand, *Melting Moments: A Collection of Punjabi Short Stories*, trans. Rana Nayar (Chandigarh: Unistar, 2005). All the subsequent references to this story as well as others cited in this chapter refer to this collection, and the page numbers of each are indicated against the quoted material.

CHAPTER EIGHT

Postcolonial *Katha*: Continuities and Ruptures in *Videshi* Punjabi Short Fiction

This essay looks at a number of theoretical issues, which we will envision as *kathas*, inherent in the study of postcolonial theory in India and, also uses these issues as contexts for reading and rereading *videshi* Punjabi short fiction. Before we begin the discussion on postcolonial *katha*, one should state the rationale behind the preference shown here in this discussion for, and insistence upon, the use of the term '*katha*'. This particular word is richly layered as it instantly evokes a cultural context that resounds with *Pauranik* tales, *Jataka* tales, *Kathasaritsagara*, etc. In short, it is evocative of a very vibrant tradition of storytelling available in our own cultural context. Narratives are essentially ways of organising and critiquing cultural traditions. Had it not been for that wonderful essay titled 'The Race for Theory' by Barbara Christian,[1] the Black American critic and scholar, perhaps our understanding of the nature and function of narratives would have remained hopelessly circumscribed. She pointed out that narratives can also be used as effective vehicles of theory, and even as ancillaries to offer resistance to—if not completely overturn—the theory over which the White race appears to exercise complete power, control and hegemony. Such attempts to create counter-discourses should be taken more seriously than they often are.

A narrative is not only a way of offering resistance to theory or a mode of undermining and critiquing it, but it is also a way of constituting a counter-discourse to theory. Narrative, as Christian theorises, is a kind of subaltern response of the Black community to the hegemony of the White-dominated theory (or the institutional practices promoted by the Western academies) and for that reason alone, it could be posited as a form of metatheory as well. Much more significant is the fact that this kind of interrogation is not marginal but central to the task we have on hand—the task of reassessing, revisioning and re-interrogating postcolonialism, especially in the context of both *desi* and *videshi* literatures.

Before the ruptures and continuities of our *videshi* or diaspora literatures are mapped out in some detail, it is necessary to understand some of the ideological contradictions and confusions inherent to postcolonial theory in general.[2] As the classroom is often the most preferred location of any intellectual discussion or debate on postcolonial theory (or for that matter, any other theory), the first *katha* we shall narrate is the one about the way in which the interaction between a teacher and a student in our context invariably takes the form of a 'colonial' rather than a 'postcolonial' encounter. Thereafter, the second *katha* shall deal with some of the institutional and market-driven practices that both facilitate and/or obstruct the promotion of postcolonial theory in our institutions. This shall uncover the exact nature of the ideological burden that the hegemony of the 'West-generated' and 'West-oriented' epistemology creates in this particular field. In other words, it would be an attempt to deconstruct the creation, production, marketing and distribution of postcolonial theory in the academia. Having gone that far, we shall then discuss the third *katha* that will seek to unfold the complex negotiations between capital and labour, White and Black, and *desi* and *videshi*, in our newly created post-industrial 'global context'. This might provide us with the necessary critical and conceptual framework we are looking for—the framework within which it may be possible for us to examine some of the ruptures and continuities that representative short fiction from Punjabi diaspora throws up for our consideration.

Examining the site of the classroom which we are all familiar with and within which we often situate the debates on postcolonial theory, we find that the strategic distance between the teacher and the student is always thought to be an absolute necessity. We are not concerned here with the psychic, emotional or the intellectual distancing but purely the physical aspect of it, as teachers are often positioned not among the students but on the other side, away from them. The physical space of the classroom is ordered and structured in such a way that it creates an oppositional discourse in terms of the 'self' and the 'other', in which the teacher always constitutes the 'self', and the students are posited as the 'other'. The entire Western discourse rests upon the substratum of this binarism—this dualistic, divisive, exclusionist mode. Our classrooms, as derivatives of a Western-oriented system of education, also tend to promote this dualism and this exclusionary politics of location. On account of this kind of structuring, a teacher is often perceived to be the superior, ideal, all-knowing 'self', whereas students are regarded as no more than the debased, contemptible, ignoramus or the inferiorised 'other'.[3]

This form of negotiation, in the language of postcolonial theory, could easily be described as a transaction between Prospero and Caliban. We often use the critical framework of postcolonial theory to re-examine Shakespeare's *The Tempest* and/or reread the Prospero–Caliban transaction in colonial terms in our classrooms. But we rarely ever extend its boundaries to re-evaluate the complex nature of teacher–student relationship, which is structured along the same lines. More often than not, teachers are willing participants in the process of legitimising these intensely hierarchy-conscious, unequal relationships of power/knowledge. So long as the teacher (Prospero) continues to be engaged in the process of civilising, and therefore, controlling, dominating and hegemonising students (Calibans), the ideological contradictions of our institutional practices will remain hopelessly unmasked. In such an eventuality, while we might succeed in cramming the minds of our students with the intricacies of postcolonial theory/history, there is no way we can succeed in providing either them or ourselves with a liberatory narrative, which is presumably the ultimate teleological goal of postcolonial theory/knowledge. Unless postcolonial theory turns inwards and becomes truly self-reflexive—reflecting and refracting the contradictions/complexities of our institutional practices and unmasking such unequal processes of appropriation, possession and distribution of power/knowledge in our classrooms—it would perhaps continue to destabilise and deconstruct itself into a series of *kathas* of 'de-empowerment' and dispossession. These discrete *kathas* are essentially part of the undocumented history and the unrecorded life histories that shall always remain under erasure—their self-exposure always threatened with the burden of oppressive silence. It is not only within the restrictive confines of the classroom that a teacher—by virtue of her/his position, status and placement—compels the whole of the postcolonialist project into regressive, colonial postures. The story, unfortunately, is not very different even outside the classroom.

The relationship between the centre and the margin, as envisioned in postcolonial theory, could also be understood in terms of the politics of location as it operates between the shifting margins of the *mofussil* town and the metropolitan centre. The relationship between Prospero and Caliban is echoed in the negotiations between a teacher/researcher located in a *mofussil* college or university and her/his counterpart in a metropolitan college or university. Further, a Black teacher/researcher in a metropolitan centre of learning enters into a similar praxis with her/his White counterpart located in a Western institution/academy. On looking through the history of 'postcoloniality', we discover that the initial efforts in this direction were essentially made and will continue to be made by Western institutions and academies, and that too, by White scholars (read, the colonial masters), and not by the Blacks (the colonised slaves) dispersed across the continents of India, Africa and the Caribbean islands.

How far is it possible to hypothesise that postcolonial theory—as it is being taught, researched and practised in our institutions—is purely a subaltern's response or a counter-discourse designed to offer resistance to the hegemony of colonial institutional practices and procedures? The conceptual framework is as much an expression of colonial practices as are the epistemological structures/practices or the complex processes of their circulation across the globe. Gauri Viswanathan's *The Masks of Conquest*—the seminal work that put some genuine postcolonial concerns on our agenda—took some nine years to get published in India. Oxford University Press, New Delhi, brought out the Indian version in 1998, whereas the publisher's New York office had already brought out the first edition way back in 1989. Does it not mean then that it is not simply a matter of creating knowledge, but also of setting the agenda, controlling the market forces and also the processes of circulation, dissemination and distribution of knowledge? This may sound rather bizarre, especially in our times where the critic is certainly not perceived to be an obscure entity or an anonymous hack but has become a 'star', riding on the crest of poststructuralist thought. Postcolonial theory/discourse, being the latest bugbear, does offer a very bright prospect of easy and quick stardom. In his very interesting book *Dead Artists, Live Theories and Other Cultural Problems*, Stanley Aronowitz has, at length, dealt with this phenomenon of a 'critic as star'. Analysing this phenomenon, he says,

> When the writer and the painter can only reproduce object relations, because they have lost the categories of mediation and have retained only technique, when culture no longer expresses an intrinsic meaning, except in so far as it expresses, unwittingly, certain linguistic and semiotic codes, then the act of interrogation becomes the source of signification. Hence, the critic as a star.[4]

What is interesting here is that a critic becomes a star only in a culture that has either lost its intrinsic meaning or is unable to reclaim it.

Perhaps this process of cultural depletion and impoverishment is best illustrated through the third *katha* that is being narrated here. This is the *katha* of unequal distribution of labour and capital, which can be narrated only if one situates oneself neither in a *mofussil* town, nor in a metropolitan centre—neither as a Prospero nor as a Caliban, neither as a staunch supporter of postcolonial theory nor as its sternest critic, neither as a producer of *desi* nor as a consumer of *videshi*. This part of the postcolonial *katha* begins neither within the restrictive confines of the classroom nor in the complicated jargon-ridden postures of theorists or critics, but somewhere in a downtown market of a relatively modern city of Chandigarh, where this writer is presently living. I once used to live in the vicinity of Sector 19 of the city—where the first draft of this essay was written in 1999—which can be described as one of the oldest, if not the largest, markets in Chandigarh. The reference here is not to the main market frequented by the very rich and the upper-middle-class (and, occasionally, by the middle-class 'yuppies' as well), but a *rehri* market located on the fringes of the Sector, hidden away from the public view. Without going into the symbology of '*rehri*' and its associative links with the market, let us emphasise that this market is nothing more than a cluster of ramshackle, tin-roofed, 8 ft by 10 ft cubby-holed shops where all kinds of people go shopping. If people like this writer saunter in occasionally, it is only because by virtue of being what we are, the middle-class bourgeoisie, we tend to situate ourselves literally in the 'middle' of these two markets. At some level, being middle-class is all about managing the contradictions of the polished exterior of the well laid-out main market with the ramshackle, almost choking, interiors of the *rehri* market.

Once, wandering through the maze of the *rehri* market, this writer came across a placard outside a makeshift shop that proclaimed, 'PICK ANY SWEATER FOR ONLY 75'. It was the middle of December and winter was well on its way. I had not done our customary winter shopping for the family. It was with the idea of being able to strike a good bargain that I had walked into the shop. Under a canopy of tarpaulin sheets supported by two large bamboo sticks lay a pile of sweaters of all shades and colours. A horde of customers stood all around, rummaging through the pile. Struck by this strange manner of displaying wares, I asked the shopkeeper if he was selling 'seconds', cast-offs and rejects. Offended by my query, the shopkeeper immediately set about giving me a long explanation, telling me how these sweaters were actually manufactured in India. They were meant to be sold in the international market, but often, on being rejected, they found their way to the domestic market. What was indeed surprising was that before finding their way back into the domestic market, these goods had acquired labels that proclaimed them as 'imported'. He further told me how difficult it was for him to obtain these goods, elaborating on some of the hardships he had to undergo. Watching people literally drool over the goods, pushing, jostling and tripping over one another, I suddenly felt as if the discontinuities of the colonial and postcolonial history/theory were enacting themselves out, right there, in the backwaters of Chandigarh.

Was not colonialism, after all, about this unequal relationship between labour and capital? Was not it about a trade-off between the colonies that provided cheap labour and/or raw material, as also a cheap market for the goods which were always manufactured elsewhere? History bears witness to the fact that ultimately an exploitative system was set in motion, which always served the best interests of the empire, to the detriment of the colonies and the people residing there. Most of the former colonies have supposedly gained their political freedom, kick-starting the process of national reconstruction. It is also claimed, very often, that these emergent or emerging nations have even put the ideology of the empire behind. Now, after over sixty years, in what way has our situation altered materially? In what manner has the altered, political context helped in renegotiating or redefining the economic terms of this unequal relationship? The concept of cheap labour has come unstuck and so has the concept of cheap raw material or cheap markets. The location of the capital has not changed. It has simply acquired a new face, which appears both familiar and accessible, but is neither. The formerly colonised states are neck-deep in this pile of surplus, rummaging through this pile, hoping to gain a new respectability by donning the export surplus. And this surplus, one may argue, is the surplus of theory, the intellectual baggage from the West inscribed in the modifier 'post-' which is absolutely redundant, as the old story of unequal distribution of labour and capital plays itself out in the post-industrial, global context, with marginal variations. In the colonial context, everything was well defined—the face of the labour, the profit motives of the capital and the location of the market. But now, with the free and unregulated dispersal of labour and capital, all this has become rather fluid and indeterminate, leaving us with the surplus of modifiers such as 'post-'.

Bearing in mind the complexities of colonialism and postcolonialism we should cast an angular look at the short fiction produced by the Punjabi diaspora. Some of the concerns that must preoccupy us here are the relationship between the colonial past and the postcolonial migration; the centrality of the English language, and its society and culture vis-à-vis the marginalised status of a Punjabi immigrant writer; the unequal distribution of their intellectual labour and the flight of capital in reverse.

Short fiction from the Punjabi diaspora, however, must be placed within the larger historical context that has both helped shape and constitute the community in the United Kingdom (UK). It is equally imperative to understand the dynamics of the unequal relationship between English, the dominant language (*margi*), and Punjabi (*desi*), especially in the *videshi* context. In this context, *margi* and *desi* are essentially being posited as two distinct, though interrelated, traditions or systems of knowledge production. The central tradition, associated with Sanskrit or Pali is referred to as *margi* and its regional, folk or local variant is identified as *desi*. The *margi*, often monopolised by the upper castes, works as the master-text or theory, while the *desi* functions as the practice or the *kuldharma* of the lower castes.

While the formation of the Punjabi diaspora in the UK could easily be traced back to the last few decades of the nineteenth century, by the mid-twentieth century it witnessed a phenomenal and exponential growth. According to an estimate made in 1999, the total population of the Punjabis in Britain was somewhere in the range of four hundred thousand or even more. Though the trigger points of the Punjabi migration to the UK were very different in the pre- and the post-Independence phases, the general pattern of migration has remained more or less the same. While Punjabis never moved to England as indentured labourers, they became an inalienable part of the work force in English society. In the post-Partition period, however, a good number of Punjabis who had either been uprooted or displaced from Western Punjab or other areas of what is now known as Pakistan, decided to move across the shores, especially to the UK, in search of better economic opportunities. This process was further accelerated by the expansion of the education base, the near-absence of industrial infrastructure, and limited opportunities in the job market coupled with the slow shrinkage of land holdings. While these local factors had started a slow trickle, soon enough, it turned into a veritable deluge, what with the British government revising its visa policy requirements in the early 1960s.

Though Britain has now long been perceived as a multiethnic, multicultural society, a major paradigm shift in the policies of the British government vis-à-vis the ethnic minorities was first witnessed only in the early 1960s. Recognising that racism had become the principal instrument of social tensions and conflicts, the British government decided to set up the Race Relations Board and the Community Relations Commission, both of which were later merged into the new Commission for Racial Equality. The government's White Paper of 1975 pointed out that, apart from strengthening the anti-discrimination laws, there was an urgent need to evolve a broad strategy to combat 'a cumulative cycle of disadvantage' made worse by racial discrimination 'send(ing) the entire groups of people into downward spiral of deprivation'. Around this time, when British society was poised on the edge of self-redefinition, the process of massive exodus and emigration of the Punjabi community to England got underway. As it recovered from post-war recession and plunged itself into a massive reconstruction exercise, British society and economy felt the need for educated, semi-skilled and skilled labour force, and so the doors were generously thrown open. Ironically, even the educated and well-qualified Punjabi migrants had to ultimately settle for semi-skilled and skilled positions in factories, post offices, local transport services, etc. Most of the Punjabi diaspora writers were, at some stage, lured by the prospect of not-so-hard-to-find teacher permits, though ultimately, only a few managed to garner teaching positions in schools at various levels.

It is no wonder that more than a mere fact of physical dislocation or displacement, most of the Punjabi diaspora writers prefer to think of migration as an incarcerated though livable memory—an eminently forgettable act of betrayal or treachery. The race riots in Nottingham or at Notting Hill, London, in the 1950s, the horrors of Enoch Powell's rhetoric in the sixties and the riotous eruptions in the British cities in the eighties tell their own story of a 'multicultural failure' and the subsequent rise of an aggressive brand of identity politics. However, despite all these constraints, by granting official recognition to the Punjabi language, the British government did acknowledge the contribution of the Punjabi community towards realising the dream of multiculturalism. Thanks to this recognition, it is now possible for young students of Indian origin to take their A-levels with Punjabi as one of their main subjects. Incidentally, Punjabi also happens to be the second most widely spoken language in England, second only to English in its geographical reach and/or user-friendliness.[5]

While helping us negotiate the process of cross-cultural migration that went into the making of the Punjabi diaspora in the UK, the foregoing analysis also tells us, quite unambiguously, that *videshi* Punjabi writers are essentially victims of the politics of location and exclusion. That they share the same transaction with the multicultural British society (of which they are now an integral part) that obtains between Caliban and Prospero (of course, in reverse). Despite the presence of a large number of Punjabi writers and the ever-growing visibility of the Punjabi diaspora, writing in Punjabi remains an isolationist and exclusionary activity, and not a mode of internal communication within the community or the multicultural space. Unable to find patronage among their own community in terms of sustained and committed readership in the metropolitan centres of England, most of our *videshi* Punjabi writers turn to the *mofussil* publishers in Jalandhar or Amritsar to get their works published. While their works have not found recognition, official or otherwise, in the country of their adoption, *videshi* Punjabi writers continue to enjoy a fairly decent readership back home, within the (*desi*) traditions of Punjabi literature.

As the relationship between the Punjabi and English communities has been both colonial and postcolonial, it would be worthwhile to explore the historical connections between the two as well as between the two languages. The Punjabi people as well as their language could be said to have shared an uneasy and troubled relationship with the English and their language. In a way, this goes back to the days of colonial rule in India and more significantly, in Punjab. It is a matter of recorded history that the British found it much easier to succeed in the western or eastern parts of India rather than in Punjab. They had to face severe opposition on Punjab territory, and the region also proved to be the last outpost to fall within their dominion. Punjabis did not accede to colonial control until after the death of Maharaja Ranjit Singh (1780–1839), when the annexation of Punjab became imminent. Though, ultimately, they had to submit to the superior military and strategic powers of the colonial rulers, they continued to resist the hegemony of the British rulers in various characteristically defiant ways—ways that were both explicit and implicit. The various 'local rebellions' that the Punjabis sought to engineer periodically against their colonial masters—whether it was the Kuka Movement in the early 1860s or the Singh Sabha Movement of the eighties—were merely symptomatic of their deep-seated resentment of the alien rule. Of course, the Ghadar Movement began with the specific aim of overthrowing the British rule in India.[6] To a large extent, it was this resentment, coupled with their natural instinct for aggression and dissent that propelled several thousands among them to plunge headlong into the national struggle for independence. An expression of their inherently rebellious spirit and injured pride, their revolt against the alien rulers was as much an expression of their nationalistic spirit as it was a proof, if one was needed, of their constant search for identity and sub-nationalistic aspirations.

While the nationalistic spirit acquired more overt forms, the sub-national identity took on, as it always does, covert and subversive modes of assertion. The first church had been set up in Punjab as far back as 1835. However, proselytisation among Punjabis proceeded at a much slower pace than it did, for instance, among Bengalis or Keralites. It also remained, to a large extent, localised. Even the spread of English education was not as rapid in Punjab as it was in Maharashtra or the then Madras. It was almost as if, realising their own inadequacy in an actual, physical battle, Punjabis were busy fighting a psychological warfare by constantly resisting and even militating against the imposition of another language, religion or culture. Even during the Mughal rule, Punjabis had put up as much resistance, if not more, to counter what they had perceived to be a genuine threat to their own sub-national culture. And this subterranean hostility and antipathy to the English language and culture, beyond a doubt, continued to define the identity or self-assertion of Punjabis, right through the extended phase of colonial rule and even later.

This extremely complex negotiation between Punjabi and English can be easily established through the material available in the cultural domain. An entire range of cultural signifiers can be located in the archives of Punjabi language/literature, which help in defining the contours of this negotiation. Grounded in the popular consciousness, such signifiers have often taken on forms as varied as idiomatic phrases, expressions, folk songs and cultural stereotypes. It is quite common to come across such idiomatic expressions in Punjabi folk songs: *Kale Kismet wale*, *Gore Goonh De Bore* or *Kala Shah Kala*, *Mera Kala Hai Sardar*, *Goreyan Nu Dafa Karo*, etc. ['The Blacks are the lucky ones, and the Whites nothing more than a stinking dung-heap,' or 'So what if my husband is Black as soot, damned be the Whites'.] In his famous *Jungnaama*, Shah Mohammed, a nineteenth-century Punjabi poet, has offered a graphic account of the last battle fought between the Sikhs and the British on the soil of Punjab. What is significant about this ballad is the way in which he represents the British—the aggressors. Often he uses such euphemisms as *Toonda Jat* (the 'Third Caste') to describe the White aggressors. Interested in presenting the people's view of history, Mohammed was simply giving expression to the popular sentiments when he sought to reduce the British to the much hated 'other'.[7]

To put it differently, each time the Punjabi community perceived a threat, real or imaginary, to their own language/culture, it thought of newer strategies of resistance to the hegemonic culture. While in the colonial phase, it often took on defensive, literary forms, in the postcolonial phase, it struck a more aggressive posture in expressing antipathy towards, or while rejecting, the English language. It is largely reflected in the ambivalent postures that Punjabis and their politics and government have struck over the past fifty years on the question of the relative status of English vis-à-vis Punjabi at different levels of education—primary, middle and secondary school, college as well as university. Curiously enough, even after living in England for over forty years, only a very small proportion of the first-generation, educated immigrant Punjabis are known to use English as a language of self-expression in their private and public discourses. The vast majority looks upon any attempt to acquire skills in English as a serious act of capitulation, an act of abject surrender to the dreaded 'alien' culture. It is no wonder that most of them simply refuse to learn the language or even after acquiring it, refuse to make it a part of their daily interactions. However, realising the benefits of the British education system and the manifold advantages of integration, second-generation immigrants appear to have moved on ahead, succumbing to the pressures of assimilation. They tend to look upon the whole problem of dual identity as an asset and not as a liability. They treat it as an expression of cultural replenishment, not of cultural deprivation. However, the first-generation immigrant continues to look back to her/his cultural roots, drawing emotional sustenance through multiple filiations with the mother culture in terms of possession—both material and linguistic—and remaining relatively more resistant and less amenable to the overtures of assimilation.

The first-generation Punjabi diaspora writers and even those of the second generation to a limited extent, make gestures of protest or defiance towards the host culture. They consciously challenge and even undermine the multiple strategies that the protagonists of assimilation have adopted over the years to integrate them into mainstream culture. One of the visible forms of this silent protest is their stubborn and unyielding desire to write in their own language, despite heavy odds—it does not afford them readership, fame, money or recognition as writers. In this respect, the *videshi* Punjabi writers appear to be ruled by a single passion—an overwhelming desire to redefine the contours of identity politics. Aware that their decision to write in Punjabi would only push them further into self-limiting, self-restrictive postures, they would much rather reclaim and replenish their own linguistic/cultural sources than sing hosannas to the pretences of multiculturalism. Even if relative anonymity within the culture of their adoption is the price they have to pay for such resistant strategies, it is preferred to acquiescent silence or assimilation through weak-kneed capitulation. To put it differently, it may also be seen as a total refusal on part of the first-generation Punjabi diaspora writers to engage with the host culture, thus ruling out the possibility of initiating a dialogue over several issues such as the alienation of the community, racial discrimination and social exclusion—questions that need to be directed at the host culture if they have to be effectively negotiated. The choice of language does, to a large extent, push these writers into a position of self-marginalisation too.

It is against this backdrop that the process of the slow but sure evolution of the Punjabi short fiction in the UK ought to be examined and critiqued. In a manner of speaking, every immigrant has a story to tell. And as far as this goes, an immigrant writer is almost doubly blessed. Residing in a dual cultural space, she/he constantly swings back and forth, forever extending the margins of her/his existence, forever creating newer metaphors of survival. More than mere personal statements, their stories ought to be seen as 'creative interventions' or 'disruptions' in the contemporary history of English society. Documenting the ups and downs of an extremely crucial and even vibrant (and should we also say, considering the recent political developments, violent) period in its recent history, the short fiction under discussion here maps out the struggles of a society that is constantly seeking to reinvent itself.

Since this discussion does not have the scope to go into a detailed examination of the thematic/narrative concerns of the three generations of *videshi* Punjabi writers, we shall restrict ourselves to a specific analysis of three stories, each of which is representative of the generation to which it belongs. Though Raghbir Dhand, Tarsem Nilgiri, Shivcharan Gill, Baldev Singh, Pritam Sidhu and Swaran Chandan, among several others, are some of the well-known and deeply respected writers among the first-generation short story writers, we will concentrate on Darshan Dheer's (b. 1935) story *Kakhan Kanian Da Ghar* (A Nest of Straw).[8]

That we have selected *Kakhan Kanian Da Ghar* for an analysis of the first-generation writers does not suggest that it is the best among Dheer's oeuvre, or that the story is the best possible representation of first-generation Punjabi writing. But in this story, Dheer has used the trope of journey in an extremely ingenuous manner and has also succeeded in portraying both the spatial/temporal 'in-betweenness' of the immigrant and her/his multiple dilemmas and conflicts. At the level of the narrative, it is a simple story of a young man, Harpal, who boards a train from Birmingham station to go to Manchester. Though the protagonist undertakes a physical journey in time–space, it becomes a pretext for another journey, which is internal and psychological, and even historical and cultural. Having left his 'home', the protagonist is quite simply living in a permanent state of 'homelessness'. His journey between the two stations characterises his own condition of 'in-betweenness' as an immigrant. Having left his native country, his home, Harpal experiences no obvious traces of nostalgia. His memories of his native country are not centred so much around his parents or the members of his immediate family, but around his young beloved with whom he has failed to honour his commitment. Somewhere, this repressed sense of guilt and failure has taken on the substitutive form of a fantasy. And certainly, there could not have been a better mode of capturing this duality between realism and fantasy than through the 'in-between-ness' of a train journey. The journey emphasises again and again, the separateness, isolation, and the lack of warmth and intimacy among the passengers. No words are ever exchanged among the passengers and situations of 'hail-fellow-well-met' geniality and bonhomie that often characterise train journeys in India are, of course, virtually nonexistent.

On the contrary, the vast emptiness of the space that the protagonist confronts in the compartment becomes a cultural code of the unlimited social space and the resultant freedom available within the adopted country. It is another matter that this social space does not give Harpal any opportunity to either define himself in concrete terms or seek filiations or relationships within its alien, anomie-like framework. Though his paranoia and diffidence about taking a seat next to a White woman is rooted in a purely personal mythology, it is also an enactment of the historical relationship between the two races—the Black slaves and the White masters. By serving as a reminder of how Mahatma Gandhi had once been thrown out of a train compartment in South Africa, it becomes an effective effort at reclaiming history. At the same time, it becomes a statement on how the relationship between the Blacks and the Whites remains frozen in space as well as in time. Though Blacks are no longer thrown out of train compartments, their distrust of White co-passengers and the consequent self-imposed isolation are largely forms of cultural deviancy—the by-product of a long-drawn-out history of racism. Despite the fact that Harpal carries this burden of history, at least subliminally, he is not quite able to resist the pull of the White skin and ultimately does succumb to the miasma of desire. His unfulfilled desires and dreams explode in the form of his abrupt decision to sit right next to a White woman, regardless of the consequences. Though he manages to overcome his diffidence to some extent, the signs of paranoia persist much longer, and perhaps, never quite leave him completely.

Harpal's inability to make a simple overture to his fellow passenger and thus cross the cultural divide brings the whole question of 'identity politics' into focus. An acute consciousness of his own 'difference' from the White woman in terms of skin colour, race, history and culture pushes him deeper into postures of self-defence. And ultimately, when the White woman literally pulls him towards herself, the entire mise en scène of colonial history, with all its hegemonic, cannibalistic and appropriating strategies, enacts itself out through the resultant encounter. While history enacts itself out as a subliminal text in this unexpected and latent manner, Harpal is shown reflecting upon historical monuments such as Ajanta, Ellora, Taj Mahal, etc., in the process of externalising his erotic desires, and even seeking desperate justification for them. But the fulfilment of these desires, at best, remains an interlude between two journeys, a temporary process of instant gratification that enjoys the sanction of the commodified culture. It is in this sense that Harpal's personal situation becomes a site of multiple predicaments latent in the situation of every immigrant. His search for a permanent home must be constantly thwarted; he can, at best, build nests of straw that would not take long to blow away, and even a mild gust of wind is enough to do the necessary damage. Structured around the twin poles of fantasy and reality, home and homelessness, personal and historical, White and Black, the story does ultimately succeed in locating the metaphors of 'identity politics' within the dual spatial and cultural framework.

The second story that we have chosen for exegesis is titled *Dhooaan* (The Smoke)[9] by Harjit Atwal (b. 1952), whom we can place among the second-generation writers. Over the years, Atwal has definitely established himself as a gifted storyteller, one with a distinctive voice and métier of his own, qualities that his other contemporaries are still struggling to discover. Often spoken of with great respect and admiration among the critics as well as readers, Atwal shows impeccable control, judicious craftsmanship and a fairly incisive understanding of human experience. Much more than just exhibiting a promise of mature creativity, his story, 'The Smoke', manages to become a living testimony to his resourcefulness as a storyteller. In this story, Atwal has explored the little-known world of an 'illegal immigrant' with a rare sensitivity, compassion and inwardness. His preference for the first-person narrative lends a sense of urgency, immediacy and authenticity to his writing.

Often in a state of perpetual flight, an illegal immigrant is a fugitive who does not want to confront either the 'self' or the 'other' and yet, never ceases to aspire for a permanent settlement of some kind. Poised on the edge of this predicament is the narrator of the story, who, in the initial stages, keeps floating in and out of settlements, but ultimately lands himself in a job as a bus conductor with London transport services. One day, he meets a young passenger, Manisha, who happens to be working in a factory along the same route where the bus plies. On learning that she enjoys legal status as a British citizen, he decides to hitch his wagon to her star. Driven into making this choice through sheer circumstantial necessity, the narrator ultimately clinches the matter only when he gets to know that Manisha is of the same caste as he is. The baggage of caste consciousness that he has carried from his native country is still an instrument of self-oppression for him. Not only that, he is also tied to his mother culture through multiple bonds of filiation and kinship. Though he is prepared to date, woo and court a young girl of his own choice, he must seek his parents' consent for marrying her. However, a sudden discovery about the girl's past throws him off balance, sending his entire secret plans swirling into smoke. The discovery about the 'other', however, fails to materialise into a discovery of the 'self'. The duality persists as hypocrisy and duplicity of the male attitude comes in for severe criticism. Ironically, it is among the billowing clouds of smoke that we ultimately get to see the real face of the narrator and recognise all the contortions of his tradition-bound, caste-ridden, orthodox self. Atwal's message is clear enough: moving ahead in a highly industrialised society is not simply a matter of manipulation, it is first and foremost a matter of shedding one's agrarian, retrogressive, feudal and patriarchal mindset in favour of a truly modernist outlook.

Veena Verma's (b. 1960) story *Libri Hoi Chaddar* (A Soiled Sheet)[10] is a good example of third-generation Punjabi writers. She is a feminist with a strong, self-assertive voice, whose well-crafted stories consistently attack, debunk and critique false assumptions about women as well as stereotypical and traditional notions about women's roles and their sexuality along with their multiple misrepresentations often bred by patriarchal systems. Though Verma simply refuses to entertain any viewpoint other than that of her women characters, her stories reveal no penchant for shrill polemic or strident radicalism. Rarely does she carry the baggage of ideology in a very explicit manner, and never does she allow herself to be cramped by its constraints. She is persistently engaged in locating newer metaphors for her liberatory narratives in the country of her origin. Marking the culmination of such a search, 'A Soiled Sheet' brings us face to face with the processes aimed at commodifying women as well as their desires.

A powerful cultural signifier, 'sheet' is a metonymic 'absence', speaking of woman in different voices such as a wife, a mother, a mistress and a prostitute—something that hides her 'presence' behind the cloak of invisibility. Sujata is just another name for such an eternal woman, another face of a woman who has as often been betrayed by men down the ages as she is by her own instincts or impulses. All through the story, the crumpled 'sheet' is repeatedly smoothed out, folded up and put away in the closet. But in the last scene, the objectification of Sujata is complete as it brings home to the reader the real significance of the 'sheet'. Only after Kumar peremptorily tells Sujata to take the 'soiled sheet' away, does she begin to identify herself with it. Ironically enough, the moment of her objectification is also the moment of truth. The moment of 'absence' is also the moment of 'presence'. Ultimately, the 'sheet' turns into a 'shroud' within whose folds all the dreams, desires, voices or memories of Sujata, and even she herself, must now lie buried, eternally. It is apparent that, in her portrayal of a woman's experiences, Verma does attach a good deal of significance to cultural particularities. This is also reflected in her keen desire to abandon conventional methods of storytelling in favour of other modes, intrinsically better suited to the communication of the experience. Though it may appear to be no more than a simple, framed tale on the surface, 'A Soiled Sheet' is essentially a complex narrative, constantly resisting all attempts at framing, constantly readjusting the limits of self-definition—which, in turn, becomes a benchmark of the writer's diasporic experience and/or subjectivity.

Our attempt to map out the ruptures and continuities of *videshi* Punjabi short fiction as well as the contradictions and confusions inherent in postcolonial theory has been chiefly aimed at problematising both categories. Some of the *kathas* narrated in this context may not appear to have any direct bearing upon the subject on hand. But this discussion was specifically designed to be different from usual debates on such issues. This essay has been neatly fractured into two halves discussing the theory and practice of postcolonial *kathas* and *videshi* Punjabi short fiction in such a way that each half reflects and refracts upon the other. One hopes that the discussion has been able to create a framework within which some of the theoretical issues raised by postcolonial theory can be re-interrogated, and to generate a new perspective for first recontextualising and then re-examining the *videshi* short fiction in Punjabi.

Notes and References

1. Barbara Christian, 'The Race for Theory', in *Gender and Theory*, ed. Linda Kauffmann (Oxford: Blackwell, 1989), 225–36.
2. Some of the early investigations into postcolonial theory are presented in the following works: Bill Ashcroft, Gareth Griffiths, and Helen Tiffin, *The Empire Writes Back* (London: Routledge, 1989); Elleke Boehmer, *Colonial and Postcolonial Literature: Migrant Metaphors* (Oxford: Oxford University Press, 1995); Bart Moore-Gilbert, *Postcolonial Theory: Contexts, Practices, Politics* (London: Verso, 1997); Dennis Walder, *Postcolonial Literatures in English: History, Language, Theory* (Oxford: Blackwell, 1998).
3. Paulo Freire, *The Pedagogy of the Oppressed* (London, New York: Penguin, 1972).
4. Stanley Aronowitz, *Dead Artists, Live Theories and Other Cultural Problems* (New York, London: Routledge, 1994), 94.
5. For detailed discussion see, Rana Nayar, 'Introduction', in *From Across the Shores: Stories by Asians in Britain* (New Delhi: Sterling, 2002); K.S. Dhindsa, *Indian Immigrants in the UK: A Socio-economic Analysis* (New Delhi: Concept Publications, 1998); Darshan Singh Tatla, ed.,

Sikhs in Britain and America (British Centre for Research in Ethnic Relations: University of Warwick, 1987); Pashaura Singh and Gerald N. Barrier, eds., *The Trauma of Sikh History in the Diaspora* (New Delhi: Manohar, 1996).

6. For a more extended discussion of the Sikh history, see, J.S. Grewal, *The Sikhs of the Punjab* (New Delhi: Cambridge University Press, 1999).

7. Shah Mohammed, *Jungnaama* (Jalandhar: Chetna Prakashan, 1993), 30–8.

8. In this case, reference is being made to the translated version of the story, Darshan Dheer, 'A Nest of Straw', in *From Across the Shores: Stories by Asians in Britain*, trans. and ed. Rana Nayar (New Delhi: Sterling, 2002), 30–8.

9. Nayar, *From Across the Shores*, 137–47.

10. Nayar, *From Across the Shores*, 170–93.

Section Three

Reading Translation(s)

CHAPTER NINE

Author as Translator: Paradigms and Possibilities in the Indian Context

At the outset, it would be useful to outline the theoretical and contextual contours of this essay because any discussion of this kind cannot be carried out in an essentialist or universalist manner. The prepositional phrase, 'in the Indian context', therefore, is used to demarcate the boundaries of this discussion. It may also help to state that this is not an attempt to create or construct an alternative theory or discourse of translation. The intention is much less ambitious and much more modest. It is merely to identify, locate and set up, if possible, various 'tropes of translation' within the Indian context/tradition, so that we may be able to reflect upon our own processes in our own language(s) and metaphor(s).

The process of translation in India is as old as the history of various Indian languages—classical as well as modern—and this in itself is ground enough for us to, at least, start reflecting on just about how we could indigenise our theories of translation. However, the hold of Western/Euro-centric theories/ideas is so strong on our minds, imagination and sensibility that often, in our search, we willy-nilly fall back upon these very theories to explain away all our cognitive and critical processes, including translation. Since the discourse of translation in the Indian context, like so much else in the English language, is heavily complicit with the ideology of colonialism, our search for metaphors to describe the process of translation often turns egregiously imitative and even derivative. In our postcolonial context, where the indigenisation of the process of translation has come a long way, it would be worthwhile to reclaim or retrieve indigenous metaphors in order to articulate and mediate our experiences.

Indian Tropes of Translation

Our search for indigenous metaphors will lead us first into the broader framework of Indian cultural tradition(s) and then into regional variants available in the Punjabi language, literature and culture. Let us preface our discussion with an observation. In her essay 'The Race for Theory', Barbara Christian emphasises that the only way in which the Blacks can possibly escape the hegemony of the 'White-dominated' literary theory is by taking recourse to indigenous narratives, which, she further stresses, can serve as effective tools of theorisation.[1] This should encourage us to make an effort to source indigenous metaphors from native myths, which are often regarded as natural reservoirs of even the most primeval forms of metaphorical articulations.[2] It is in the substratum of myths, legends, *pauranik* (mythological) tales and the diverse though rich folk material that one may discover some of these tropes of translation.

This writer's own experiences as a translator for over twenty years prove that the process of translation is in some ways similar, if not identical, to the process of *kaya kalp* or metamorphosis/transformation.[3] Here, we will try to excavate some of the 'narratives of transformation' available in the Indian and Punjabi cultural contexts, the ones that may serve as effective tools, and even vehicles, of translation theory.

We could begin by referring to one of the most gifted of all the protean characters in Indian mythology—none other than the (in)famous Narada. It would be instructive to look into the narratives available in various Sanskrit texts that help us understand the unique role of Narada as a cosmic messenger across different worlds. He possesses this special gift of moving in and out of shapes, characters and situations; of hiding behind the authority of Vishnu or Shiva; of ferrying divine messages across different worlds; and of creating understanding (and, at times, wilful and mischievous misunderstanding) between persons, both human and divine. It seems that in Narada, we not only have one of the earliest mythical images of a mediator, a communicator, an interventionist and/or a disruptionist, but also a translator who combines all of this and so much more in an amazing manner and variety. Rather than present the process of communication in an unproblematic way, Narada's presence (by asserting his authority) or absence (through its opposite) and his several incarnations problematise the processes of communication as well as translation or linguistic and cultural *kaya kalp* (transformation).[4]

Let us now turn to another 'narrative of transformation' available in the ancient Sanskrit epic, the *Mahabharata*. This largely concerns Yayati, a character whose story has been a subject of perennial interest to playwrights and short story writers alike.[5] Yayati, who was cursed with old age in the prime of his life, regained his youth through his son Puru's willingness to exchange his youth for his father's old age. Apart from the transformational aspect, what makes Yayati's story significant for anyone theorising about translation is how it asserts the constant need of the 'old' to 'renew' and 'rejuvenate' itself through contact—here, through an actual physical exchange of bodies—with the young. This idea has special relevance in relation to ancient or medieval texts that are translated into another language in a context other than the one in which they were originally written. Walter Benjamin's concept of how an act of translation imparts 'afterlife' to a given text located in a particular historical context offers perhaps the best endorsement of this.[6] This 'afterlife' is nothing but a process of renewal and renegotiation of cultural texts across a time–space continuum. Benjamin believes that this ensures for long-forgotten cultural texts, a sense of continuity within the source language and culture and also ensures the process of initiation of these texts into an entirely new target language and culture.

The third narrative is about Trishanku, whose story is found in the *Puranas*—the secular, non-scriptural texts of Hinduism—and also in the 'Bala Kanda' portion of the *Valmiki Ramayana*. This strange story, which is an inseparable part of the Indian mythical folklore, is about a man who wanted to enter the portals of heaven in flesh, without renouncing his mortal frame. His extraordinary wish was granted by Lord Shiva, whose attendants did their best to push Trishanku into heaven, only to be stoutly opposed by the attendants of Lord Indra, the sovereign monarch of heaven. As the story goes, Trishanku remains suspended between this world and the 'other world', between the earth and the sky, unable to return to his native land and unable to enter into the longed-for land. This mythical figure is a superb illustration of the problematic of the translator and the translation. Like Trishanku, it is the fate of all translators and translations to remain suspended between two languages, worlds and cultures, to belong eternally to the 'third space'[7] or the 'third language'[8]—to remain as 'deterritorialised' subjects and texts in an epistemological and ontological sense. In the 'third space' or through the 'third language', languages or cultures are not fully appropriated or transferred. They are only negotiated or renegotiated. Thus, translation becomes an interesting site of multiple transformations (replete with mediations, interventions and disruptions), an exchange or transaction effected through the materiality of language/history/culture, and a project that forever remains inconclusive, incomplete and provisional.

It is much the same story when we turn to Punjabi literature and culture. Stories of 'transformation' abound and so do the tales of 'nowhereness'. One is reminded of a folk tale that features in Gurdial Singh's novel *Parsa* that tells us of a young girl who is married off to a farmer's son. This young man is mentally challenged and has no idea how their relationship is to be consummated. In their immediate neighborhood lives a young, robust wrestler, who does push-ups in his courtyard in the mornings and in the evenings with unfailing regularity. The young girl occasionally peeks through the crevices of the common wall to catch a glimpse of him, and she is attracted to his youthfulness. One day, unable to rein in her impulses, she climbs the wall and jumps into her neighbour's courtyard. When she falls at his feet asking him to satiate her passion, the wrestler is dumbstruck. Saying that he thought of her as no more than a sister, not only does he refuse to oblige her but he also helps her climb back over the wall, without touching any part of her body except her feet. Soon afterwards, the young wrestler's skin breaks out in a rash that just refuses to heal. When he finally approaches a faith healer, he is asked to obtain the sweat from the palm of a woman whose body has not been defiled by human touch. As fate would have it, he ultimately has to turn to the same woman whom he had once refused, to get his rash healed.

This story has implications for our understanding of the process of translation. Experiencing a sense of incompleteness and inadequacy, the source language or culture seeks fulfilment through intrusive mediations into the target language(s) or culture(s). While the contact does take place, it is more in denial (on the part of the target language) than in affirmation, and for that reason, the contact remains peripheral, never complete or fulfilling. Ultimately, there is a backward impulse or a wash-back effect—in the sense that the target language, too, falls back on the source language for its own enrichment, plenitude and healing—a symbiosis of sorts that emphasises that target languages and cultures are as hopelessly dependent upon the source language and culture. This symbiotic union, this deliberate act of interrogating linguistic hierarchies, gives the process of translation its therapeutic, redemptive and liberatory powers. We can regard this particular narrative in *Parsa* as a metanarrative of the process/theory of translation.

Paradigms and Possibilities

The discussion we have had so far may help us draw inferences that have a direct bearing upon the question of how the mutual relationship of an 'author' and a 'translator' is to be mediated. One of the first conclusions one may draw is that the distinction between an 'author' and a 'translator' is 'real' at one level and yet 'unreal' or even facetious, at another. It is real in the sense that we often use two distinct terms/categories to describe the processes that an author and/or a translator are engaged in, which makes these two mutually exclusive though not entirely unrelated pursuits. To put it differently, this also extends the conventional, hierarchical notion that the author is a primary agent, whereas the translator is a secondary one. Perhaps, at the epistemological level, it not only appears to be so, but it *is* so, as both an author and a translator appear to be constructing two distinct forms of knowledge—one from abstract to concrete and the other from concrete to concrete.

However, at the metaphysical level—which is why we brought in all those narratives of *kaya kalp*—this distinction becomes quite irrelevant, especially when we realise that both the author and the translator are engaged in a similar process—an author in 'translating' thoughts into language (with warts and all) and a translator into translating 'thought content in one language/culture' into another. This is not just another semantic puzzle or a conundrum. It is a way of interrogating the false distinctions we often make about an author and a translator, and also a way of projecting newer possibilities in delimiting their roles/functions and mediating their mutual relationship. So, much of what we have discussed about Narada, Trishanku, Yayati and *kaya kalp* can easily be transferred or extended to understand the roles and functions of an author too, but of course, with its own set of qualifications.

The second conclusion that we can draw here is that both an author and a translator are engaged in a similar and equally complex, mediated and material process of 'communication' (with all its mediations, interventions and disruptions). However, we must also bear in mind the fact that 'translation' or 'creativity' cannot simply be reduced to 'metaphysical categories', as both are implicated in very real, material and historical processes of writing, editing, publishing, marketing, sales and/or distribution. Apart from that, there is a whole network of material forces such as advertisements, publicity, copyrights, authorship and the contested claims of royalty, originality and/or imitation that impinge upon this complex relationship between the author and the translator. Once we take cognisance of this materiality, the 'metaphysical similitude' disappears, giving way to an ever-progressive, yawning gulf between the author and the translator. Be it India or Europe, the history of translation almost anywhere is replete with several instances of how these material and/or historical differences have been negotiated in the past or could possibly be renegotiated in the future.[9]

It is equally important to stress the fact that the material/historical differences are only to be seen as 'deviations' from the Platonic norm of 'oneness' where the author virtually becomes indistinguishable from the translator. However much we want to posit this 'equality' and 'oneness' as a categorical imperative, there is no way we can possibly escape from the fact of 'material differences' and the manner in which these not only affect but quite literally constitute our understanding of 'translation as a process' and also that of the author–translator dialectics. It is no wonder that when we start reflecting upon different paradigms or possibilities in this regard, the only route open to us is the historical one. These paradigms and possibilities, as we will discuss them here, derive themselves largely from our understanding of the history of translation. It is only within the specifics of the history/archaeology of translation that such paradigms can possibly be located or sited—either in the form of 'archival traces' or 'archetypal images'. Our effort now would be to reclaim and/or reconstruct some of these paradigms, develop an outline of each and also share, if possible, the problematic of each with respect to the issues at hand.

Author as Translator

Translating his own work

Let us first start with the problematic of what is sometimes referred to as 'auto-translation' or 'self-translation', a situation in which an author, for whatever reasons, refuses to hand over her/his 'work' to a translator, and insists upon translating it into, say, her/his second or third language. Apart from other facetious questions that have largely to do with her/his linguistic competence in languages other than those of self-expression, it also raises certain 'ideological' questions of how and why must a writer continue to maintain her/his hold over the work. To put it a little differently, regardless of the method a writer may adopt—rewriting, adapting, trans-creating, transcribing or simply translating the 'work' into another language/culture—the question whether the 'work' ever becomes a 'text' in this kind of a situation is always an open issue. We may argue that when the author is also the translator, the 'work' may acquire an 'afterlife' without being able to cut off its umbilical cord.

In this situation, the 'work' may continue to be treated by the author as her/his exclusive property or acquisition, with its usual mechanisms of controls and copyrights, and its distinct brand consciousness. However, in such a situation, the 'work' simply fails to become an independent 'text' with a distinct identity of its own, ready to be located within the larger public space/domain, with its attendant problems and distinct advantages. To make it a little more specific, let us cite the case of Gurdial Singh, a novelist whose three major novels have been translated by this writer.

Though Punjabi is his preferred mode of self-expression, Singh continues to translate most of his novels into Hindi himself. Without commenting upon the quality of his translations, one could argue that in his Hindi translations, the interference of the mother tongue is so intrusively strong that it often makes us wonder whether they are Punjabi novels written in Devnagari script. Such and other related questions could be raised in relation to other writers in other Indian languages too. In such a situation, not only do the 'author' and the 'translator' fuse together into a single entity, but the 'work' itself continues to draw upon the 'person' or the 'personality' of the author and even her/his linguistic oddities for its continuation and/or sustenance. In other words, the proverbial 'death of the author' does not ever occur, and the 'work' remains author-centred and author-centric—a 'readerly', not a 'writerly', text despite all its efforts to reinvent itself through the controlled act of trans-creation or trans-substantiation (which is what *kaya kalp* is, at some level).

Author as Translator

Translating another author's text

The history of translation, both in our context and in the West, is replete with instances of how successive generations of writers have taken recourse to translation as a form of *alaap* (self-practice or self-training), and even as a way of acknowledging their debt to the previous generations of writers. It would be no exaggeration to say that this was perhaps one of the most important factors that provided both the initial thrust and the later impetus to European Renaissance. This was also the time when various European languages, in the advanced stages of their development, were on the verge of breaking away from classical languages. They were all poised to acquire distinct cultural identities and/or formations of their own. Though this process of an author translating another author's work started during the Renaissance, it continued through the later periods. This happened largely through the mediations of such prominent writers as John Dryden, Alexander Pope, Thomas Carlyle, William Morris, Dante Gabriel Rossetti, Edward Fitzgerald, Robert Graves, Cecil Day Lewis, Ezra Pound, etc. However, in the later stages, the rationale for this activity was not so much the development or evolution of what were once called 'the vernaculars', but a constant search for established literary styles and/or conventions, aided by an equally dominant impulse for constituting or reconstituting literary discourse(s).

While reflecting upon this phenomenon, it is important to point out that, unlike the other possibility debated earlier, such a situation does not demand any proprietorial hold over the 'work'. This is one of those situations where the translated work has the potential to turn into an independent 'text', complete with its ideological baggage. As the translator in this case works quite independently of the author, far removed as she/he is from the cultural context or the historical contingencies of the author, the process of selecting, editing or translating a work becomes more of an individual enterprise (if it is not already guided by a complex web of market forces). In the case of this paradigm, the question of 'authorship' coupled with allied questions of the translator's identity, class, gender, ideology, methodology, royalty, visibility/invisibility, etc., become the main problematic. It is rather difficult to say whether such translations are prompted by a desire to exorcise the 'anxiety of influence'[10] or are motivated by a more altruistic agenda of cultural replenishment of one's own linguistic or literary resources. But what one can safely deduce is that in this case, the 'otherness' of the text is accepted as fait accompli and so, translation becomes a matter of how this otherness is to be negotiated.

We can identify three possibilities within this paradigm. However, we shall refrain from going into a detailed discussion of all the three since these may just as well be seen in other paradigms too. For now, let us just enumerate the possibilities we have in mind so that we can establish the rationale of our argument. These three possibilities are:

1. Translator as an independent author

2. Translator as a collaborator of the author
3. Translator as subordinate to the author

If you look close enough, you will discover that these possibilities exist not only within the paradigm under discussion, but within other paradigms too. So it would not be desirable to talk about further possibilities or segmentations within this paradigm.

Our argument here is that, for the purposes of theorising or constructing knowledge (about translation or otherwise), we cannot escape the strategic essentialism of well-ordered, well-structured models or paradigms of classification and/or theory. But this does not necessarily mean that such structures, wherever they are created, are sacrosanct. We create such watertight structures of knowledge with the realisation that they often have a latent, inherent tendency to turn porous and fluid, dismantle themselves, and thus even spill over into each other. It is with this consciousness that we go into our next paradigm.

Author as Translator

Translating from one Indian language to another

In this paradigm, the question of who is translating—an author or someone other than the author—becomes peripheral and the question of the language 'from' and 'into which' the translation is being done becomes the central concern. This happens in all cases where translation takes place from one Indian language to another. Here, are we returning to the ancient Indian concept of an author, which not only minimises her/his role/function, but also reduces her/him to a non-entity—an anonymous Vyasa— more of an institution than an individual? (In this ontological sense, the only real author is God and the rest of us are mere shreds of platinum—the medium of transference or catalysts in the process of metamorphosis or *kaya kalp.*) The answer is a firm 'no'. This discussion does not intend to invoke this kind of 'construction' (or should we say, quintessential 'deconstruction') of an author as a category or an institution.

The emphasis here is on the fact that far from being author-centric, this particular paradigm tends to become language-centric. The concept of 'Indian languages', as posited here, is inclusive of the particular variant called Indian English, used and practised in our context. Despite the fact that most Indian languages, except those belonging to the Dravidian family, share a common genealogy with several European languages, this discussion defines its own problematic. Now, another question arises: Given this scenario, what kind of problematic do we envision? The first point that needs to be underlined here is that this situation definitely compels us to think in terms of the relative positioning, ideology, status and value of various Indian languages vis-à-vis each other, and also vis-à-vis English. Within the spectrum of Indian languages, we often valorise English and Hindi more in comparison with, say, Punjabi or Dogri, or perhaps Marathi, Gujarati, Bengali and Tamil more in comparison with Manipuri, Bhojpuri or Konkani. To put it differently, we have not so far succeeded in creating a sovereign, democratic and non-hierarchical 'Republic of Indian Languages', where all languages can possibly enjoy equal status, opportunity, value and patronage. Translators, either individually or collectively, may become emissaries of goodwill in such a Utopian but laudable mission.

Returning to our argument, let us say that regardless of whether the author is translating an ancient, medieval or a relatively modern text, she/he has an obligation to address the historical relationship that one Indian language shares with another. The author should also ask whether any kind of 'linguistic homology' exists between the two. Apart from this question, the choice of methodology or strategy in 'either/or' terms—for instance, 'foreignising' or 'domesticating'—also contributes towards outlining the problematic of this paradigm. Factors such as how and why the choices are made or whether we tilt towards the source language or the target language, go a long way towards defining and even determining the politics of translation in our context.

Author as Translator

Translating from a European language into an Indian language

Let us start our discussion of this paradigm with some observations on the economics of translation. This relates to some recent trends in publishing translations, especially by local publishing houses in Punjab. Shifting their focus away from bringing out original works in Punjabi, many of them have now begun publishing books in English and also offloading translated versions of Western 'best-sellers' into the local/regional market. And this has, no doubt, paid them rich dividends. In this kind of a situation, where translations are driven almost completely by market forces, the author becomes perhaps as redundant or disposable as the translator.

Going beyond the politics of language (which we have already discussed in the preceding sections), this subversive form of cultural politics erases the finer distinctions between the 'original' and the 'translation', reducing both of them to 'saleable commodities'. In such a scenario, all debates about the 'rights/privileges' or 'authority' of the author or that of the translator become redundant, and the author or the translator ceases to have any say in either the process of selection of a particular text or the final quality of the product. Such translations are profit-driven and they are simply rolled off the conveyor belt, to be passively consumed by the 'brand-conscious' and largely naive readership. In short, the author, the translator and the translation are subsumed or swallowed by the ever-bourgeoning 'translation industry'. For this reason, the role of the publisher, his location, the modes of production and distribution, and marketing networks become the determining factors of what is to be translated, why and how.

Of course, there are several other questions that shall continue to have definite bearing upon our reflections on 'author as translator', especially when we think about this kind of 'orientalism-in-reverse'. These questions include, whether the translator is a 'cultural insider' or an outsider, whether she/he translates for herself/himself or others, whether the target audience of the translator is located within her/his own culture or another, whether she/he is translating an ancient, a medieval or a modern text, a sacred or a secular text, and whether she/he is also aware of the history of translation either of the source language or that of the target language or of both.

Through this essay, we have sought to speculate on the subject at hand and to form some tentative hypotheses. These hypotheses need to be carried further and even turned around before things begin to fall in place. We have also attempted to map out various configurations of the theme 'author as translator' that emerge through the history of translation, define their contours if possible, posit some theoretical issues and problems arising from their exclusivism or inclusivism, and also engage with the problematic of each. However, we should bear in mind that this is only an attempt to initiate a debate, not to conclude it.

Notes and References

1. Barbara Christian, 'The Race for Theory', in *Gender and Theory*, ed. Linda Kauffmann (Oxford: Blackwell, 1989), 225–36. In this article, Christian has made a strong case for opposing hegemonic and Euro-centric theories and has also suggested that it is possible for us, especially in the Third World context, to structure an alternative/oppositional discourse by using culturally specific narratives in innovative and creative ways.

2. I owe this understanding to Claude Levi-Strauss, who is of the view that myths are the richest source of cultural paradigms. He believes that myths, which always have antinomies built into them, often function like languages and facilitate our understanding of cultural subtexts.

3. After I had already envisioned this idea in its present form (as having affiliation with the process of translation), I came across it in Jacques Derrida's writings (*Positions*, 1981). Among several metaphors for translation that Derrida has used, he also describes it as 'transformation'. Otherwise, the concept of transformation is available to us in Ovid's *Metamorphosis* and the story of Yayati recounted in the *Mahabharata*.

4. Wendy Doniger O'Flaherty, *Hindu Myths* (London: Penguin, 1985), 46–53.

5. Among others, Girish Karnad, the famous Indian playwright, has made very creative use of this story and crafted it into an extremely successful play (*Yayati*, 1961).

6. Walter Benjamin, 'The Task of a Translator', in *Illuminations*, trans. Harry Zohn (New York: Schocken Books, 1969).

7. Homi Bhabha talks about the 'liminal space' in terms of the diasporic imaginary, which is the 'third space' where the creative energies of the immigrant writer ultimately seek gratification and fulfilment. According to him, the act of writing becomes an act of translating the culture to which the immigrant essentially belongs. In his scheme of things, the distinction between the 'original' and the 'translation' virtually disappears, as he de-privileges both. See his *Location of Culture* (London: Routledge, 1994).

8. For an extended discussion, see George Steiner, *After Babel: Aspects of Language and Translation* (London: Oxford University Press, 1975). Steiner is of the view that translation is never done in the second (target) language, which invariably goes through a series of mutations, thus giving rise to what he prefers to call the 'third language'.

9. For a discussion on the history of translation see, Susan Bassnett, *Translation Studies* (London and New York: Routledge, 1980); Mona Baker, *Routledge Encyclopedia of Translation Studies* (London: Routledge, 1998); Susan Bassnett and Andre Lefevere, eds., *Translation, History and Culture* (London: Pinter, 1990).

10. Harold Bloom, *The Anxiety of Influence: A Theory of Poetry* (New York: Oxford University Press, 1997).

CHAPTER TEN

Punjabi and English: Mediating the History of Language, Literature and Translation

Any attempt at reconstructing the history of translation becomes, by implication, an exercise in the reconstruction of the historical links between the two languages—or the two cultures—involved. Reconstructing the history of a single language is, in itself, a fairly complicated enterprise, but when two languages—especially, two dissimilar languages such as Punjabi and English—are involved, it becomes all the more daunting and even problematic. This enterprise presupposes that some effort would be made to map out the historical congruencies and incongruencies between the two languages and cultures and their literary forms, thus locating ways in which they have interacted, intersected and overlapped with each other in the past.

This essay will take some tentative steps towards formulating the historical relationship between Punjabi and English in terms of language, literature and translation. However, it does not construct its understanding of history in orthodox terms. The effort will be to locate the gaps and fissures in the conventional historical frame, as well as to find support for its arguments in the cultural matrix that often lies embedded in literary and cultural archives and/or in the collective, popular consciousness. The contours of this historical frame coincide broadly with the extended phase of British colonial rule in India, when most Indian languages and literatures, including Punjabi, began to develop their multiple points of conjuncture and disjuncture with the English language, literature and culture. During this period, Indian languages and literatures underwent an extremely complex negotiation—often characterised as 'resurgence'[1] or even 'amnesia'[2]—which has remained, for the most part, somewhat sketchily mapped out. Interestingly, this process of negotiation, thought to have coincided with colonial rule, has continued uninterrupted in the postcolonial phase of Indian history. So, in this sense, despite their share of ruptures and discontinuities, colonialism and postcolonialism can be said to constitute a single, uninterrupted time continuum—at least in the context of Punjabi and English.

Common Ancestry, Different Trajectories

Before exploring the complexities of this negotiation, we should discuss briefly how Punjabi and English have evolved historically. Punjabi evolved out of Sanskrit and Prakrit *Apabhramsha* through its historical contact with Persian and Arabic,[3] whereas English originated out of Latin and Old English, under the strong influence of Anglo-Saxon and Scandinavian literatures. However, their common ancestry can be traced back to the Indo-European family of languages.[4] This common genealogy is not reflected, however, in the two languages' historical evolution or geographical spread, or in their linguistic patterns or homologies. Although they started out on their journey at roughly around the same time—the tenth century CE—the two languages have followed vastly different trajectories in the course of their evolution. While both can boast of a history spanning a thousand years or more, Punjabi is today no more than a regional language, apologetically rooting for survival and space in the northwestern plains of Punjab, the place of its birth. By contrast, English, by virtue of its hegemonic, imperialistic expansionism, has not only spread across several continents but also emerged as a dominant global language.

If the inequities of historical and geographical space have dangerously tilted the matrix of this relationship against the Punjabi language, these inequities have been further exacerbated by notions of status, power, dominance and hierarchy, weighing rather heavily in favour of English. Our understanding of the relationship between these two languages is further complicated by the wide-ranging, irreconcilable (phonetic, morphological, lexical and semantic) differences between their linguistic systems and structures, and the clear divide in their sociological and cultural matrix, often reinforced by differences inherent in the ideologies inscribed within each language.

Anti-hegemonic, Anti-authoritarian Punjabi Mindset

Now that we have understood the impulses behind the relationship between Punjabi and English, it would be useful to look into the dynamics of how this relationship has functioned historically between the two peoples. Here we should go for a synchronic, not a diachronic, study of the relationship, and operate from within the framework of colonialism. When commenting on the complex nature of the coloniser–colonised relationship, postcolonial theorists often talk of how this at best reflects ambivalent, and often self-contradictory, patterns. This is characteristically articulated in the form of confrontation and collaboration, resistance and subversion, and opposition and complicity.[5] It is in the light of this theoretical premise that we will discuss the relationship between Punjabi and its literary forms and their English counterparts.

Historically, Punjabis—as a people, race and *quam* (community)—have shared an uneasy and troubled relationship with the British. It is a matter of recorded history that the British found it much easier to establish their dominion in the western and eastern parts of India than they had in the northwestern frontiers of Punjab. To understand the dynamics of this process, we need to examine some of the ways in which Punjabis have reacted to structures of authority, domination and the consciousness of hierarchy. Traditionally regarded as an outpost and a frontier Indian state, Punjab has always stood guard like a sentry, protecting its borders and opposing enemies and marauders. In a way, its history is a saga of confrontations and resistance, directed initially against the Mughals and later against the British.[6] This history of dissent, social protest, non-conformism and ideological resistance dates as far back as the Punjab-born founder of Sikhism, Guru Nanak Devji (1469–1539), although its archival traces could also be found in the *banis* (scriptural texts of Gurus and medieval saints) of Baba Farid (1173–1266), a Punjab-born Sufi poet. Despite being a religious preacher, Guru Nanak did all he could to raise a banner of revolt against the repressive regime of Babur (1483–1531), the Mughal emperor. When Babur invaded Punjab in 1521, Guru Nanak reacted vehemently, saying, *'Paap Di Janj Leh Kabulon Charya, Jori Mange Daan Weh Lalo'* (Oh, Lalo! Accompanied by his sinful *barat* [marriage party, a metaphor for Babur's army], this aggressor has landed from Kabul, and now is forcing us to give away our daughter [the land] in marriage to him). As Babur's atrocities became more blatant and barbaric, Nanak's protests grew more strident and vociferous. Similarly, Guru Gobind Singh (1666–1708), the last of the Ten Sikh Gurus, set up the *Khalsa Panth*—a theocracy which was largely a response to the exigencies of his times. In the last quarter of the seventeenth century, he felt that only a strong spiritual, moral and military force could offer effective opposition to the 'tainted' authority of Aurangzeb (1618–1707), the Mughal emperor. In a way, the entire history of the Sikhs, their evolution as a *quam* and that of Punjab is replete with counter-hegemonic, resistance movements.[7] It was this long history of hostility towards all overt and covert forms of domination that ultimately led Punjabis to develop an anti-hegemonic, anti-authoritarian mindset.

Subterranean Hostility between Punjabi and English

It is against this background that we need to assess the historical relationship between the Sikh *quam* and the British rulers in Punjab. History shows that the British had to face their severest opposition ever on the soil of Punjab and that it proved to be the last outpost to fall under their dominion. Not until after the death of Maharaja Ranjit Singh in 1839 did Punjabis accede to colonial rule, and it was only in 1849 that annexation of Punjab became an inescapable reality. Although they had to ultimately submit to the superior military and strategic powers of the colonial rulers, Punjabis continued to resist British hegemony in ways which were both explicit and implicit. The Ghadar Movement, initiated in the early decades of the twentieth century, was a significant milestone in this history of dissent and resistance, specifically aimed at overturning British rule in India.[8] Their anti-hegemonic stance coupled with a natural instinct for aggression propelled thousands of Punjabis into the national movement for freedom. Their revolt against the alien rulers was as much an expression of their nationalistic spirit as it was proof of their constant search for identity and Punjabi sub-nationalism.

As we have discussed in an earlier chapter on *videshi* Punjabi writing, the complex interaction between Punjabi and English can easily be corroborated through archival material and the whole range of cultural signifiers therein. It often finds its expression in the popular consciousness through idiomatic phrases, folk songs and cultural stereotypes. In Punjabi folk songs, for instance, we come across idiomatic expressions such as *kale karamawale, gore goon de bore* ('Blacks are the lucky ones, and the Whites a stinking dung-heap), or *Kala shaa kala, weh kala eh sardar, gorian nu dafa karo* ('So what if my husband is black as soot, damned be the Whites).[9] We have also seen how Shah Mohammed's graphic account of the last battle between the Sikhs and the British in *Jungnaama* represents the White aggressors using euphemisms such as *Toonda Laat* (lord with a lopped-off arm), *Firangi* (foreigner) and *Teesri Jaat* (the third caste).[10] Thus, whenever the *quam* perceived a threat, it devised new strategies of resistance. This resistance has taken a more aggressive form in the postcolonial phase. The antipathy towards English language and English education is an instance of this overt resistance. This is reflected in the fact that in the sixty years since Independence, the various governments who have been in power in the state of Punjab have failed to evolve a long-term, consistent policy on English education at the primary school level. Apart from being an expression of severe myopia and resulting in policy confusion, this reflects how the Punjabi mind has always wavered over its attitude towards the English language and culture.

Collaboration between European and Indigenous Literary Forms

While the Punjabi language clearly became a site of conflicting ideologies, it was literature, with its multiple formations, that offered the possibility of both collaboration and internalisation. Until the latter half of the nineteenth century, when the impact of English education, administration and policies slowly began to manifest itself, the most popular forms of literary expression had been purely indigenous in identity and character. These included local forms of heroic poetry and narratives popular in the medieval period (*varaans*), inspirational forms of semi-religious literature derived largely from the life of Guru Nanak Devji (*janam sakhis*), Sufi forms of secular and literary expression (*masnavis* and *quissa kavyas*), and various other forms of popular literature such as folk stories and folk songs. It was R.C. Temple, a British official and scholar posted in Punjab, who towards the end of the nineteenth century, made the first ever attempt to compile and translate folk tales popular in the region.

The spread of English education and literary culture, especially among the Punjabi elite, slowly and almost imperceptibly began to change all this. Aided by the hegemonic state machinery and the forces of cultural production, the Punjabi mindset not only experienced self-alienation and a sense of cultural inferiority, but also began to participate in the accelerating process of collaboration with, and assimilation of, English literary/cultural practices. While the popular mood and sympathies remained largely hostile to the colonisers, the educated bourgeoisie began to gravitate towards them by internalising their forms, styles and literary formations. Being the beneficiaries of English education, most members of the elite tended to develop a natural propensity towards, and a belief in, the superiority of English literary/cultural practices.

For instance, the novel as a genre did not emerge in Punjabi literature until the end of the nineteenth century. When it did, it bore a definite impress of the English novel. Bhai Veer Singh (1872–1957), widely recognised as one of the pioneers in this field, began by experimenting with historical romances, a subgenre within the European novel, which he clearly developed under the influence of Walter Scott and others. Although Singh's novels such as *Sundari* (1898), *Bijay Singh* (1899), *Satwant Kaur I & II* (1900, 1927), *Baba Naudh Singh* (1921), etc., were rooted in the soil of Punjab and derived raw strength and energy from their local character and earthiness, the literary form was certainly borrowed and imitative. It was Singh's exposure to English education and literature that made him gravitate towards the English Romantics and the literary forms they popularised.[11]

Singh had begun his career writing poetry steeped in the native traditions of mysticism, which harks back to the *bani*. But when he chose to write novels, instead of turning to native narrative traditions such as the *varaan* or the *quissa*, Singh adopted historical romances. However, later developments of the Punjabi novel show how this European form was subsumed or assimilated into more indigenous narrative forms. The question of how the Punjabi novel assimilated the aesthetics of the English novel, synergising it with native narrative forms, is beyond our scope here, but this extremely complex process of cultural negotiation was nothing short of what is often described as subversion or collaboration—a process consequent upon the internalisation of the hegemonic ideology and its strategies.

The same process governed the emergence of the short story as a literary form in Punjabi. However, in the case of the Punjabi short story, the process got underway only in the first decade of the twentieth century. The pioneers of the Punjabi short story were inspired as much by Russian writers as they were by English and American writers. It was a strange case of internal colonialism—a fascination for the ideology of revolution inherent in much of nineteenth-century Russian literature—that made Punjabis gravitate towards Russian writers or to the short story as a form in which most Russian writers had already excelled. Maxim Gorky, Leo Tolstoy, Fyodor Dostoyevsky, Anton Chekhov and a host of other nineteenth-century Russian realists influenced a good number of Punjabi practitioners of this form. Significantly, the pull of the Russian short story for the Punjabi creative mind was not purely aesthetic, but ideological.[12] This is particularly true of the writers like Gurbaksh Singh Preetlari, Sant Singh Sekhon, Sujan Singh, Santokh Singh Dheer, Kulwant Singh Virk and Gurdial Singh. To an extent, the Punjabi short story could easily be described as an extension and modification of the modern short story that emerged out of the Euro-Russian context, especially in the middle of the nineteenth century.

We have so far demonstrated that literary genres and sub-genres in Punjabi are largely the offshoots of a complex negotiation between European and indigenous forms of literary expression. What can safely be deduced is that in the context of Punjabi, the language and literary forms constitute an internal schism and an irreconcilable dichotomy. While Punjabi appears to constitute an oppositional discourse with English—as language often operates at the ground level of folk consciousness—its literary forms have apparently had a more collaborative and complicit function in relation to English literary forms. Literature, being an elitist formation, often allows its various forms to be incorporated and assimilated. This process may be perceived either as an expression of Punjabi cultural schizophrenia or as cultural synthesis and hybridity. Whatever the case, it is certainly a valiant expression of the strength and resilience of Punjabis and of their ability to absorb and assimilate a wide variety of foreign influences—a tendency they have displayed right from or even before the Mughal invasions.

Translations of *Sri Guru Granth Sahib*

Now that we have understood the historical relationship between Punjabi and English in terms of both language and literary forms, we shall proceed to an understanding of how this relationship has, in the past, actually impacted the processes of translation, both of scriptural and secular texts. For this purpose, we will take up two texts—*Sri Guru Granth Sahib* (1469–1708, hereafter referred to as the *Granth*) and *The Last Flicker*, the English rendering of Gurdial Singh's magnum opus, *Marhi Da Deeva* (1964). The purpose here is to problematise, and if possible, even theorise about the translation process, particularly as it governs these two languages. To begin, we will examine some of the popular translations of the *Granth* and then take up the issues related to Singh's novel.

In the context of Punjabi literature, *Sri Guru Granth Sahib* occupies the same canonical position that is often conceded to the Bible in English literature. Philosophical in intent, mystical and spiritual in content, this holy text of the Sikhs is regarded as the ultimate repository of the collective wisdom of the Sikh Gurus and other proponents of the Bhakti (religious) Movement. Therefore, it makes sense to look at the historical process through which some of the important translations of this scriptural text have passed. The

Granth contains 1,430 *angs* (pages) and 3,384 hymns, with 15 *Bhagats* (saints) and 17 *Bhats* (folk singers) contributing 937 hymns. Apart from Punjabi, which is the language in which most of these hymns are presented, the text brings together a number of other languages and dialects including Hindi, Persian, Sanskrit, Gujarati, Marathi, various dialects of North India, and even some Arabic words. This plurality of languages and voices, which might otherwise be celebrated as an expression of a composite culture, poses the toughest challenge to the English translators of the *Granth*.

The heteroglossiac nature of the *Granth* highlights not only the eclectic character of this sacred text but also the fact that it is quintessentially a confluence of various linguistic and cultural traditions. The writers came from different corners of the Indian subcontinent and belonged to various castes and creeds, signifying the egalitarian character of the *Granth*. It represents an excellent record of social, political and religious thought in India between the twelfth and seventeenth centuries, and can truly be called a 'spiritual dictionary' or an 'encyclopaedia of philosophy'.

In 1869, Ernest Trumpp, a German missionary, attempted the first-ever English translation of the *Granth*. Published in 1877, Trumpp's *The Adi Granth* failed to gain broad acceptability among the Sikhs, who felt that it was both poor and untrustworthy. Another reason for the rejection was that Trumpp had left the work incomplete. He managed to translate only 5,719 stanzas out of a total of 15,575. Max Arthur Macauliffe (1841–1913), a British administrator posted in Punjab, completed another translation in six volumes titled *The Sikh Religion*. Regarded as the first correct English version of the *Granth*, it was published by Oxford University Press in 1909.

Both these translations essentially belonged to the colonial phase. Truly postcolonial endeavours in this direction did not begin until 1960, when eminent Sikh scholar Gopal Singh produced the first complete English translation of *Sri Guru Granth Sahib*. Published in a four-volume set, this translation enjoyed wide publicity and distribution, so much so that the World Sikh University Press decided to bring out its international edition in 1978. Singh's translation provides extensive paratextual material in the form of elaborate footnotes that explain legendary figures, Hindu mythology and local folk idioms. They facilitate the revelation of the true meaning of the Guru's Word. In certain cases, Singh explains the linguistic derivations of a word or an idiom. Drawing on a thorough understanding of comparative religion, he brings to light the common threads that run through Sikhism and other religions. However, Singh's language, grammar and syntax are rather antiquated and distracting. For instance, the translation contains expressions like, 'For several births thou wert a mere worm'; 'He, (whose way is this) knows his master and compassion comes into him, and becomes eternal he: he dies not thereafter', etc. Singh apparently sought to locate his translation in the sixteenth century, when the original work was compiled. His archaic (almost Shakespearean) diction and deliberately convoluted syntax clearly suggest that he was not translating for the contemporary readers.

This raises an important theoretical issue that could be posed in a variety of ways: should the choice of the target language be specific to the period in which the work was originally created or to the period in which it is being translated? As both the source and target languages are almost always caught in the process of change, accretion and renewal, how acceptable is it to 'de-historicise' or 'domesticate' the translation in such a way that it ceases to develop an 'afterlife' and appears to come into existence simultaneously with the original, almost like the birth of twins in two distinct, separate languages? As Singh's translation amply demonstrates, in all such cases, the translated text is, for all the wrong reasons, given the same authority and legitimacy that the original text is believed to have possessed.

Well before Gopal Singh thought of translating the *Granth*, Sardar Manmohan Singh, another devout Sikh, had started working on a translation of the same text around 1948. He took nearly twelve years to complete his work, finishing around the same time as Gopal Singh. His was an eight-volume set with the original Gurmukhi script placed side by side with the English translation, with nearly every word individually cross-referenced in both languages. Published by the Shiromani Gurdwara Prabandhak Committee (SGPC), which brought out the first volume in 1962 and the final one in 1969, this translation was treated as an authoritative one.

Both Gopal Singh and Manmohan Singh produced their translations in free verse, retaining the poetic element of the original hymns. Manmohan Singh's work represents a distinctly more accurate and direct translation of the Guru's Word, although it includes a large number of antiquated and idiosyncratic expressions more common to eighteenth- and nineteenth-century British India. For instance, he uses words like *mammon* (for 'Maya'), *myrmidon*, *collyrium*, *mumpers*, *gnosis* (for 'knowledge'), *apostates* and *sans* (French for 'without'). Much of Manmohan Singh's grammar is so dated that it is distracting and even confusing for the modern reader—for instance, 'Raising the embankments of my mind's field, I gaze at the high sky or mansion. When divine devotion enters bride's mind-home, the Friendly Guest pays her a visit.' Although Manmohan Singh's translation has a much deeper impact and is more accurate than the earlier one, it raises much the same questions.

In 1977, Gurbachan Singh Talib (1911–86) of Punjabi University, Patiala, was commissioned by the university to translate the *Granth*. His translation (published in 1988) is grammatically the least satisfying and the most distracting of the three translations cited so far, as is evident in the following examples: 'In listening to laudation of the Name eternal find I life.'; 'To whomsoever the vision of unicity does grant, propped by the holy congregation, of the Lord's love has joy.' Despite many useful footnotes added by the translator in order to shed light on the Guru's teachings, this translation fails to supersede either of the previous attempts.

One of the problems common to all these translations of the *Granth* is that the English renderings, regardless of how competent they are, tend to homogenise the content, blurring all distinctions of faiths and creeds, and erasing the plurality of languages and voices. This prevents the translation from becoming an independent and autonomous text, and also destabilises and dislocates it, both historically and culturally. Translations of contemporary Punjabi texts pose much the same problems. For instance, while translating Gurdial Singh's *Unhoye* (*The Survivors*), this writer was daunted by the vast array of dialects and idiolects in the original. Apart from the *Malwai* dialect that Singh usually uses in his novels, the novel also made extensive use of *Baghri*, a dialect popular in backward regions of Rajasthan (since one of the characters hails from this area), and also a hybridised variety of Punjabi and *Baghri* (as spoken by another character). There are no easy solutions when it comes to this tendency towards homogenisation, especially when the target language happens to be English. Like other languages, Punjabi has a rich variety of linguistic subsystems, and these come under heavy assault—and even under the threat of erasure—in all acts of translation, ingenuous or otherwise. Closely allied to this is the problem of domestication, whose risks multiply each time an effort is made to translate a text from a local or regional language into a dominant, global one. The inherent inequities of the two languages operate in and through the process of translation, guiding or imposing choices and decisions upon the translator. Such conditions often push the translator into taking ad hoc, arbitrary and inconsistent decisions, thus increasing the possibility of capitulation to the ever-present pressures exerted by the dominant language and/or ideology.

The Last Flicker: A Case Study of Cultural Dislocation

In this section, we will discuss a relatively contemporary work in translation, as an illustration of how the tendency towards domesticating and homogenising texts sometimes results in completely unexpected and even bizarre acts of cultural dislocation. *Marhi Da Deeva* (1964), Gurdial Singh's path-breaking first novel, was translated into English by Ajmer Rode and it was published as *The Last Flicker* in 1991. Rode, an immigrant Punjabi settled in Canada, chose to translate into English (a European language) a novel written by a regional writer in Punjabi (a non-European language). That these two languages have long had an unequal and problematic relationship has already been stated above. But we need to investigate the circumstances in which linguistic structures turn hegemonic and authoritarian, especially in the context of translation. Other questions connected with the process of 'cultural transfer', which is what translation is in its simplest sense, are equally important here. These questions often become manifest in the form of skewed registers, distortions in speech rhythms, erasure of kinship culture, repression of cultural content and specificity, and subsequent dislocation of the source culture in and through translation.

The following excerpts from Rode's translation will help us contextualise our discussion:

1. 'You dirty nigger! What do you think you're doing? Playing tricks on me?' Jagseer, as he approached the *sheesham*, heard Bhanta's voice seething with anger . . . 'You think, you're very smart? What do you think I've been doing all my life, grazing sheep?' Bhanta continued in the same angry tone (56).
2. 'Here comes Jago . . .' Jagseer heard a line of the Jago marriage-song coming from the far end of the village. Taking advantage of the opportunity, he changed the subject.

   'Yeah, the elder son of Sohna Tunda, from the other side of the village.'

   'That oaf, big-boned like a bullock?'

   'Yeah, yeah, the same one, Goddam dumb ox with dripping eyes and sticky cheeks like the rotten sides of the water-channel. See, some asshole will wed his daughter to him. Shit! The girl will sure be better off tied to a bull instead . . . Such sinners who wed their daughters without any mercy on them die the death of a leper, Jagsia' (67).
3. 'Want to know something, *Bapu*?' Bhilee asked, looking around with suspicious eyes, as if going to tell him something very secret.

   'Yes, honey,' said Dharam Singh.

   'Mother and brother, Bhanta, were muttering yesterday, Right? And . . . and mom said, "Get your share of land from your father, because he'll give it away to others", right? . . . and Bhanta said, "we would live together here and I'll make a shack for *Bapu* in the barn . . ."'

   'Yes! Okay, I'll be coming to see you,' Bhilee said with such assurance that Dharam Singh couldn't help smiling.

   'Okay, *Bapu*, you have your meal, I'm going to clean this place. What dust and rubbish!'

'What do mom and sister-in-law do when they come here? "Look, look at the piles of dirt everywhere."' (89)

4. 'Fucking nigger! Full of hot air! No use talking to darky! Huh, rites of the old hag! Big deal! . . . king shit!' (114)
5. 'But I tell you, Jagsia, a man like him is not born every day. Even fucking God goes after nice guys like him . . . and those Goddam scoundrels who hustle through life day and night, who bullshit around everywhere, even He dare not touch them; He's afraid of them bloody big daddies, how can he go near them . . . ?' (119)

The novel is set in an insulated village in Punjab, inhabited mostly by unlettered or partially educated characters. While conversing with one another, most of these characters do not even use standard Punjabi. Instead, they use the *Malwai* dialect, popular in the Malwa region, which is where the village is located. From the extracts above, it is apparent that Singh has a definite preference for the 'dialogic' (showing) mode over the 'narrative' (telling) mode. Playing the part of an unobtrusive narrator, the novelist appears to be portraying characters and situations through the adroit use of his characters' speech rhythms and the rich cultural resonance these rhythms invariably evoke. As cultural specificities can hardly be ignored in this kind of narrative, a translator cannot afford to hedge on questions of methodology. Ultimately, these questions are bound to influence, if not determine, the success or failure of the translation, regardless of whether it is oriented towards the source or the target culture.

Even a casual reading of these extracts points to the absence of a well-defined methodology or strategy. As a result, we have this somewhat incongruous, if not anachronistic, situation where characters residing in a remote village in Punjab speak the same idiom that inhabitants of New York or Montreal often use. For instance, it is nearly impossible to decode the 'voice' behind the words in excerpt 5. One cannot really distinguish whether it is that of a 'rustic dowdy' or an 'urban rowdy'. Though largely rustic and unlettered, these characters mouth expressions that make them appear far more educated than what they are and, what is worse, these expressions project them as products of a metropolitan subculture that is unlikely to have even the remotest of connections with them or their cultural matrix. Rather than create a context within which the cultural and speech specificities of these characters can become real and meaningful, the translator has sought to relocate them in a cultural context that is ideologically so different that it appears almost alien to their world.

Lexical markers such as 'king shit', 'fucking piece of land' and 'asshole' clearly point to a specific cultural context which is completely at variance with the one within which the novel was conceived. Moreover, the newly created context is overladen with Christian ('Goddam') and racist ('fucking nigger') ideologies which are clearly in conflict with the ideology of the characters and the novelist. It is almost as if, dispossessed of their immediate surroundings, the simple-minded, uneducated characters surviving in the distant rural parts of Punjab have, through this bizarre process of *kaya kalp*, suddenly acquired the accents and mannerisms of street smart, educated Whites living in an affluent metropolis. While erasing the oral speech rhythms of *Malwai* dialect, the translation also imparts to these characters an identity that is completely at variance with the one that the novelist had presumably imagined or intended.

Closely allied to this is another problem, which largely stems from skewed registers. The translation, one can argue, presents a narrative where American colloquialisms, Punjabi twang and British crispness are mixed in a hotchpotch of registers. Moreover, not much thought appears to have been given to whether the kinship markers, culturally overloaded as they often are, should be consistently replaced with their English equivalents or retained in their original form and distinct emphasis. For instance, *Bapu*—a term used for father or an elder—has been preserved in its original form, while the overtly anglicised 'mom' and 'aunty' have replaced *Maa* and *Chachi/Tayyi*. In actual social praxis, the use of *Chachi* or *Tayyi* depends on whether it is a younger or an elder aunt who is being addressed. Moreover, in Punjabi society, kinship markers are not only lexical markers, but have a definite ideology of their own. They are inextricably bound up with notions of hierarchy, status and power. The use of certain forms of salutation also reveals the nature and degree of the affective content inherent in a particular relationship. For this reason, inconsistent use of these terms might prove to be misleading in two distinct ways. First, it might dilute the emotional content; second, it might subvert the hierarchical structure in a village community. It is obvious that both these contradictions are inscribed in the translated passages quoted above.

One can argue that through his inappropriate choice of swear words, inflections and endearments, the translator displaces the characters, thus reinforcing their cultural alienation. Even among educated, English-speaking, urban middle-class Indian fathers, it is not at all common to use such endearments as 'honey' when they address their daughters. Likewise, 'yeah' or 'huh' comes naturally to only those trained in the inflections of the American idiom or speech mannerisms. Use of such colloquialisms as 'nice guys' and 'big daddies' or expletives such as 'Goddam scoundrels', 'bullshit', etc., is certainly not the best way to capture the cadence of the spoken word of illiterate villagers. Apart from dislocating them spatially, this also 'dislodges' the characters in terms of their class, status and ideology. It is almost as if the translator has recast them in his own ideological frame, overwriting their class, status and linguistic markers with his own. In his efforts to relocate a typical Punjabi novel within the cultural frame of his adopted country, the translator has merely succeeded in dislocating it from the source culture. While this particular translation might have worked as a 'linguistic transfer', it certainly fails to qualify as a 'cultural transfer'.

The real question here is not whether an English rendering of a Punjabi text should be heavily interlarded with Punjabi words and expressions. It is whether a translator should take these decisions arbitrarily or work out a careful strategy that is applied consistently and self-consciously. For instance, kinship markers, forms of salutation, exclamations and, at times, the names of plants, trees, seasons, rituals and ceremonies, etc., are so deeply embedded in the specificities of the source culture that all efforts at translating them into the target language are bound to prove self-defeating. In this context, it makes sense to remember Walter Benjamin's famous argument that it is not just translation but all forms of writing that necessarily form a deflection away from 'the purity of the original'.[13] Seen from this perspective, translation is never completely done in the target language, as is often assumed, but in what George Steiner calls the 'third language',[14] and it is often mediated in what Homi K. Bhabha describes as the 'third space'.[15]

If the search for the 'universals' in specific human experiences makes translation possible, the cultural specificity adds to the innumerable challenges facing a translator. Gayatri Chakravorty Spivak, an eminent critic and a distinguished translator herself, has pointed out the need to recognise the whole area of 'untranslatability' embedded in the archaeology of each seemingly translatable text. This clearly suggests that far from being a mechanical activity (or simply a matter of finding lexical and/or semantic equivalences in two different language systems), which is what sums up the popular understanding of translation, it is a highly self-reflexive, political act.

The political nature of translation is inevitable in a situation where the source and target languages are as highly differentiated as Punjabi and English, which are inequitably placed in terms of their spread and power. As a global language, English is inherently privileged. If a translator, by accident or design, starts colluding in this process of domination by adopting a 'domesticating'—and not a 'foreignising'—method, de-culturation of the source language and culture is inevitable. And this, in turn, is bound to defeat the very purpose for which translations are often undertaken. By scrupulously adhering to the foreignising method and refusing to make egregious concessions to English, a translator may not only reflect her/his own ideological and methodological preferences, but also demonstrate how her/his 'politics' essentially functions.[16]

This essay had set out to explore the problematic of Punjabi and English and its historical variations in terms of language, literature and translation. The canvas, as we have seen, is fairly broad and, occasionally, bewilderingly chaotic. But we have, in the course of our discussion, raised a few pertinent questions and helped focus attention on a handful of theoretical issues.

Notes and References

1. The idea that Indian literature went through a phase of 'renaissance' has been suggested by a host of thinkers and literary critics, who have over-emphasised the reformist movements of the nineteenth century and attributed the growth of literary trends and movements in different Indian languages to their symbiosis with European languages, cultures and literary forms.

2. Ganesh Devy, essentially a nativist, has constructed an oppositional discourse on colonialism, perceiving it primarily in terms of a rupture of our historical consciousness. In *After Amnesia: Tradition and Change in Indian Literary Criticism* (New Delhi: Orient Longman, 1992), he points out how this encounter worked to the detriment of Indian languages and Indian literary and critical traditions.

3. For a historical understanding of Punjabi, and its growth and development, see Pyara Singh Padam, *Punjabi Boli Da Itihaas* (Patiala: Punjabi University, 1964) and Prem Parkash Singh, *Punjabi Bhasha Da Itihaas* (Patiala: Punjabi University, 2002).

4. For a historical understanding of the English language, see Charles Barber, *The English Language: A Historical Introduction* (Cambridge: Cambridge University Press, 1993) and Barbara A. Fennell, *A History of English: A Sociolinguistic Approach* (Oxford: Blackwell Publishers, 2001).

5. A number of postcolonial theorists such as Ashis Nandy, *The Intimate Enemy: Loss and Recovery of Self under Colonialism* (New Delhi: Oxford University Press, 1983) and Leela Gandhi, *Postcolonial Theory: An Introduction* (New Delhi: Oxford University Press, 1998), have pointed out that the interaction between the coloniser and the colonised is not a unilinear but a multilinear process, a complex negotiation that ensures simultaneous collaboration and subversion.

6. Punjabi opposition to the Mughals was mainly directed at the hegemonic policies of the invaders, not at their religion, as Sufism, supposedly the benign face of Islam, was conveniently subsumed and incorporated into popular Punjabi folk literature and consciousness.

7. For an elaborate discussion of this idea, see H.R. Gupta, *History of the Sikhs* (Simla: Minerva Book Shop, 1952); Khushwant Singh, *The History of the Sikhs* (New Delhi: Oxford University Press, 2003); N.K. Sinha, *Rise of the Sikh Power* (1936; repr. Calcutta: A. Mukherjee, 1973); W.H. Mcleod, *The Evolution of the Sikh Community: Five Essays* (New Delhi: Oxford University Press, 1975); and J.S. Grewal, *The Sikhs of the Punjab* (New Delhi: Cambridge University Press, 1999).

8. For the history of the Ghadar Movement, see Hugh Johnston, *The Voyage of the Kamagata Maru* (Vancouver: University of British Columbia Press, 1979) and Harish K. Puri, *Ghadar Movement: Ideology, Organization, and Strategy* (Amritsar: Guru Nanak Dev University Press, 1983).

9. For a more detailed exposition, see the introduction of Rana Nayar, *From Across the Shores: Punjabi Short Stories by Asians in Britain* (New Delhi: Sterling, 2002).

10. Here *Teesri Jaat* refers to the third caste in the caste hierarchy—the *bania* caste, a much-hated caste in Punjab because of the longstanding unequal economic relationship between farmers (growers) and *banias* (money lenders). Owing to their economic dependence upon the *banias*, peasants developed a deep-seated hatred for them. In the context of Punjabi popular culture, the peasant–*bania* relationship has a distinct sociology of its own that has endured through history, despite far-reaching changes in the sociology of caste structures over the years. For a more detailed exposition, see the introduction of Rana Nayar, *From Across the Shores*.

11. Incidentally, the first college in Punjab to offer an MA in English literature was Khalsa College in Amritsar, which started offering this course way back in 1892 and later emerged as an important hub of Punjabi culture and its dissemination. Although Bhai Veer Singh never took an MA degree in English, he was a product of this institution and came under the influence of the Singh Sabha Movement, of which Khalsa College, Amritsar, was a significant nucleus. The foremost objective of this movement was to reform the Sikhs from within, and towards that end, it aimed to provide the Sikhs with education along the lines of English education. This represents an attempt to indigenise English education to suit the needs of the local population.

12. In his famous 'Ideology of the Aesthetic'—Terry Eagleton, 'Ideology of the Aesthetic', in *The Politics of Pleasure: Aesthetics and Cultural Theory*, ed. Stephen Regan (Philadelphia: Open University Press, 1992), 1–32—Eagleton discusses the mutual relationship between ideology and aesthetics. My understanding of this relationship derives largely from this work, and in my introduction to *Slice of Life: Punjabi Short Fiction 1901–2000* (Chandigarh: Unistar, 2006), I have further developed it in the context of the Punjabi short story.

13. Walter Benjamin, 'The Task of the Translator', in *Illuminations*, ed. Hannah Arendt (Glasgow: Fontana, 1973), 78.

14. George Steiner, *After Babel: Aspects of Language and Translation* (London: Oxford University Press, 1975).

15. Homi K. Bhabha, *The Location of Culture* (London: Routledge, 1994).

16. In his well-known work, *The Translator's Invisibility* (London: Routledge, 1995), Lawrence Venuti offers an extended discussion of these two strategies of translation. Each strategy has its distinct ideological slant, and so a translator's preference for one over the other betrays his or her ideological leanings.

CHAPTER ELEVEN

Bhisham Sahni's *Tamas*: Multiple Historical Perspectives and Literary Art

1

It is important that we begin this discussion on the complexities of the relationship between, and internal contradictions of, history and literary art by looking into certain questions pertaining to historiography. In the past few decades, historians appear to have shown more interest in historiography than they have in history per se. From which perspective should history be told or narrated? What kind of historical contingencies must define the contradictions or ambiguities in terms of its representation? Why has history ceased to be an objective science and become instead a subjective fiction? These are some of the questions that have, in the recent past, provided the necessary stimulus for the revaluation of historiography. It would be no exaggeration to say that such developments in the arena of historiography are largely responsible for creating a new consciousness of history among contemporary historians. It is neither possible nor desirable to go into the intricacies of this multifocal debate on the subject within the scope of this essay.[1] Yet, a few facts in this regard will have to be addressed.

In the context of this increased focus on historiography, Francis Fukuyama's *The End of History and the Last Man* has claimed more than its share of attention in the past decade or so. Published in 1992, this book, in fact, originated in the form of an essay that Fukuyama had earlier published in an American journal called *The National Interest*. According to Fukuyama, we are stepping into a phase of globalisation where ideological conflicts and contradictions have ceased to exist, or even if they do exist, these do not really amount to anything much. It is noteworthy that Fukuyama made these observations at a critical historical juncture—in the post-Cold War period when the entire world was reeling under the collapse of the Soviet Union. On the strength of such a premise, he offers a prognosis of the future, and claims that ultimately, liberal democracy is the only system of governance that must inevitably triumph in all the countries around the world. According to him, liberal democracy is the only answer to all the manifest forms of totalitarianism. Behind this belief lies a set of assumptions that can only be understood when they are unmasked. One of Fukuyama's assumptions is that the impact of modern natural science is fairly uniform all over the world. He further argues that consumer culture has spread through the globe like a worldwide campaign, so much so that unlimited accumulation of wealth has become the life mission of almost every citizen of the world. Rejecting the Marxist view, he says that Hegel's non-materialist notion of history is more purposive for our times as it is based on the struggle for recognition. It is on the basis of such assumptions that Fukuyama has sought to bring the Hegelian dream of the 'Universal History of mankind' back into the discourse of history. Defending his position, Fukuyama says, 'By raising once again the question of whether there is such a thing as Universal History of mankind, I am resuming a discussion that was begun in the early nineteenth century, but more or less abandoned in our time because of the enormity of the events that mankind has experienced since then.'[2]

It is nothing short of an anachronism that Fukuyama has chosen to talk about the 'Universal History of mankind' at a time when serious doubts are being voiced about its philosophical lineage and, therefore, its legitimacy. Writing some two decades ago, Jean Francois Lyotard, the French philosopher and literary theorist, had, in his article 'The Postmodern Condition', questioned the very raison d'être of grand narratives in our times. Ruling out the possibility of searching for grand narratives, Lyotard says that in our times, such a search would be nothing more than a self-defeating exercise. Michel Foucault, whose writings reconstituted the discourse of history, repeatedly emphasises that the 'temporal dislocations' and 'discontinuities' which, in the past, have been the source of anxiety to historians, could now very well become the starting points of an inquiry into history. Mikhail Bakhtin has gone so far as to suggest that in history as well as literature, 'continuity', 'linearity' or 'unidirectionality' (a term which recurs through Fukuyama's analysis) could only give birth to a 'totalising narrative'.

The real question is not whether the Hegelian view is to be given preference over the Marxist view of history or vice versa and what should be the basis of either. Once the breakdown of consensus on the unidirectional view of history is almost accepted as a fait accompli, the only question that remains is this: How far is it justified to first construct and then legitimise yet another grand narrative using the concept of 'Universal History', which, in any case, appears too worn out, clichéd and decontextualised to be serviceable? In recommending the US brand of liberal democracy as a panacea for the political ills facing countries very different from the US, Fukuyama is either guilty of being ahistorical or has fallen an easy prey to historical amnesia, or both. He makes it convenient to forget that despite the American Revolution, Afro-American Blacks continued to fight and struggle for recognition in this very liberal democracy. Moreover, the consumer culture which, he believes, would be instrumental in restoring human dignity to all citizens across the world, already appears to be threatening the humankind with the dehumanising potential of commodification. Fukuyama even chooses to overlook the fact that despite the global spread of science and technology, neither its distribution across the globe is uniform nor is its 'transfer' ever done on equal terms. He does not recognise the internal contradictions of capital and labour and he is not interested in externalising or investigating the conflicting claims of both. A die-hard, almost unsparing critic of fascism and communism, Fukuyama, ironically enough, ends up becoming a spirited advocate of another kind of ideological totalitarianism, which he neither perceives nor understands.

When they are read and understood in their respective contexts, both Fukuyama and Bakhtin appear to be supporting the cause of two very different, rather divergent viewpoints on history. Fukuyama, it appears, attempts to create a grand narrative out of human history by homogenising it and by erasing specific historical differences as well as ubiquitous economic inequities intrinsic to various nations.

The main objective of such a view of history is to give legitimacy to the hegemonic and neo-imperialist designs of the American culture. Going beyond this, Fukuyama also seeks to project the American society, polity and culture as a paradigmatic model worthy of emulation for all developing countries, glossing over the internal contradictions of globalisation in the process. If carried to its logical extreme, such a unilateral and lopsided view of history can easily turn monopolistic, totalitarian and oppressive. And, for that very reason, it can hardly be used as a mode of negotiating the interrelationships/internal contradictions between a nation's—least of all, a developing nation's—history and literature or the point of artistic convergence of the two. As opposed to this, Foucault and Bakhtin have a firm logic for giving legitimacy to multiple perspectives.

In his writings, Bakhtin has clearly pointed out how multiple perspectives first surfaced in the novels of Fyodor Dostoyevsky, that too, in the form of a particular type of novel he chooses to describe as 'polyphonic'. Such a novel, Bakhtin believes, can be seen as a potential battleground for conflicting ideologies/voices, with its structure supporting the unresolved contradictions embedded within. If the polyphonic novel was a kind of counter-discourse—Bakhtin's answer to the totalitarianism of Stalin's hegemonic discourse—so was Foucault's 'historical discourse', perhaps a shade braver at knocking down the very basis of the Western project of enlightenment that valorised rationality. It is equally important to note that both of them arrived at the conceptual understanding of multiple perspectives independent of each other—mainly through an attempt to counter the mechanics of oppression in their respective contexts. If seen against this backdrop, the claim that multiple perspectives are an extremely valuable tool for negotiating the mutual relationship of history and fiction in a developing country should not sound entirely untenable. Perhaps, this is one of the several ways in which an emancipatory narrative could possibly be created.

2

Bhisham Sahni's (1915–2003) Sahitya Akademi Award winning novel *Tamas* (Darkness) can be considered as an emancipatory narrative—the kind that we have discussed in the previous section.

Published in 1973, this novel bears a living testimony to a dark, tainted phase of contemporary Indian history, which despite all attempts at description or analysis, would perhaps never fully reveal the hidden depths of its multilayered reality. *Tamas* is a reflection of the bloodstained days of Partition, which shall perhaps, forever, remain dispersed in our collective memory. It is an extremely sensitive and graphic portrayal of those nebulous historical memories out of whose dark womb both India and Pakistan had leapt into existence, albeit after a Caesarean. The most outstanding achievement of Sahni's art of characterisation is its exuberance and rich vitality. Ripping off the grotesque masks, he manages to bring out some of the long forgotten faces wrapped in the dense fog of memories—both personal and collective—and he succeeds in making them eminently memorable. It is perhaps for this reason that *Tamas* could well be seen as an important link in the long chain of historical novels in Hindi.

There is near unanimity among scholars of Hindi literature over Kishori Lal Goswami (1865–1932) being a pioneer of sorts as far as the historical novel in Hindi is concerned. With the medieval period of Indian history constituting their backdrop, he created such immensely popular novels as *Rajkumari* (1902), *Lal Kunwar* (1912), *Razia* (1915) and *Tara* (1917). Explaining the rationale behind his historical novels, in the introduction to *Tara*, Goswami says,

> In most of the historical novels that I have created so far, my constant effort has been to foreground imagination and push history into the background. Occasionally, I even go so far as to allow history to bow meekly before the power of imagination. That is how it shapes into a novel, not a slice of history. In a novel, it is imagination and not historical or documentary realism that ultimately reigns supreme.[3]

Apparently, Goswami never tried to achieve—or he was never able to achieve—that enviable, delicate balance between history and fiction, which a creative writer often aims at. Behind this failure lies his schematic division, compelling him to regard 'truth' as the territory of history and 'imagination' that of literature. His view of history appears to draw its legitimacy from religion, since he claims that he uses his narratives, primarily, for 'restoring or reinstating the inherent pride of the Aryan people'.[4] Rather than help us understand the dynamic relationship between history and fiction, such a one-sided view will only serve to fulfil the intensely personal and whimsical objectives of the writer. To an extent, the novels of Devaki Nandan Khatri (1861–1913), too, evoke a vaguely similar response.

Although Babu Ganga Prasad Gupt (1874–1938) has also written such celebrated character-based novels as *Noorjahan* (1902) *Veerpatni* (Brave Man's Wife, 1903) and *Jaimal* (1904), he does not regard the historical novel as a work of pure imagination. According to him, it is much better to create a historical novel under the 'shadows of history'. Elaborating upon it, Gupt describes these 'shadows' (which he mentions in the preface to his novel *Hameer*) as a sense of actuality in the presentation of historical situations and/or characters which often turn a novel into 'a crystal clear mirror of religious, social, political ideas as well as man's inner nature'.[5] It was perhaps this that prompted Gopinath Tiwari to concede, in his book *Itihasik Upanyas Aur Upanyaskaar*, that Gupt can be viewed 'as a trailblazer among the critics of modernity such as Premchand'.[6] Vrindavan Lal Verma (1889–1969), who created such monumental works as *Jhansi Ki Rani* (1946), *Satran Sau Unees* (1946) and *Ahalyabai* (1956), too, was a sympathiser of the same brand of idealistic realism that Munshi Premchand (1880–1936) often practised. In one of his articles published in *Sangam* on 26 January 1950, Verma quipped, 'Only if the right kind of facts were to mix with idealism in the right proportion, would it be possible for the historical novel to play a positive role in the process of social reconstruction.' What makes his approach to history somewhat different from that of his predecessors is the fact that, for inspiration, he often turned to popular, folk sources and not so much to historical documents. For instance, Verma's *Padmini* (1933) and *Kachnaar* (1946) borrow their material extensively from popular and folk traditions. Therefore, it would not be wrong to say that Gupt and Verma were primarily responsible for bringing social consciousness into the historical novel in Hindi.

Despite their social consciousness, the absence of dialectical, human conflict in the narratives of Gupt and Verma often proves somewhat exasperating, if not intriguing, for the reader. Though Verma uses the backdrop of human conflict in most of his novels, he ends up valorising the love stories developing against such backdrops. One can say that these novelists were so completely wrapped up with the notion of idealism that despite being rather deft at the presentation of reality, they were unable to either analyse or critique reality. To a large extent, Acharya Chatursen Shastri's (1891–1960) novel *Vaishali Ki Nagar Vadhu* (1948) did succeed in filling up this gap. Written with the avowed purpose of popularising and disseminating the theoretical principles of Buddhism and Jainism, this novel launches a scathing attack on the advocates of mainstream Indian culture. Even if one were to agree that this novel was not written to promote a specific agenda, one could raise serious doubts about Shastri's sense of objectivity. As critics have noted, instead of looking for the 'traces of history', this novel appears to be searching for 'the *rasa* of history'.[7] Probably, this is what inspired Prabhakar Machwe to say, 'What a historical novel should not be. This 787-pages-long novel set in the war period is a brilliant testimony to the *rasa* of history.'[8]

At this point, one may ask how far would it be right on the part of a historical novelist to become not just a producer (creator) of historical *rasa* but its main consumer (*rasika*) as well. Under these circumstances, is it possible for a novelist to present the events, situations and characters with complete objectivity, without showing any favour towards or bias against a particular viewpoint? After all, what is the main purpose of a historical novel—to enable a writer to present either her/his religious or secular viewpoints or to create the space within which the tensions, conflicts and contradictions of human society can possibly be dramatised? Is the historical novel merely a scientific tool of analysing, dramatising or critiquing human values or is it a site of artistic or aesthetic plenitude as well?

Sahni's *Tamas* not only wrestles with some of these and other related questions, but seeks to answer them, albeit tentatively. *Tamas* is perhaps the first ever historical novel in Hindi literature that can be said to exemplify the Bakhtinian notion of a dialogic novel. This novel captures the anguish of realism with as much sensitivity as it displays in delineating the inspirational mode of idealism. Striving towards a balance between 'historical traces' and 'historical *rasa*', *Tamas* does manage to foreground those internal and external contradictions or conflicts, which are intrinsic to all human situations. Despite being its creator, Sahni is, in a way, 'absent' in the narrative. Perhaps, it became possible only because, apart from being a novelist of repute, Sahni was a playwright of considerable training and experience. He has not only authored such classics among Hindi novels as *Basanti* (1980), *Jhorokhe* (1988), but also penned some well-known plays such as *Hanush* (1977), *Kabira Khara Bazar Mein* (1981) and *Madhavi* (1982). It appears that in *Tamas*, Sahni has made use of the artistic strategies and procedures readily available to a dramatist. It is no wonder that the multiple historical perspectives tend to become the focal point around which the artistic design of *Tamas* has assiduously been created.

Now the question arises: how and in what different ways does this multiple perspective manifest itself in the novel? At this stage, all one can say with some degree of definitiveness is that it takes on four distinct, discrete forms: 1. ordinary people's or the victim's viewpoint; 2. non-sectarian, nationalist viewpoint of the secular forces; 3. religion-inspired, obscurantist viewpoint of the destructive forces; and, 4. the viewpoint of the ruling class or the imperialist forces.

Each of these viewpoints is grounded on a distinct ideology, and it also seeks to demonstrate the distinctiveness of its character. The novelist has shown an impeccable sense of objectivity in presenting these multiple viewpoints and they often tend to operate in an autonomous, self-regulatory manner, speeding up the course of events and continually exacerbating the ideological conflicts. Set against the backdrop of India's Partition, Sahni has created such a narrative space in the novel that it has the power to dramatise the ideological conflicts in a rather unobtrusive way. To put it another way, the novelist has reserved his liberty to mount a systematic attack on each viewpoint, pointing out the inherent flaws and limitations of each, without being partial to any single one. Despite the fact that he has affiliation to Marxist ideology, Sahni has not allowed his personal preferences to dominate the novel. Of course, there are only two distinct ways in which the personal ideological stance of the novelist becomes manifest. One, in his artistic treatment of dialectics that easily transforms the novel into a battleground of a rag-bag of ideologies, and the other, in his unimpeachable commitment to humanistic values or codes that comes through in his delicately sensitive characterisation. To understand this better, we need to put each viewpoint to a more sustained scrutiny and comprehensive expostulation.

Viewpoint of the Ordinary, Common People

In a manner of speaking, *Tamas* is a novel without a hero. Still, if anyone is to be regarded as the hero, it is none other than the masses who, despite being exploited by the inexorable forces of history, fail to make it even to its back pages. They neither understand the significance of history nor do they have the real power to break through its vicelike, cyclic pattern. Though these common men and women are always at the receiving end of social, economic and historical conditions, and are often persecuted by them, they invariably fail to raise a banner of revolt against them. Haunted by the sheer longing to live and survive, they find themselves reduced to hapless observers or spectators. And when the circumstances are not propitious, they either die a silent death or are brutally killed. Nathu, the Chamar, Ibrahim, the *ittar*-seller, Harnam Singh, Banto, Iqbal Singh, Jasbir, Prakasho, Natha Singh, etc., have been conceived as representatives of these common masses. Within the space of the novel, the existence of most of these characters remains confined to, at best, two or three events or situations. In a way, these characters never quite progress beyond becoming more than just footnotes of history. The situational exigencies or circumstantial compulsions turn them into victims with as much ease with which they make victimisers out of them.

In the opening chapter, Sahni has presented a ferocious struggle between Nathu and a pig with such synecdochic effect and skill that, while obliterating all the facile differences between the victim and the victimiser, he manages to prefigure other such instances in the novel. Not only does Nathu persecute and wound the pig, but is also persecuted, in turn, by its bestiality. He fails to understand why Murad Ali, despite being a Muslim, first gives him this assignment to hack a pig to death and then, on the completion of the job, refuses to even recognise him. Nathu Chamar's perplexity is largely the creation of those religion-inspired, destructive forces that are forever ready to make sacrificial lambs out of the common masses. These forces ultimately kill Ibrahim, as mercilessly as Nathu had earlier dispensed with the pig. Ultimately, these sectarian forces do succeed in sparking off the blazing fire of communal riots that reduces as many as 103 villages to a heap of ash and dust. It is the circumstances created by these very forces that first compel Harnam Singh to seek refuge in his friend Ramzan Ali's house, and then be robbed by him as well. When Iqbal Singh is forced to convert into Islam and become Iqbal Ahmed, and when Jasbir jumps to her death in a blind well, neither history nor religion is able to offer consolation and solace. All that remains is the child-like innocence of Natha Singh's hollow laughter, spilling out of his care-worn, creased eyes. Apart from revealing his frenzied state of mind, it also brings his latent, suppressed pain and anguish to the fore.[9]

If there is untold pain, agony and uncertainty in the lives of the masses, there is a delicate balance of music as well. Sahni does not fail to remind us that much before the communal riots broke out, the 'mutual relationships among the masses were poised on the edge of an uninterrupted stream'. It is described by the novelist in an artlessly poetic manner:

> When Ibrahim, the *ittar*-seller, with bottles of varied shapes and sizes hanging from his shoulders, would pass from one end of the street to another, beckoning people to buy *ittar* or *gulel*, striding forth at an even pace, it would appear as though he were lifting his feet to the rhythmic tune of this town. Propelled by this very tune, the women would make a beeline for the municipal tap, lifting pitchers on their slender heads. It appeared as though this sweet rhythm set the clock for the entire business to be transacted, and that if this rhythm were to get disrupted even temporarily, the entire chain of activity would grind to a sudden halt. Or you could even say that the humming of the routine chores, creating rare, harmonious sounds, struck a chord in each and every heart. It was as if on hearing this music, the people of this town would blossom into youth, ripen into years, so much so that the generations together would go away, swaying to this very tune . . . (92).

It is apparent that there is no conflict or contradiction in the lives of the common people. For their lives, quite simply, revolve around an overpowering sense of warmth and closeness, belonging and completion, all of which is imperceptibly transformed into a lyrical tune or harmonious music. If at all there is any conflict or contradiction, it is in the social and historical contingencies that enmesh and define their lives. The greatest tragedy of history is—and here Partition is no exception—that such contingencies often tend to mutilate and snuff out these eternal notes in the ordinary lives of the common people. In *Tamas*, such contradictions manage to find a crystallised, chiselled expression.

Non-sectarian, Nationalist Viewpoint of the Secular Forces

In *Tamas*, the secular and nationalist viewpoint finds its votaries among those Congress workers who have helped strengthen and consolidate the spirit of nationalism. Des Raj, Sher Khan, Jarnail Singh, Master Ram Dass, Bakshiji, Kashmiri Lal, Mehtaji and Shankar Lal belong to this category. It is obvious that, within the frame of the novel, most of these characters are simply engaged in promoting the Gandhian brand of nationalism. They take out *prabhat pheris*, undertake community work, do their utmost to douse the raging fires of communal hatred, and when the looming threat of communal riots assumes alarming proportions, they even call on the deputy commissioner and seek his intervention for bringing the situation under control. This is the way in which their collective identity manifests itself. The real achievement of Sahni's art of characterisation is that he has managed to set up a dialectical opposition between the collective identity and the individual attitudes/attributes of his characters. Once these characters are put through a microscopic scrutiny, we realise that as individuals, they demonstrate heterogeneity rather than unity of purpose.

Though Jarnail Singh gives the impression of being a somewhat eccentric Congressman, he always speaks out his mind with a rare candour and forthrightness. Despite being a committed Congress worker, Ram Dass is rather proud of his Brahmanical identity. Mehtaji is a corrupt and degenerate Congressman. A strong votary of communal harmony and collective unity, Bakshiji does not think twice before using politics for his personal ends, especially when his overriding ambition gets the better of him. Shankar Lal, a young Congressman, has no patience with either duplicity or hypocrisy, and is always willing to speak his mind out against all this. It needs to be pointed out here that Sahni's purpose behind all this is not to offer a critique of Gandhian philosophy or that of the Congress Party. Rather, his purpose is primarily to offer a realistic portrayal of all those circumstances and situations which led to the slow fragmentation of the Congress-sponsored nationalism. This process of dissolution had been set into motion much before the Partition. If the ever-widening gap between Gandhiji and Subhash Chandra Bose was just one of its manifestations, its other face was reflected in the growing sympathy or natural tilt of the Muslims towards the Muslim League after it had come into existence. One of the questions to which the novel, directly or indirectly, returns rather insistently is this: how far could the Congress Party have championed the cause of the Muslims, especially in the altered historical context where the existence of the Muslim League had already become a living reality? Rather than put a question mark over why the Congress Party persisted with its policies and its agenda even in the altered historical circumstances, such questions create for us both the space and the opportunity for re-evaluating and re-assessing the Congress brand of nationalism.

The novel is replete with instances where an oppositional discourse sets itself up between the Congress Party's monumental view of nationalism and its antithesis in the common masses' perception. For instance, Shankar tells Kashmiri Lal, 'This community work is nothing but trash . . .', and that 'cleaning up drains won't help us win Swaraj' (52–3). In another instance, we hear one labourer tell another, '*Ganjmandi ton ik babu di pand chuki aa riha si, je babu kahan laga, "Azadi awan wali hey," Mein haas ke kiha, "Awe Azadi, babu sahoon ki, Asan hun wi pand chakkani ain, pichon wi pand chakkange."*' (101) ['I was walking back with a babu, carrying his sack on my head, when the babu suddenly said, "Freedom is round the corner." I laughed and said, "Let this freedom come or not, babu, how does it matter? Until yesterday, we carried the sack on our back, and again tomorrow, we'll have to carry the same sack."']

Religion-inspired, Obscurantist Viewpoint of the Destructive Forces

It might appear to be an anomaly that the maximum narrative space in *Tamas* has been allocated to the destructive forces. But given the context of the novel, it is not really so. There are two reasons for it. One, the novel unfolds itself against a sequence of events where the destructive forces were marching headlong towards the Partition of the country. Two, by thus allotting more narrative space to this viewpoint, Sahni has managed to overturn it, inviting us to question the very basis of its rationale and legitimacy. In a way, it goes to the credit of the novelist that he has managed to present a variety of viewpoints grounded upon various religious doctrines and ideologies, without in the least straining his sense of objectivity and fair play. Rather than lash out against any specific religious doctrine, he has ripped the mask off all ideologies, without being partial to one or unnecessarily harsh on another.

Tamas chooses to focus upon three main subcontinental religions—Hinduism, Islam and Sikhism. Vanprashthji is the controlling spirit behind Hindu Maha Sabha. A scholar of Indian culture and Sanskrit language/literature, he has not only studied the *Vedas*, but also reels off mantras from the *Upanishads* and the *Gita* with felicity and elan. When he does the *shanti paath*, it appears as though 'the entire atmosphere is set aglow with peace in its transcendental aspect' (60). Ironically, this sagacious exterior is only a pretense, a mask that conceals the real face of Vanprasthji. Often during the sermons, he gets 'somewhat excited and charged', especially when he spews the poison of communal hatred against the Muslims. He is unable to understand the conflicting demands of his emotional states. During the same *satsang*, he claps and sings, '*Sab par daya karo Bhagwan/Sab par kripa karo Bhagwan*' [May God shower His mercy upon all/May God shower blessings upon all], and then in an equally charged voice, he chants the following lines: '*Falaye ghor paap Musalmin ne/Nemat falak ne cheen li, daulat zameen ne*' (60). [Muslims spread the worst of all sins/They snatch away the land and money of the poorest among the poor.] Due to his excitable temper, he often starts conjuring up visions that are hardly grounded in reality. Even when the situation in town was very much under control, though somewhat delicately poised, he had already started saying, 'All the members should keep a canister of mustard oil in the house. Boiling oil can always be poured over the enemy's head, smouldering embers can also be hurled from the roof-top . . .' (62). His logic is that everyone except the Hindus and Sikhs are '*malechh*' and for that reason, deserve both contempt and hatred.

Fifteen-year-old Ranveer is a raging flame of communalism, a living embodiment of this consuming passion. He is an ardent devotee of his teacher, Master Dev Dutt, and has almost internalised his self-destructive, anarchic mindset. Not only does Dutt teach Ranveer the first lesson in the philosophy of hatred but is also responsible for his initiation into violence. At the time of his initiation, Ranveer is almost in the same state of mind that Nathu had been through, earlier when he was called upon to hack a pig to death. The only difference is that while Nathu does go through a bout of penance, Ranveer has no qualms whatsoever about leading a murderous assault against a *halwai*, his coreligionist. The most glaring discrepancy in the viewpoint of the religious forces is that they invariably invoke the authority of the scriptures for legitimising the most brutal and inhuman of their deeds. The obscurantists often indulge in wilful distortion of scriptures or invoke the *Pauranic* stories and even anecdotes from the *Mahabharata* to whip up communal passions and flames of hatred. Dutt very deftly narrates an anecdote about how a yogi had, through his spiritual powers, burnt a *malechh* to ashes, just to instil in Ranveer's heart a deep-seated hatred for the '*malechhs*'. Sahni illustrates that the obscurantist's historical viewpoint is essentially grounded on mythological sources. Perhaps this is how they manage to decelerate the process of history, without in the least slackening the tight noose of unwarranted dogmas around their neck. This is one of the several reasons why, in the recent decades, fundamentalist forces have reared their ugly head. For most of these forces, the march of history stopped the moment their respective religions came into existence. They are not in a position to understand the mutually exclusive, and often contradictory, characters of mythology and history.

Such obscurantist ideologies bring people like Karim Khan to the forefront. He appears to treat his 'White rulers' with the same respect that he reserves exclusively for the Prophet. Inspired by such sentiments, Khan relates the *quissa* of the Moses and Khijjar, as he sits among other people at Fazal Din's shop (95–8). For him, religion is merely a tool for legitimising the policies of the ruling classes. In a way, the same attitude led to the slow corrosion of the spirit of nationalism, and helped the cause of separatists and divisive forces. Once this ideology had gained ground among the common masses, they not only began to look upon the imperialist rule as their destiny, but also capitulated to its hegemonic control without any uproar or protest. For this reason, the policies of the obscurantists indirectly became instrumental in the spread of imperialism and they also helped undermine the collective strength of the common people. On learning about the outbreak of communal riots, Khan says, '*Quran Sharif* says that the crops shall stand in the fields so long as I Will it and if I don't, even the harvest in full bloom could burst into flames and be destroyed . . . Ultimately, it's His Will that must prevail' (101). People sitting all around him simply nod their heads approvingly. Just as the contradictions of Hinduism are reflected in the discrepancy between Vanprashthaji's mask and his real face, the conflicting claims of Islam are encoded in the architectural design of the mosque. The novel describes the mosque like this:

> Behind Nanbai's shops rose the imposing Jama Masjid. In the declining afternoon sun the mosque looked clean and white. Beggars sat on the steps lower down and further up labourers lay sprawling. Worshippers cautiously picked their way through the people sitting or lying on the steps (194–5).

In Chapter 15 of the novel, while depicting the growing differences, distrust and hatred between the Muslims and the Sikhs, Sahni says,

> Gurdwara was packed to the capacity, and the *sangat* was swaying in rhythm. It was simply a supernal hour. With their eyes shut, *Raagis* were singing hymns in a self-absorbed manner . . . '*Tum bin koi nahi Gosain*' . . . everyone in the *sangat* was sitting with hands folded, eyes shut and heads swaying in reverence . . . Across the time barriers of centuries, this clarion call for martyrdom was reverberating in the air. Three hundred

> years ago, this very song was heard much before the gauntlet was thrown across to the enemy. Soaked with the spirit of self-sacrifice, all of them were oblivious to everything else. In this supernal hour, it was as though their souls had been reunited with those of their ancestors, and they had regressed into the past, once again. It was time, again, to meet the challenge of the Turks. The Sikh race was under an assault, and once again, the threat had come from the Turks . . . (173).

The implications of this passage are clear enough. The religious point of view is inimical to history—nothing but an ironic reversal of history, regardless of how we choose to understand history. Rather than inspire the common people to put up a spirited fight against the inhospitable historical conditions, all it can offer them is phoney consolations. Without making any effort to understand the real conditions around them, the Sikhs choose to adopt the same medieval strategy of warfare that Guru Gobind Singhji had adopted while fighting the Mughals. Perhaps, this is why Sahni says that 'the fighters had their feet in the twentieth century, but their heads wrapped up in the medieval age'. Their defeat and consequent persecution and mayhem was almost inevitable. The main reason for their persecution and destruction was their inability to analyse the specific historical conditions determining the past and the present. It is this attitude that often puts the religionists on the path of self-destruction, which makes them self-propelled agents of mass destruction, too. Pointing out the glaring contradictions in the religious viewpoint, Sahni manages to expose their monologic and non-historical character.

Viewpoint of the Ruling Class or the Imperialist Forces

This viewpoint in *Tamas* is represented by Richard, the deputy commissioner. His character has two different facets, one public and the other private. Commenting upon these facets, Sahni says,

> Seeing him walk about these rooms, no one could say with certainty that he was the senior most officer in the district. Here, he was an authority on Indian history, a connoisseur of Indian art. Yes, when he sat upon the administrator's chair, he was nothing but a representative of British imperialism. And in that capacity, he would be overeager to implement those policies, which were hammered out in London. It was a special

> quality of his training, his temper that he never allowed one set of duties to cast a shadow over the other (41).

And the most prominent contradiction in Richard's character is that he is both a witness to the process of 'history-in-the-making' and also its creator—both a scholar of Indian history and its chronicler. At one point, Richard, who displays this remarkable quality of being able to 'keep his avocation apart from his vocation', concedes, 'When I'm out of the bungalow, I'm in just one of the towns of Hindustan. But when I return to the bungalow, I return to the entire Hindustan' (40). One of the rooms in his bungalow was adorned with 'all kinds of statues and samples of Indian folk art and the almirahs stuffed with books' (35). It is somewhat anomalous that Richard, who, on the face of it, is so well entrenched in Indian history, prefers to look at the common people, struggling hopelessly against historical forces, with the eyes of a voyeur. It is in this context that his following statement becomes extremely important: 'These people here know next to nothing. They know as much as we tell them. These people don't know their history, they simply live it out' (36).

It was nothing but this voyeurism that turned Richard into a silent spectator, especially when the town was in the grip of communal tension. Despite the fact that a delegation of respectable citizens of the town had met him, urging him to take necessary preventive measures, he neither imposed curfew nor asked the police or the army to patrol the town. Behind his voyeurism lies concealed a Euro-centric viewpoint that compels him to say, 'The subject of history is ours' (35). Such grandiloquent assertions provided the main stimulus for the spread of imperialism across the world and also helped in establishing the hegemonic control of the Whites over much of Asia and Africa.

The presence of Lisa, Richard's young wife, helps to call the imperialist designs into question, since she is the one who ultimately has to bear the burden of Richard's anarchic policies. Almost in the manner of the common people, Lisa, too, has to bear the brunt of Richard's administrative policy decisions. As he gets more and more preoccupied with his administrative duties, she finds herself succumbing to the pressures of the 'emptiness syndrome'. As destructive, anarchic forces make their presence felt with renewed vigour, Richard finds less and less time for her. Consequently, Lisa finds herself poised on the edge of an inner fragmentation, a nervous breakdown. The first indication of this is available in the section of the novel where, exasperated with her state of loneliness, she starts feeling 'suffocated inside the rooms', or 'seeing the statues carved in stones . . . she would go from one room to another, feeling utterly helpless' (86). We get the second indication of her troubled mind when, from very close quarters she sees a lizard 'lying face down upon her dressing table, writhing and struggling in acute pain' before finally 'breathing its last'(86–7). Unable to understand the reasons behind the hatred between the Muslims and the Hindus, Lisa fails to come to grips with the logic of communal tensions. Her confusion is not very different from that of an ordinary person in the street who prefers his ordinary, contingent pleasures of the world to a sustained engagement with any grand design or narrative.

Though the voice of the ordinary men and women fails to get across the walls of Richard's bungalow, Lisa's presence inside those very walls continues to launch a systematic assault on the ideology of the ruling class and those of the imperialist forces. In the early parts of the novel, when he tells her about the communal tension building up in the city, Lisa asks, 'So, what do you propose to do about it?', and when he says, 'Then I'll administer, what else?', she simply dismisses it lightly. She is unable to comprehend why despite being an able administrator and a historian, Richard chooses to ignore the raging flames of communal passions. He simply says, 'I'll tell them, religious matters are your personal affairs. You must sort them out on your own.' Through Lisa's character, Sahni has launched a tangential attack on the imperialist forces. Once the riots break out, she asks Richard, 'How could it happen with you around?' (114) She is completely oblivious of the politics of administrative manipulations and communal subversion. She knows fairly well that she has to choose between her husband and the ordinary people, yet she feels that 'the real significance does not lie so much in human values as it does in the values of the ruling class' (115). There could not have been a more strident, more sarcastic denunciation of the ruling class's ideology. Not only does this particular statement emblematise Lisa as a spokesperson of the common people, but it also brings to the surface, albeit obliquely, the internal contradictions within the ideologies of the ruling elite and the ruled masses.

Tamas serves to externalise the latent contradictions within each viewpoint and also the contradictions between and across different viewpoints. One is prompted to ask a couple of questions at this juncture: Why did Sahni project these multiple viewpoints in the manner that he did? Why did he have to make it into the raison d'être of his novel? It is apparent that Sahni prefers not to cast a historian's conventional look into history. He prefers a novelist's creative and innovative gaze. His primary interest is not in historical verisimilitude or the representation of a monumental view of history. Rather, it is the worm's-eye view of history—the one that looks at the processes of history from below and epitomises the painful tragedy of its victims, the common people—that appears to fascinate and engage him, and this he portrays with all the artistic sensitivity and eloquence at his command. In this sense, *Tamas* is a fine example of how the ideological conflicts can be given non-partisan, objective representations within the fictional space. In this regard, one is tempted to mention Bertolt Brecht's well-known modern classic *Mother Courage and Her Children*. This play, too, was conceived and written against the backdrop of a historical conflict, popularly known as the Thirty Years' War, which raged in most parts of Europe from 1618 to 1648. By projecting the internal contradictions of this sordid event in purely human terms, Brecht managed to create a powerful play which sets up a process of inter-animation between the past and the present. Commenting on the nature and function of history, in his book *What is History* (1961), E. H. Carr says that history is merely a tool of activating a dialogue between the past and the present. By thus initiating a dialogue, Brecht has, in his play, managed to expose the latent and manifest contradictions and dichotomies of history. And it was made possible mainly because of his efforts to mediate history, not through 'linearity' or 'continuity', but through 'temporal discontinuities'.

It may not be possible here to conclude whether or not Sahni was in any way influenced by Brecht's creative symbiosis of history and fiction. But one can safely say that much in the manner of Brecht, Sahni, too, has made an effort to set up a dialogue between the past and the present. *Tamas* is a living testimony to all such successful efforts in the realm of fiction. In a way, Brecht has only set up dialectical opposition between the mutually conflicting viewpoints, while Sahni goes a step further by presenting multiple viewpoints. If on the one hand, it gives a certain stolidity and complexity to his narrative, on the other, it gives his reader an opportunity to re-assess or re-evaluate the complex historical processes with a degree of autonomy. Therefore, it would not be wrong to say that *Tamas* is, to borrow the expression of Roland Barthes, a *writerly* and not a *readerly* text. Lacking in the pretensions of a grand narrative, it is, at best, a local narrative, which while demonstrating its unswerving allegiance and commitment to basic human values that common people live by, gives readers the autonomy to sympathise with whichever viewpoint they may choose. It is quite another matter that our choices could, through an ultimate ironic reversal, become the barometer of our own responses, our commitments, our ideologies, and even our psychological dispositions. And this undoubtedly, is a fine justification, if one is needed, for fashioning or structuring an emacipatory narrative.

Notes and References

1. For a discussion on this theme, see Hayden White, *Metahistory: The Historical Imagination in Nineteenth-century Europe* (Baltimore, Md: John Hopkins University Press, 1973); Fernand Braudel, *On History*, trans. Sarah Matthew (Chicago III: University of Chicago Press, 1980); Dominick LaCapra, *History and Criticism* (Ithaca, NY: Cornell University Press, 1985); Keith Jenkins, ed., *Postmodern History Reader* (London: Routledge, 1997); Michael Bentley, *Modern Historiography: An Introduction* (London: Routledge, 1999).

2. Francis Fukuyama, *The End of History and the Last Man* (London: Hamish Hamilton, 1992), xiv.

3. Introduction to *Tara*, as quoted in Gopinath Tiwari, *Itihasik Upanyas Aur Upanyaskaar* (Agra, 1960), 82.

4. *Itihasik Upanyas Aur Upanyaskaar*, 82.
5. Preface to *Hameer*, as quoted in *Itihasik Upanyas Aur Upanyaskaar*, 96.
6. *Itihasik Upanyas Aur Upanyaskaar*, 95.
7. *Itihasik Upanyas Aur Upanyaskaar*, 156.
8. *Itihasik Upanyas Aur Upanyaskaar*, 168.
9. Bhisham Sahni, *Tamas* (New Delhi: Hind Pocket Books Prakashan, 1973), 231. All subsequent textual references are also from this edition. However, the translations of the extracts are mine.

CHAPTER TWELVE

Mahasweta Devi's *Hajar Churashir Ma*: A Narrative of Healing

Before we begin the discussion of Mahasweta Devi's (b. 1926) *Hajar Churashir Ma* (Mother of 1084, 1974), it would be useful to take a look at the different narrative possibilities that are either available to, or are exercised by, women writers for 'narrativising' their stories. Let us take up a hypothesis that is central to our analysis, and look at, without any intention of essentialising, four different possibilities with regard to women and the narrativisation of their stories.

The first possibility is the 'narrative of oppression or captivity'. These conditions of oppression or captivity are created by a male or a female authority, imposing restrictions on women and projecting them as tradition-bound creatures—not as individuals—defined stereotypically and symptomatically in terms of social, historical and cultural forces. The second one is the 'narrative of self-liberation', which projects the woman as a social rebel who raises a banner of revolt against the tyranny of social laws, conventions and standards, defining her distinctive, and sometimes existential, value system in the process. Third one is the 'narrative of emancipation', within which the woman becomes an instrument of change. She works not just towards her own liberation but that of her race, religion, community or sisterhood. Fourth is the 'narrative of healing'—strategically positioned half way between the 'narrative of oppression' and the 'narrative of self-liberation'—which helps a 'woman' ultimately become a 'person' or an 'individual'.

Narratives of healing constitute an important stage in the evolution of women's consciousness, and they presuppose that much before a woman is able to raise the banner of revolt, she needs to recover from several inflictions of the narrative of oppression. For this reason, the narrative of healing is an intermediate form which looks back to the narrative of oppression and forward to the narrative of liberation. Though it combines the elements of both, it is unable to acquire the character or function of either. Despite that, it often transcends the limitations of both.

Both as a writer and as a social activist, Mahasweta Devi has never fully positioned herself within the domain of her *bhadralok*, bourgeoisie background or within the space of tribals, among whom and for whom she does most of her work. Situating herself in the 'third space', she has always tried to mediate the differences and negotiate the troubling questions arising from the clashes and conflicts between the familiar, civilized world of the *bhadraloks* and the less known, subliminal world of the tribals. In a conversation with Gayatri Chakravorty Spivak, she has stated, 'The tribals and the mainstream have always been parallel. There has never been a meeting point. The mainstream simply doesn't understand the parallel.'[1] It is no wonder that her interventions as a writer, journalist or an activist have been somewhat in the nature of an interlocutor who, gifted with social conscience and commitment, is forever seeking to create newer meeting points, forever building bridges across the parallel lines. This explains, to a large extent, why the intermediate form of the narrative of healing has almost become the stock-in-trade of Mahasweta Devi, who heals as she narrativises and narrativises as she constructs the discourse of healing.

Hajar Churashir Ma is essentially a narrative of healing, positioned strategically both within the realm of Mahasweta Devi's corpus of work—in her literary oeuvre consisting of forty-one novels, fifteen short story collections, some plays, five collections of children's short stories and two historical biographies—and that of Indian fiction, not necessarily of the Indian English variety. Originally written as a short story for the periodical *Prasad* in 1972 and adapted for the stage by the writer herself in 1973, it grew into a full-scale novel a year later, in 1974. Govid Nihalani made it into a film in 1998. Interestingly, in its journey of rapid transformation from a play into an extended narrative, *Hajar Churashir Ma* has sought to reverse the traditional mode of adaptation, in which usually a play originates or grows out of a familiar or popular story, legend or myth. The revolutionary potential of this narrative is, therefore, inscribed in the very process of its creation. Not without reason has

Mahasweta Devi described it as a narrative about 'the awakening of an apolitical mother'.

The narrative of *Hajar Churashir Ma* focuses on Sujata—a middle-aged woman belonging to a *bhadralok*, bourgeoisie Calcutta (Kolkata) family—and is strikingly rich in its layered intensity and complexity. Born into a conservative, affluent family, Sujata is allowed to do her BA so that it helps her marriage prospects. She is ultimately married off to Divyanath Chatterjee, a chartered accountant, despite the fact that his financial situation is far from encouraging. In the thirty-four years of her married life, Sujata gives birth to four children—two sons (Jyoti and Brati) and two daughters (Nipa and Tuli). When the novel opens, two of her children are already married—Jyoti to Bina and Nipa to Amrit. In the eyes of the world, all of them are leading perfectly happy and settled lives, but as Sujata goes on to discover later, this happiness is only skin-deep. Significantly, Sujata makes this and several other such discoveries only after the sudden and mysterious death of Brati, her younger son, with whom she had always shared a very special relationship. For instance, she discovers that during the thirty-four years of her married life, she has been living a lie, as her husband, being an incorrigible philanderer, has been cheating on her with his mother's and worse still, his children's tacit approval.

If Divyanath had found Sujata a petty bank job when Brati was barely three years old, it was not out of any consideration for her economic independence, but essentially to help the family tide over a temporary financial mess. As soon as the tide turns, he wants her to give up the job, something that Sujata simply refuses to do. She also discovers that her children, too, are leading lives very similar to her own. If there is someone who has dared to be different, it is Brati. Sullenly rebellious right from his childhood, Brati has made no secret of his disregard and even contempt for familial codes and value systems.

Turning his back on this decadent and defunct code, Brati decides to join the Naxalite movement sweeping through the state of West Bengal in late 1960s and early 1970s. Unaware of his secret mission, Sujata is not even able to dissuade her son from taking the plunge. During his period of struggle, he comes into contact with a young girl, Nandini, who is also a member of the underground movement and with her he shares his vision of a new world order. On being betrayed by one of his comrades, who is bought off by the state, Brati and three of his close associates—Somu, Parth and Laltu—are brutally murdered by the goons hired by police. Later, the police call up his father, asking him to come and identify the dead body of his son, who has in the meantime been divested of his identity as an 'individual', and given another dehumanised identity as 'corpse number 1084'. Not only does the father refuse to go, but he also forbids other family members from doing so. Outraged at the manner in which his associates, his immediate family and the state have abandoned the dead Brati, his mother, Sujata, decides to go, throwing all pretensions to false social respectability and the fear of public censure to winds.

In a way, *Hajar Churashir Ma* is the story of Sujata's multiple oppressions within a stifling, familial, patriarchal and feudal order. However, it can also be read as a story of how Sujata moves out of her cocoon of social respectability and civilized façade, only to discover the little-known, primitive, underground world of Naxalites or that of her son, about whom she knew very little while he was alive. Going beyond, it is also the story of how an 'apolitical mother', ultimately pushed over the threshold, is compelled to recognise the basic human need to formulate or re-formulate her moral/political/ideological position in a crass, narcissistic and utterly commercial world of *bhadraloks* such as the Chatterjees. If it is any indication of what Mahasweta Devi actually wanted to communicate, her position is unambiguously clear. It is only in the process of formulating or defining one's moral/political/ideological position that an individual could possibly hope to heal several inflictions of oppression, or prepare herself/himself to fight the mechanics of oppression at personal or collective level, thus paving the way for self-liberation.

It is important to note that this particular work stands apart from the rest of Mahasweta Devi's oeuvre, in more ways than one. Unlike some of her earlier short narratives such as 'Standayini', 'Draupadi' and 'Gohumni', which are focalised around tribal women, this particular novella is centred on an upper middle-class, bourgeoisie, 'apolitical' woman. Moreover, unlike so many of her stories, which by virtue of their location in the oral/folk tradition often betray the stark simplicity of folk narratives, *Hajar Churashir Ma* possesses a rare sophistication in its handling of temporal/spatial designs as well as in the complex structuring of events and situations. Conceived on the lines of Virginia Woolf's *Mrs Dalloway* (1925), the entire action of *Hajar Churashir Ma* is confined to a single day. And if the comparison is extended a little further, the narrative also makes use of the stream of consciousness technique the way Woolf often does. The only difference is that Mahasweta Devi has schematically divided the entire span of twenty-four hours into four timeframes—dawn, afternoon, evening and night—one succeeding the other. Superficially, it may even be seen as an oppressive, linear narrative that has been so designed as to project the multiple oppressions Sujata is made to suffer in the Chatterjee household. But a closer examination shows how the linearity is constantly ruptured and disrupted through a series of memory snapshots and flashbacks which not only help Sujata in reclaiming her personal memory, but also provide her the much-needed psychic healing. By thus consciously disturbing the chronological, sequential and linear pattern of the narrative, Mahasweta Devi is clearly pointing out that the narrative of *Hajar Churashir Ma* is anything but a narrative of oppression. As Sujata ultimately collapses into a heap, much before she can walk out on her husband (unlike Nora in *A Doll's House*), hers is not a narrative of self-liberation either.

Each of the four chapters in the narrative marks a new stage in the evolution of Sujata's consciousness, as it enables her to reorder her fragmented and chaotic life in search of a cohesive identity. Each time she visits either her own past or that of Brati, Somu's mother or Nandini, her long-suppressed personal loss and grief is slowly released into the ever-widening, eddying spirals of a collective framework of betrayal, guilt and suffering. Now, whether it is a question of becoming acutely conscious of other people's suffering or that of her own situation, or simply gaining a more enlightened understanding of the circumstances that compelled Brati to make the kind of choices he did make—all these do facilitate Sujata's transformation. From a weak-willed, hopelessly dependent and a non-assertive moral coward, Sujata is transformed into a morally assertive, politically enlightened and socially defiant individual.

The novel begins on the dawn of 17 January, the day Sujata's youngest daughter Tuli is to be engaged to Toni Kapadia, an exporter based in Sweden. As it was her son Brati's birthday, and as he had died barely two years ago on the night of 16 January, Sujata cannot help but walk down the memory lane. As a new beginning threatens to collapse into the memory of a tragic end, Sujata's mind races back to the day Brati had come into her world. She remembers how she had packed her bag, hired a taxi and rushed to the hospital on her own, with no assistance from her mother-in-law or husband. Indifference of her husband, hostility of her mother-in-law and her own isolation in the Chatterjee household hit her in a single momentary flash. With epiphanic clarity, it dawns on her that her husband only lusted after her, never loved her. He was willing to impregnate her with child after child, but was never around to own up the responsibility or to care for her. Soon after marriage, he had started a secret liaison with a typist in his office, for whom he had later rented out an apartment. As a result, all her children were born out of a combination of lust, hatred and self-disgust. But Brati's case was somewhat different.

When she learnt that Brati's life was in danger, her heart 'melted with maternal affection', thus forging a special bond with him while he was still in her womb. He was a fear-stricken child who clung to his mother for security and comfort and was often dubbed by his father as 'Mama's boy'. She clearly remembers how twenty years later, the news of Brati's death had thrown 'the settled life of Chatterjees into a state of turmoil and confusion'. Disowned by his family, Brati had died in a state of disgrace. The family even refused to cremate him, locked up all his memories into an attic room, and did not even allow Sujata the luxury of articulating her grief. Now, Sujata realises that her son was no criminal, as his only crime was that he refused to 'accept the code of a decadent society'. She also realises that 'death is the only punishment for those who lose faith in the system' (27).[2] In the first chapter, significantly titled 'Dawn', Sujata primarily returns to her interior, private world of personal suffering, torture, betrayal and loneliness. Negotiating the inner space/time in relation to her immediate familial situation, she becomes aware of how she and Brati were not just fellow sufferers but also soul mates.

In the second chapter, 'Afternoon', Sujata's visit to the bank to take out jewellery from the locker is only a pretext for her intended visit to the house of Somu's mother. A close associate of Brati, Somu had been killed in the same encounter. More significantly, before his sudden, mysterious disappearance, and later death, Brati had spent his life's last night in Somu's house. While Sujata goes to Somu's mother with the specific aim of retrieving the memories of Brati's last few hours, the journey turns out to be her entry and initiation into another world altogether, which is simply beyond her comprehension. It is a world of primitive squalor, filth, poverty, degradation and subhuman existences that only hovers tentatively on the margins of the *bhadralok* consciousness. Breaking the glass ceiling of her cloistered, though unprotected, existence in a false, hypocritical world of *bhadraloks*, Sujata enters into this little-known world of slum dwellers. The sight of Somu's ageing mother, her disgruntled daughter and that of their ramshackle tenement with a straw roof is enough to complete the rituals of initiation. While talking to her, she suddenly discovers that Somu's mother remembers Brati's 'spontaneous, tingling laughter', something that she, as his biological mother, had never known. It was only in the company of his associates that Brati recovered his primeval innocence and spontaneity. He always maintained a studied façade in the presence of his family. Across the class and caste divides, a strange bond develops between the two suffering mothers, which enables Sujata to see the chaotic nature of her personal loss, suffering and grief within a much wider framework of social and historical injustice and/or denial. Recovering from her over-romanticised and narcissistic notions of self-pity and grief, Sujata suffers the assault of reality and internalises the sufferings of those who are less privileged than her, and thus, she heals herself—at least partly—through gestures of empathy and compassion.

This process of healing is not only about recovering memories—both personal and collective—but is equally about becoming a moral/political being. For Mahasweta Devi, political naiveté is as much a sin and a social crime as political indifference or an immoral political choice. For this reason, Sujata's healing process runs a complete circle only in the third chapter, titled 'Evening', when she visits Nandini, who apart from being Brati's comrade-in-arms was also his beloved. It is Nandini who reconstructs for Sujata the events leading up to Brati's murder. In the process, she also initiates Sujata into the little-known world of underground movements, explaining to her the logic of an organised rebellion, giving her a first-hand account of state repression and its multiple failures. It is through Nandini that Sujata is finally able to understand the reasons for Brati's political convictions and his rejection of the bourgeoisie code. All this leaves her so completely bewildered that she openly admits to Nandini, 'I didn't really know Brati' (87). Mahasweta Devi has captured the impact of Sujata's meeting with Nandini in very poetic terms. Commenting upon it, she says:

> With the flow of time, the grief and pain settle into layers of sedimentation. Then one day, penetrating these layers, new buds sprout forth, stretching out their little fingers. These fingers ache to touch the sky. The buds of hope, sorrow, joy and bliss—the buds with little aching fingers! (81)

This healing is possible only because the dynamics of grief, loss and pain is finally understood and accepted by Sujata, and, in doing so, she manages to break the vicious cycle, and even transcends it.

Once the healing is over, it remains to be demonstrated how far Sujata can go now in re-adjusting her priorities and reordering her life. In the last section of the novel, titled 'Night', therefore, we meet a transformed Sujata, one who is more self-assured, morally confident and politically sensitive. She decides to leave the house in which Brati never felt at home, where he was not valued while he was alive, where his memory is not respected after his death. Having found a soulmate in Brati, she turns her back on Divyanath and his decadent value system. Bound by a sense of moral responsibility, Sujata does go through all the rituals and ceremonies connected with Tuli's engagement, but during the party, she maintains a stiff, studied silence. Her insistence on wearing a plain, white saree for the party is also a significant gesture. Though she had earlier promised all her jewellery to Tuli, now she changes her mind, refusing to part with what her father had given her, passing on to Tuli only those that Divyanath had gifted her. Had Sujata been somewhat younger like Nora, she would have possibly made a dramatic gesture of shutting the door in her husband's face. But being physically weak and fragile—for a few years, she has been living with a rotten appendix inside her—and traumatised by her younger son's death and subsequent repression of her grief, Sujata simply gives up on life. When she screams and collapses into a heap, her husband is quick to speculate that her 'appendix has burst'. One may read this statement as symbolic. She certainly succumbs to the slow process of inner/outer rot and decay. Finally, as she herself says, 'Now that Brati is dead, I, too, wouldn't like to go on living.' She recovers her humanity, but loses her will to live and survive. Had she lived, hers would have been a narrative of self-liberation or even that of emancipation.

However, as it stands, *Hajar Churashir Ma* ends up essentially as an intermediate form—as a narrative of healing. In this bi-focal narrative, time constantly swings back and forth, and so does the pendulum of two interconnected, intertwined lives—that of Sujata and her son Brati. Interestingly, it is death that unites them both, irrevocably asserting the authenticity of their lives. Death, as the existentialists often believe, is the ultimate form of transcendence. Not only does it put us beyond the pale of class or caste conflict, but also dissolves the compulsions of politics or history into an endless spiral of nothingness. In this realisation lies our survival, or perhaps our redemption too.

Notes and References

1. 'The Author in Conversation' in Gayatri Chakravorty Spivak, ed., *Imaginary Maps: Three* Stories *by Mahasweta Devi* (New York: Routledge, 1994), ix–xxii.

2. Mahasweta Devi, *Hazaar Chaurasi Ki Maa*, trans. Mahadevi Verma (New Delhi: Radhakrishna Prakashan, 2008). All the English translations used in the text are mine.

SECTION FOUR

Power, Hegemony and Mass Media: Case Studies in Popular Consciousness

CHAPTER THIRTEEN

Of Language, Consciousness and Mass Media

This essay attempts to investigate the interrelationships among the three constituents of discourse—language, consciousness and mass media—and then locate this entire question within the overarching framework of contemporary Indian reality. As a prelude to this investigation, we will also attempt to arrive at a definitive, critical position with respect to the paradigmatic relationship between language and consciousness. Apparently, this, in turn, presupposes that the archaeology of the philosophic tradition be excavated in order to historicise this whole question. For this reason, the first section of this essay shall seek to hypothesise a philosophical position over this fundamental question. The second section will attempt to historicise this relationship by presenting a worm's-eye view of various philosophical positions available to us. In the third section, the relationship between language and mass media will be considered with special reference to some of the developments in India in recent times. And finally, an attempt will be made to locate the ideological grids of both English and vernacular newspapers in an attempt to establish how, as the purveyors of mass culture, newspapers often indulge in linguistic distortions, resulting in grotesque portrayals of reality. Following this logic, an attempt will be made to unmask the contradictions of mass culture and its dangerous ideological implications for both language and consciousness.

1

Philosophers down the ages have been intrigued by the epistemological question of how to negotiate the relationship between 'consciousness' and 'language'. Beyond a doubt, philosophers have repeatedly engaged with this question, but somehow the results of their investigations have been less than satisfactory. There are several reasons for this. One, both consciousness and language are often mediated as absolutist, abstractified categories, constituting two distinct, well-differentiated discourses with only peripheral contact and/or intersection. Two, this tends to introduce a sense of essentialism into our understanding of these two categories, which comes in by way of a binarism, and even a dualism, that sets off one category against the other as an oppositional discourse. So long as the debate remains mired in this kind of binarism, it is almost impossible to avoid the pitfalls of the 'either–or' reasoning. What is needed here is not a structural but a relational understanding of these two categories, in which each serves to delimit, define, demarcate and constitute the other. From this standpoint, the real question is not whether it is language that precedes consciousness or vice versa, but rather how and under what conditions the intersection or interpenetration of both language and consciousness becomes possible. Three, it leads the entire discussion into the familiar trope of Western epistemology that aims at constituting or reconstituting hierarchical structures out of these two categories, often making it difficult, if not impossible, for us to perceive them in purely relational terms. (Hierarchy, one may argue, does not really help constitute a relationship. It simply deconstructs it.) Four, it pushes us deeper into that classic impasse which raises the question whether it is consciousness that is a priori to language or it is language that can be said to delimit the nature and function of consciousness. This question of 'a priori-ness' further brings us up against the all too familiar epistemological impasse, sealing off the limits of discourse, and blocking off all possibilities of arriving at definitive positions.

My purpose in enumerating these epistemological problems in relation to both consciousness and language—and that too, right at the beginning of this essay—is simply to underscore the problematic of this complex issue we are trying to address, examine and perhaps interrogate in different situations. Now, we will take a brief look at Western philosophy in an effort to identify the shifting paradigms of this problematic relationship. However, this is not meant to initiate an extended debate on each of these paradigms, but merely to sketch out their outlines or contours.

We can start off our overview of Western philosophy by looking at the rationalist construction of consciousness, as has been put forward by Rene Descartes (1596–1650). Descartes believed that nothing could really exist outside the mind or consciousness and went so far as to say that '*Cogito ergo sum*'—'I think, therefore, I'm.'[1] Not only did he valorise consciousness, but he assigned to it an all-enveloping, all-subsuming function. In his scheme of things, language is no more than a necessary adjunct to, or an attribute of, consciousness, and it has no extensionality of its own and exists only to facilitate its multiple functions.

For John Locke (1632–1704), the English empiricist, more than the mind and/or consciousness, it was the idea of self-consciousness that was extremely important. His concept of mind, which he described as a kind of *tabula rasa*, emphasised not only its transparency but also its accessibility to the 'thinking subject'.[2] It is a well-known fact that Locke's model did not make any allowances for 'unconscious thinking'—which could be said to carry the imprint of language as well as culture—which had to be schematised and hypothesised by Sigmund Freud (1856–1939) in his writings, some three centuries later. Despite the essential ontological and epistemological differences between the two ideological perspectives, the empiricist model of Locke appears to be as much a product of Euro-centric binarism as Descarte's model is.

Though Edmund Husserl (1859–1938) is often recognised as one of the main proponents of modern phenomenology (another name for the science of consciousness), it was Georg Hegel's (1770–1831) *Phenomenology of Mind* that had kick-started the investigations in this field as early as in 1807.[3] Conceiving reality as a living, evolving and dynamic process, Hegel sought to identify logic with metaphysics or ontology, thus emphasising both the differentiated as well as unified nature of both thought and being, subject and object. In a manner of speaking, it was Hegel's 'phenomenological model' that offered a real possibility which had long eluded Western thought of overriding the ever-present dualism and seeking a relational, synthesised understanding of language, consciousness and reality. However, what really stood in the way of its realisation was Hegel's own ontological position that posited that 'essence is the appearance' or 'God *is* the universe'. By thus absolutising the transcendental reality, Hegel created another binarism in terms of spiritual and material realities, without actually providing the apparatus for working out their mutual symbiosis or dialectics. And that possibility had to wait until Karl Marx (1818–83) appeared on the scene with his 'materialist model of consciousness'. We will sketch out this particular model in a detailed fashion and follow it up, to comprehend the precise nature of connectivity among all the three categories under discussion here—language, consciousness and social reality.

The materialist view perceives consciousness as the 'sum total of mental processes that participate in man's understanding of the objective world and of his personal being'.[4] This view obviously postulates that it is our attitude to the world—reflected in our understanding and knowledge of objects—that constitutes our consciousness. Moreover, this model offers a real possibility of connecting language and consciousness, as, apart from being historically constituted, both are perceived as instruments of collective social and psychological transformation.

We need not take this materialist understanding of consciousness as the last word on the subject, but we find its functionalism extremely serviceable and efficacious in our analysis. Somewhere, when we do reflect upon this relationship of language with consciousness, we have an unstated expectation that the transformative power of each in relation to the other should not only be recognised but tapped as well. The materialist model does not just posit language as an extension or an attribute of consciousness but as a separate sub-system that has the potential to transform consciousness as much as it can effectively be transformed by consciousness in turn.[5] In this schematic conceptualisation, language, consciousness and social reality truly become relational categories—intersecting, interpenetrating, defining, delimiting and demarcating the boundaries of one another. Language becomes an intermediate category, mediating between consciousness on the one hand and social reality on the other. Once this intermediate quality of language is realised, it is possible for us to start exploring the middle ground, which makes a reasonable plea against the self-limiting 'either–or', and for a more inclusive and encompassing 'both–and' logic?

Though Husserl's model has not quite figured in this discussion, it might be interesting to point out that his reflections on phenomenology appeared around the time Germany was passing through an unprecedented internal crisis.[6] The growing influence of fascism upon the popular mind had split the German society almost vertically. Though it might be somewhat difficult to look upon Husserl's phenomenology as a potent weapon of resistance or a strategy of overturning the existing patterns of thought, it could certainly be perceived as a refuge for those tormented in their consciousness or a mainstay of the bruised intellects. Perhaps reflections on language and consciousness become absolutely necessary each time the hydra-headed monster called fascism slithers in imperceptibly, threatening to poison our lives and the very air we breathe. Does anybody need argue here that we, in India, are living through such dreadful times, when our consciousness is as much under an assault as are our powers of thought, expression or language?

2

By its very nature, mass media tends to make egregious concessions to the prejudices, biases, bigotry and stereotypical ideas of the masses. To put it another way, it plays a conformist and not a critical function in shaping or determining the consciousness of the people it purports or claims to serve. If the mass media were to assume the critical function and seek to interrogate, attack or overturn the established opinions of the people, it would perhaps cease to be a tool of mass media and instead become a purveyor of selective, critical information. This, in turn, would impose severe limitations upon the media, especially in terms of its wider acceptability among the people. For any mass media tool to circumscribe itself in terms of its wider acceptability would be nothing short of hara-kiri. Therefore, no mass media tool can ever afford to run against the grain of popular opinions and prejudices, most of which need to be corrected or critiqued.

It is no coincidence that in the post-liberalisation period, newspapers in India suddenly went through a radical shift, not necessarily in terms of redefining their role or function but in developing their brand image. If we look at the way in which several leading English newspapers in India have undergone a radical face-lift, it will become apparent how large scale concessions are being made to the overruling, overarching logic of the market forces. For some strange reason, it was believed that this was the only way the newspapers could have possibly survived in our consumerist culture with its ever-shifting gaze and fragmentary, spliced-up reality reducible into a million splintered micro images. It was this basic Darwinian impulse for survival in the market that had brought newspapers in line with other disposable consumer products such as tooth pastes, hamburgers and soft drinks. Among other things, this has put a big question mark over the credibility of these newspapers and the news being purveyed by them. Under such circumstances, they are almost compelled to give a sense of legitimacy to the uncritical, conformist and standardised language used for purveying or communicating information.

Let us look at an example of what we have discussed. Pick up any newspaper or magazine and browse through an article on fundamentalism, terrorism or communal riots. You would hardly ever come across an article or an analysis in which an attempt has been made either to go into the history of fundamentalism/terrorism/communal riots or to define the terms of reference. More often than not, the conceptual framework of ideas is left undefined in the hope that such terms are so deeply embedded in popular consciousness that they need no further investigation or critique. I cannot recall having read even a single article in which a systematic attempt was made to differentiate between terms such as *Hinduism* and *Hindutava*, a very important distinction that ought to be made, as each constitutes a different discourse.

Our English newspapers do not in the least suffer from the burden of 'anxiety of influence'[7] and often tend to view Indian reality in exactly the same way in which either *The Guardian* or *The New York Times* would view it. Not many self-conscious attempts are made to see how the burden of the language, English, could also, in certain cases, become the burden of the ideology and, therefore, of representation. It is no wonder that often enough, our newspapers begin to perceive our domestic situations and events through the eyes of foreign correspondents. This writer remembers the manner in which some of the foreign newspapers had reported the appointment of Sister Nirmala as the head of the Sisters of Charity Mission, on the demise of Mother Teresa. It was shocking to see how the reports had tried, very painstakingly, to privilege and foreground the fact that Sister Nirmala was essentially a Hindu, who had later converted to Christianity and was now being installed as the head of a Christian mission. How many of us would actually be bothered with the religious identity of Sister Nirmala? This is not to suggest that this kind of divisive consciousness about religious identities is the creation of the mass media. But it shows that the orientalist project of (mis)representation that started during the colonial rule has still not ended in Western academia and institutions.[8] And that they continue to create stereotypical structures of knowledge and consciousness about us, that too, in a language whose dominance over our own languages is unquestionable.

Through their refusal to critique orientalist representations and quite oblivious of its ideological implications, our newsmen, especially in the English media, often end up showing complicity with this project. This is how the Euro-centric view of India—as a primitive, undeveloped society, still struggling with its archival combination of violence, bigotry and religious identity—gains both popularity and legitimacy, eclipsing and obscuring in the process, its multifarious economic successes and development activities.

If the English language media has failed to liberate itself from the hegemonic influence of the ideology of the language in which it operates, the 'vernacular' media has largely been hegemonised by their English language counterparts. We very often see regional newspapers advertising themselves, emphasising that they offer everything that a good English newspaper can, plus other features in the regional language. It is as if apologetic for being regional newspapers, they are anxious to assume a national identity, not by competing with the best of regional dailies, but by comparing themselves with the best of English dailies available in the market. Is it not, once again, a case of internalising the ideological burden and thus indulging in self-inferiorisation?

One might turn around and say that it is not for the mass media to interrogate and critique the inferiorisation of both language and representation. Rather, its function is to lend legitimacy to it. Why cannot the mass media, going by popular sentiments and choices, proclaim a work by Shakespeare as well as a new brand of cigarettes as a 'classic'? Such attitudes are built into the very nature of mass media and all other organs of mass culture. Not only do they trivialise the serious but also vulgarise it, while at the same time, sanctifying something that deserves only a little or perhaps no notice or attention. This is how mass culture ends up giving a covert sense of legitimacy to what Shestakov, a Russian literary critic, very appropriately, chooses to describe as the 'aesthetics of the trivial'.[9]

The classic dualism of 'quality' versus 'quantity' is another anachronism that mass culture brings into play and legitimises. The strongest impulse of a mass culture is to make more and more goods and products and make them available for the consumption of more and more people. As mass culture is a quantity-oriented system—quantifying goods, products and people with the same kind of eagerness and urgency—it often becomes a pretext for the commodification of people and humanisation of lifeless objects such as computers, television sets and other appurtenances of consumerist *haute coutre*. As a result of this kind of quantification, human beings are often denied a sense of reality and subjectivity, and thus, they fall easy preys to the multiple processes of objectification.

In such a situation, gender often does not matter as both men and women are readily subjected to the processes of objectification. And when attempts at objectification become overbearing or overwhelming, the threatened subjectivity often reorders its strategies of survival by escaping into the self-structured worlds of fantasy, mythology, narcotic pleasures or narcissistic contemplations of the self. This aspect of mass culture has been very convincingly analysed by American writer Christopher Lasch in his book *The Culture of Narcissism*. Analysing all the aspects of contemporary culture—politics, art, literature, sports, advertising and education—he comes to the conclusion that each of them is characterised by the phenomenon of narcissism. All of this, in his view, is linked to the appearance of a new kind of individual for whom the world is nothing but a mirror in which he is reflected: 'Narcissism remains at its most precise, a metaphor, and nothing more, that describes a state of mind in which the world appears as a mirror of the self.'[10] This kind of 'narcissistic self', living as it does in a perpetual state of flight from reality, is certainly exposed to a greater danger than anyone else, to the multiple processes of self-mutilation, self-destruction and gradual dissolution of being. Although Lasch has essentially made the American mass culture of the 1960s the target of his attack, his analysis assumes an alarming significance for our understanding of contemporary Indian society.

One may argue that in the twenty-first century, we in India are definitely in the vice-like grip of the psychological and cultural crisis that had assailed the United States and its people in the 1960s. If we do go along with this proposition, mass media has only one consideration and one function in our consumerist culture—its growing concern to stay in the market, its losing battle for survival, and its narcissistic preoccupation with its own fantasies and mythologies. As its propensity to perceive the world in terms of its own struggles and survival has increased manifold, mass media's potential to become a mirror to the society has proportionately diminished and decreased. Only a media that is free from the clutches of the market forces can possibly serve the cause of democracy—not the one whose ideology is already underwritten by the multiple grids of various economic, social and political forces. A media that is obsessed with its own angularities and distortions cannot afford to take upon itself the onerous task of reflecting, mediating or analysing the angularities or distortions of the society it operates within.

All big, small and marginal newspapers in India—with a few exceptions, of course—owe their existence to corporate houses, business barons or political parties. For their patrons, motives of profit maximisation or power brokering clearly supercede all altruistic considerations of objectivity and neutrality. Whereas, such laudable aims do not even appear on the agenda of those ideologically inclined newspapers that unabashedly serve as the organs of various political parties.

Where does it all lead us, ultimately? As we stand at this crucial juncture of history, and look at this mishmash of language, consciousness and mass media, all thoughts of their individual or collective redemptive powers seem to desert us. An independent, credible and strong media, no doubt, is the need of the hour and our discussion has thrown up several pointers in that direction.

Notes and References

1. It was in his famous work *Discourse on the Method* (1637) that Rene Descartes had initially developed this notion of the non-corporeal, non-material nature of the 'thinking self'. It is another matter that the term 'consciousness' was never used in his writings directly or explicitly, but only implicitly and indirectly. According to him, 'thought' was not restricted to cognitive activities but included everything we often attribute to consciousness. This idea, which otherwise constitutes the core of Cartesian system, became the foundation of his epistemology, as it postulated a neat division between mind and body, thereby giving rise to the problem of mind–body dualism. However, the notion of '*Cogito ergo sum*' was propounded by Descartes in his *Meditations* (1641), wherein he clearly emphasised the primacy of consciousness. His views on language did not emerge until he wrote *Principles of Philosophy* (1644), wherein he described language as the non-material nature of the 'thinking self'. Since my understanding of these ideas is derived largely from my readings of various works of Descartes, no specific reference is being made here.
2. My understanding of the 'empirical model' of the relationship between language and consciousness is essentially based on John Locke's famous work, *An Essay Concerning Human Understanding*, ed. A.C. Fraser. 2 vols. (1894). It is in this work that Locke develops the idea of human mind as '*tabula rasa*' (II.i.2).
3. For detailed discussion, refer to G.W.F. Hegel, *Phenomenology of Mind*, ed. J.B. Baillie, 2 vols. (1910).
4. I. Frolov, ed., *Dictionary of Philosophy* (Moscow: Progress Publishers, 1984), 81.
5. Karl Marx, *The German Ideology*, ed. C. J. Arthur (London: Routledge and Kegan Paul, 1974), 47–51.

6. For a detailed exposition, refer to *The Oxford Companion to Philosophy*, ed. Ted Honderich (Oxford: Oxford University Press, 1995) or *Husserl*, ed. D. Bell (London: Methuen, 1991).

7. This phrase is derived from the title of Harold Bloom's book *The Anxiety of Influence*. In this particular work, Bloom has interpreted the whole process of creativity in Freudian terms. According to him, creative process is a way of overcoming the anxiety that literary influences create in the mind of the creative writer. The process of writing is, therefore, a process of outgrowing one's influences, and often involves the 'ritualistic killing of the father principle' (with its specific Oedipal overtones) and is seen as the only way of coming to terms with this 'anxiety'. What is significant about Bloom's conceptualisation is that he places this paradigm specifically within the matrix of Western history, thought and philosophy.

8. This is the main thrust of Edward Said's arguments in his *Orientalism* (New York: Penguin Books, 1995).

9. Vyacheslav Shestakov, 'The Aesthetic of the Trivial', in *Aesthetics, Art, Life: A Collection of Articles*, ed. A. Zis, trans. Sergei Syrovatkin (Moscow: Raduga Publishers, 1988), 212–6.

10. Christopher Lasch, *The Culture of Narcissism: American Life in an Age of Diminishing Expectations* (New York: Norton, 1979), 75.

CHAPTER FOURTEEN

Of Influence, Power and Empowerment

Every year, *Forbes* magazine publishes a list of the most influential men and women in the world. The readers often lap up such lists, without ever bothering to pause over their 'whys' and 'wherefores'. They are only interested in who has moved in or out, up or down, that coveted list. The publication of this list is treated as a celebrated and much-awaited event by the media the world over. Once the names are out, the media mills all over the world start working overtime, publishing snippets from the *Forbes*' list, either exulting over the fact that men and women from their country have made it to the top or bemoaning why some of them have slipped down the ladder of global influence.

In the next phase, the process repeats itself at all possible levels such as national, state, regional and local. Newspapers and magazines across the globe start conducting similar exercises to identify their own little pockets of power and influence, in the process pushing up their circulation and sales. *Forbes*, one assumes, conducts a world-wide survey annually to arrive at such lists. Entries are invited from readers who are not only expected to provide their own lists of influential men and women but also put them in some order of priority. The magazine develops its own parameters, which are meant to facilitate the readers' choice, which, in turn, is ascertained through an opinion poll, and its results are finally tabulated in the form of a list of influential men and women.

Now this raises a number of questions: Who are these readers of *Forbes*? What is their profile? If one were to look beneath the surface, one would discover that the readers of this magazine are essentially from a very special, privileged class, which picks up these influential men and women from amongst its own members. These readers constitute a closed club. One wonders if this is not purely, and symbolically, an incestuous activity, initiated by a group of influential men and women to keep the world informed about how their sphere of influence is spreading globally. Are those who make it to such lists—one hundred or five hundred people, at the most—not trying to tell the rest of the world—more than a trillion people—that the economic or political decisions that affect your lives and life-styles ultimately rest in our hands? Is it not a demonstration of power by the most powerful, a declaration by the mightiest of their growing might, a symbolic gesture of the rich and powerful to assert their growing power and influence over the world economy, and even politics?

The readers, who are often in the position of passive consumers, accept such lists uncritically. They also remain oblivious of the insidious ways in which the rich and powerful make preposterously loud statements about their growing power and influence. Rather than question the rationale behind such lists or their subversive logic, the readers begin to get intimidated by such unabashed declarations of power and start dreaming of how, if at all, they can possibly slip into the position of those who supposedly preside over the destiny of the mankind. In other words, these lists become the 'wish lists' of the less powerful and power crazy—all of whom begin to hitch their wagons to the stars, raising the benchmark of their expectations, dreams, aspirations and perhaps, frustration.

There are other related questions too. For instance, is money or power—or the influence that flows out of their combination—the only benchmark for assessing the influence of an individual on her/his society, nation or the world? What does the term 'sphere of influence' mean? What are some of the ways of assessing or quantifying the 'sphere of influence'? Should the influence of an individual be judged in terms of the money power s/he exerts or the actual benefits her/his presence makes available to her/his society? Is the 'sphere of influence' linked to the 'visibility' of an individual and the frequency with which s/he appears in the media or the invisible gains s/he transfers on to the less privileged sections of her/his society on account of her/his growing wealth and riches?

Let us suggest that 'sphere of influence' is essentially a sociological concept, which is extremely difficult to measure or pin down. It is extremely difficult to either define or set the parameters for, on the basis of which it could be formulated, assessed or quantified in actual, material terms. In fact, its abstruseness is one of the reasons why the media is able to take advantage of this sociological phenomenon. For instance, if the editorial team at *Forbes* wants to find out whether or not Indra Nooyi—an India-born American business executive who has figured very prominently in the prestigious *Forbes*' list—is an influential woman, one of the most obvious criteria they would go by is the fact that she is the CEO (chief executive officer) of a multinational company. In that case, they are likely to be led by certain beneath-the-surface assumptions which need to be externalised. First of all, it will matter to them that the company she works for is a multinational giant and also the largest producer of aerated drinks in the world. In other words, they will be conscious of the position (read turn over) of the company in world market, and its position in the hierarchy of companies producing aerated drinks. The moment anyone rises to the top position within such organisational structures, these editors begin to presume that the influence of that individual is now synonymous with the organisation to which s/he belongs. Moreover, they tend to attach a great deal of 'value' to the internal hierarchical structures of such organisations. For them, a CEO definitely does wield, or is supposed to wield, much greater influence, power or clout than a COO (chief operating officer). This is true, but only partially so. Then they start seeking endorsements for their preconceived ideas (which are formed based on hierarchical and notional concepts of individual power) from the public in general by conducting market surveys or opinion polls, the results of which are not likely to be much different from what they have believed in all along. More often than not, it is this kind of circular logic that goes into a systematic process of manufacturing such images of great men and women of power, of legitimising their power as a measure of their influence.

Is there any direct correlation between the 'power one wields' and the 'influence one exerts'? Does the growing personal influence of an individual also become a logical determinant of her/his power and authority within an organisation, society or the world at large?

How much of this power that an individual wields is to be attributed to her/his personal charisma/worth and how much of it to her/his identification with an organisation? This is something rather difficult to answer. Here, it needs to be emphasised that all organisations value individuals only in direct proportion to the extent to which they can maximise the organisational benefits (read profits) or organisational objectives. Once an individual fails to achieve either the first or the second or both, s/he becomes disposable and the organisation starts looking for a more productive substitute. In all organisations, especially in multinational giants, individuals are mere cogs in a big, well-oiled machine, and what matters is not the individual worth or significance but her/his performance in enhancing the worth or significance of the organisation's productivity and/or profits, which, in turn, becomes a hallmark of the organisation's influence and power. It follows that an individual within an organisation has worth/significance only so long as s/he enjoys a pre-eminent position within the organisation. This also means that within a society, an individual commands respect, influence, power and privileges, only because of the organisation, and not in spite of it. We are not discounting the fact that an individual has to work and perform much better than other individuals within an organisation to excel and reach the top bracket. This is considering that performance and productivity are the only parameters used in evaluating an individual's worth and significance within an organisation, and are also treated as infallible indices of her/his elevation and promotion within hierarchical structures. Sadly, this is not always the case, especially in our context where mediocrity and sycophancy often thrive at the expense of meritocracy.

The media constructs images of success and fame based on such and other similar determinants. In other words, the media first considers an individual's worth (read cost) to the organisation, then comes to her/his position within the organisation and finally, the positioning of the organisation within the larger global network. One can argue that more often than not, such surveys end up producing either pre-doctored or entirely predictable results. Does it mean that such surveys are the only ways of asserting or demonstrating the growing power of money and influence for the privileged few and that the media simply becomes a convenient tool or instrument in the process? Does it mean that the media only colludes with, and for that reason, enters into a symbiotic alliance with the growing influence of money and power? Does it also mean that the media has its own intrinsic compulsions to constantly manufacture such images and fashion icons, which is what it periodically does through such surveys?

The underlying question is this: Why should the media manufacture such images of discontent and collude with the subversive forces of capitalism? First, today, media houses across the world are largely controlled by business barons. Second, the economic survival of the media largely depends on advertising, which is the largest source of revenue, apart from the direct or indirect funding it often receives from one business establishment or the other. Third, the media has this inherent compulsion to project newer images on the consciousness of its readers, if it has to sustain and/or enlarge its readership base. The logic is simple—you stay in the news only by creating newer images of consumption and/or discontent. In other words, the media is constantly engaged in this swirling enterprise of creating iconic figures, manufacturing larger than life images, which not only feed the growing aspirations and dreams of the reading public but also their appetite for novelty. It is this kind of subversive logic that often lies behind most of the surveys, such as the one that occupies us here.

While critiquing this phenomenon, one has to be convinced about the inevitability of such surveys. There is no doubt that such surveys will continue to dominate the media scene and perhaps they will get more fiercely competitive and even more ruthless with the passage of time. Does it mean that there are no options left for us? Does it mean that this entire critique is a kind of cul-de-sac? One has to concede that there is no escape from the commercial logic of such surveys, which is why they are eminently irreplaceable. But if we have to actually measure or map out the extent of influence or clout that an individual enjoys, we must change the way in which we measure this influence. Rather than relying on specious and flimsy factors, it is much better to depend on a set of well-defined criteria. For instance, if we wish to measure the exact nature of Nooyi's personal influence as the CEO of a multinational giant, it will be a good idea to see how far her elevation within her organisation has helped the cause of women's empowerment. How many women within the organisation have benefitted because of Nooyi's elevation to the top position? Another way of asking the same question is this: Has she taken a policy decision to either recruit more women or empower the existing women staff by offering them key appointments, positions and elevations? If Nooyi works only for the promotion of the organisational objectives and fails to make her organisation more gender sensitive and a level playing field for women, it would be a sheer folly on our part or that of the media to lionise her as a symbol of growing woman power within the multinationals. In the absence of a set of well-defined criteria, it is often this kind of fallacious reasoning that is used by the media to promote its icons and sell its carefully constructed and manufactured images.

The reality is that the elevation of a Nooyi is not a symbol of the growing power of women, as hundreds and thousands of women are conveniently left out of the loop. As such, her elevation only enhances the sense of helplessness among those who are excluded for one reason or the other. So long as our modes of analysing social reality remain faulty and fallacious, we will continue to lap up images that are no more than mere cardboard cutouts, hollow from within and garishly painted from without. At this juncture, if someone were to turn around and say, 'Why grumble so much about surface appearances and their facetious nature, when a postmodern, fractured reality surrounds us all?', one has no choice but to retreat into the 'habitual silence', the last refuge!

References

Berry, John W., R.C. Mishra, and R.C. Tripathi, eds. 2003. *Psychology in Human and Social Development: Lessons from Diverse Cultures*. New Delhi: Sage Publications.

Blanchard, Ken, John P. Carlos, and Alan Randolph. 2001. *Empowerment Takes More than a Minute*. 2nd ed. San Francisco: Berrett-Koehler Publishers.

Daft, Richard L. 2008. *Organization Theory and Design*. Ohio: Cengage Learning.

Foucault, Michel. 2002. *The Archaeology of Knowledge*. London: Routledge.

Ginnodo, Bill. 1997. *The Power of Empowerment: What the Experts Say and 16 Actionable Studies*. Arlington Heights: Pride Publishers.

Kanungo, Rabindra N., and Manuel Mendonca. 1996. *Ethical Dimensions of Leadership*. London: Sage Publications.

Kinlaw, Dennis C. 1995. *The Practice of Empowerment: Making the Most of Human Competence*. Hampshire: Gower Publishing.

Narayan-Parker, Deepa, ed. 2005. *Measuring Empowerment: Cross-disciplinary Perspectives*. Washington DC: World Bank.

Quinn, John J., and Peter W. F. Davies, eds. 1999. *Ethics and Empowerment*. Hampshire: Macmillan.

Runco, Mark A. 2007. *Creativity: Theories and Themes, Research, Development and Practice*. London: Elsevier Academic Press.

C H A P T E R F I F T E E N

Of Little Magazines in Punjabi: A Historical Overview

The beginnings of journalistic writings in Punjabi can be traced back to the middle of nineteenth century. Such efforts were closely bound up with the twists and turns in Sikh political history. It was the rise of the Singh Sabha Movement in the 1860s that provided the necessary impetus to the whole enterprise of Punjabi journalism. In its initial stages, magazines and journals were started with the specific purpose of promoting Sikh religious ideals and so, they had a definitive religious character. Literary journalism—essentially a secular enterprise—was apparently a later offshoot, and it became the raison d'être for the emergence of little magazines, only towards the end of the nineteenth century.

It was through the efforts of Bhai Veer Singh (1872–1957), a noted Punjabi poet and novelist, that *Khalsa Samachar*, a weekly, was started in 1899. Known for its conservative outlook, substantive financial standing and well-reasoned articles, the magazine gave a new direction to Punjabi journalism, enriching both the language and its prose in the process. It is no wonder that *Khalsa Samachar* is the longest surviving magazine in Punjabi today. Apart from publishing poems, short stories and literary reviews, the *Samachar* devoted a large chunk of its space to promoting articles related to *Gurbani*, Sikh philosophy, history and religion. Singh's novel *Satwanti* was also first serialised in the magazine.

The material and historical conditions in Punjab and elsewhere underwent cataclysmic changes in the beginning of the twentieth century. The Bolshevik Revolution in the erstwhile Soviet Union, the outbreak of World War I in Europe, growing influence of imperialism in India and sporadic acts of resistance to it resulting in the Komagata Maru incident (1914) and the Jallianwala Bagh episode (1919) were only some of the historical events that helped in shaping an emergent political and national consciousness all over India, and especially in Punjab. Shedding its religious character, Punjabi journalism was quick to adapt itself to these social and political changes. Redefining its thrust, it increasingly became a tool of mass awareness, social education and reform. Its reformist character was evident both in the content and form of Punjabi literary journalism as well as in the manner in which it developed in the early decades of the twentieth century. The exponential growth of little magazines in this period can easily be gauged from the fact that between 1900 and 1947, as many as 300 such magazines were established; out of which twenty-seven were circulated daily, 122 weekly, seven fortnightly, 130 monthly, and almost twelve of them were circulated every three months, six months or annually (M. Singh 2001).

One of the earliest magazines to come out during this period was *Pritam*—by all accounts, the first literary magazine of its kind. Conceived as a monthly, *Pritam* was brought out by S. Labh Singh in January 1923 from Montgomery (now in Pakistan). Shifting its base first to Lahore and then to Amritsar, *Pritam* continued to play an important role in Punjabi life and letters until 1947, when it ceased publication on account of the Partition. Later, the magazine was revived, and it continues to play an important role in the world of Punjabi letters. Among its prominent contributors, one could count such luminaries as Bhai Veer Singh, Puran Singh (1881–1931), Mohan Singh Vaid (1881–1936), Lala Kirpa Sagar (1881–1939), Lala Dhani Ram Chatrik (1876–1954), Mohan Singh Diwana (1899–1984) and hundreds of others. Popular for its objectivity and fearlessness, this magazine provided patronage to all known forms of literary genres, ranging from poems to short stories, specialised essays to articles of general interest, one-act plays to translations, and from biographies to novels. Besides, from time to time, several theme-based special issues of the magazine were also brought out.

In 1924, Giani Hira Singh Dard (1889–1965) started *Phulwari*, another monthly, from Amritsar. It gained immense popularity over the years, and played significant roles in both pre-Partition and post-Partition Punjab. But for a period of four years (1942–6), when it had to cease publication on account of Dard's imprisonment,

Phulwari continued to exercise its shaping influence on Punjabi literary sensibility, right up to 1958 when it finally folded up. In his early years, Dard was under the influence of Akali politics and ideology. The magazine too bore its imprint. After 1938–9, when the editor succumbed to the charms of Marxist ideology, *Phulwari* became a strong votary of progressive ideals and philosophy. Though it published all kinds of writings, short story was definitely its most favoured, privileged form. Some of the old issues of this magazine are literally a treasure trove for anyone interested in exploring the history of Punjabi short story in its nascent form.

Preetlari occupies almost a legendary status in the history of Punjabi literary journalism. Started in 1933 by Gurbaksh Singh Preetlari (1895–1977), a prominent prose and short story writer in Punjabi, *Preetlari* was initially published as a bilingual monthly—both in Punjabi and English. It became an exclusively Punjabi magazine in 1937. Right from its inception, *Preetlari* was recognised as an important organ of progressive ideology. What made for its special appeal was the open, uninhibited way in which it encouraged dissemination of information, which was otherwise regarded anathema to the conservative Punjabi society. Thanks to this little magazine, for the first time ever, subjects as diverse as human health, physiology, psychology, happiness, love and sex were openly discussed and debated in the columns of a Punjabi paper. Among several others, Amrita Pritam (1919–2005), Shiv Kumar Batalvi (1936–73), Navtej Singh (1924–83), Balraj Sahni (1913–73), Santokh Singh Dheer (1920–2010), etc., published some of their best early writings in this magazine.

In 1939, Mohan Singh 'Mahir' (1905–78), started a monthly, *Panj Darya*, at Lahore. It continued to come out from Lahore until 1947. After a gap of two years, it was revived from Amritsar, and later was published from Ludhiana and then from Jalandhar. Now *Panj Darya* is being brought out as a fortnightly from Chandigarh, as a global news magazine. *Panj Darya* aimed at fostering a sense of unity among Punjabis of all castes, creeds and religions by strengthening the sense of cultural pride in them. With this in view, it often carried Punjabi translations of essays on politics, religion and culture by Jawahar Lal Nehru, Rajagopalachari, Sohan Singh Josh, Master Tara

Singh, Gian Singh, etc. On the literary front, it published critical writings by such well-known scholars as Teja Singh, Harbans Singh, Sant Singh Sekhon; short stories of Kartar Singh Duggal (b. 1917), Rajinder Singh Bedi (1915–84); and translations of the works of Maxim Gorky, Rabindranath Tagore and Kishan Chander (1914–77); and poems by Mohan Singh (1905–78), Gopal Singh Dardi (1917–90) and several others. By promoting the spirit of innovation and experimentation, *Panj Darya* did give a definite boost to the modernist impulse in Punjabi literature.

Punjabi Sahit, another monthly magazine, was started in 1942, thanks to the efforts of S. Harbhajan Singh. Kartar Singh Duggal was on its advisory panel. It was perhaps the first little magazine in Punjabi to appear in the form of a book, as a digest. Apart from initiating several literary contests, *Punjabi Sahit* helped institute Punjabi Sahit Fund. While this magazine went out of its way to extend special patronage to folk literature and culture, it helped the cause of mainstream Punjabi literary tradition as well. Undeniably, *Punjabi Sahit* made a very special contribution to the development of both Punjabi language and literature.

One of the worst fallouts of the Partition was that, when the maps were redrawn, Lahore, which by then had emerged as the nucleus of Punjabi literary journalism, went to Pakistan. Forced to bear the brunt of dislocation and displacement after 1947, Punjabi literary journalism had to make a fresh beginning. In the post-Partition period, Amritsar, Jalandhar, Ludhiana and Delhi became the alternative sites of its location. Between 1947 and 2000, as many as 250 old and new literary magazines came out in Punjabi and they survived against all kinds of odds and pressures (M. Singh 2011). It would not be wrong to say that in this period, literary journalism not only emerged as a specialised discipline with a distinctive character of its own, but also succeeded in creating its own niche both in terms of its marketability and readership.

One of the magazines that have had an unexpected revival in the post-Partition era is *Saaddhi Kahani*. Floated in 1941, *Saaddhi Kahani* had folded up temporarily after the Partition. It was revived in 1951 as *Kahani* from Amritsar. Though this particular magazine was devoted primarily to the cause of the short story as a genre, it published poems, essays and one-act plays as well. For years, it ran a column called *Sadhe Lekhak*, the main purpose of which was to introduce young, upcoming as well as established short story writers to the Punjabi readership. *Kahani* helped its readers develop and hone a critical understanding of short story as a form. Both the traditionalists and the experimentalists were equally enthusiastic contributors to *Kahani*. Despite its immense popularity, it could be sustained only until 1964–5 when it finally folded up. Other literary magazines that folded up abruptly, after sporadic runs, include *Kavita*, *Jeewan Masik*, *Punjabi Sahit* and *Lok Sahit*.

Bhapa Pritam Singh, the renowned Punjabi writer and publisher, launched *Aarsi* from Delhi in 1956 with great fanfare. The magazine finally ran aground in June 2000. After *Preetlari*, *Aarsi* was perhaps the longest surviving magazine in Punjabi and while it lasted, it was largely perceived as a forum for some of the best writing available in Punjabi. The main reason for this was that apart from publishing literary works of enduring merit, *Aarsi* provided space for translations from other languages as well. There is not a single Punjabi writer worth the name who has not published her/his writings in this magazine—a fact that imparts great archival value to some of its old issues. The Punjabi readership, no doubt, is already feeling the absence of *Aarsi* rather acutely.

Started by Raghbir Singh in 1965, *Sirjana*, a quarterly magazine initially published from Jalandhar, ran sporadically between 1970 and 1975. Since then, it has found stability and gained a fair amount of consistency. Now published from Chandigarh, it has already brought out as many as 238 issues (by the end of the year 2010). *Sirjana* divides its space equally between creative and critical aspects of writing, and—being an organ of progressive ideology—extends patronage to both young and old writers of similar persuasion. Apart from Punjabi writers of repute, it has also published translations of such well-known writers from other languages as Mansur Kaisar, Kamleshwar, Ramesh Kuntal Megh, Faiz Ahmed Faiz and Hazari Prasad Dwivedi. Over the years, *Sirjana* has definitively managed to create a niche readership for itself.

Started from Delhi in 1966, *Nagmani*, a monthly magazine, bears an unmistakable stamp of its lifetime editor and the renowned dame of Punjabi poetry, Amrita Pritam. Its distinctive character lies in the way in which it illustrates all literary writings with artistic images and pencil drawings, most of which are done by Pritam's companion, Imroz. Its readership has declined over the years. However, that has not made any dent into the magazine's quality of material or production. What really makes this little magazine stand out is its truly cosmopolitan character. Apart from the who's who of Punjabi literature, it has published the writings of Alberto Moravio (Italian), Abraham Saleshki (Israeli Jew), Kumar Sanyal (Bengali), Nirmal Verma (Hindi), Ismat Chugtai (Urdu) and several Russian, African, Spanish and Bulgarian writers, in translation. More than a literary magazine, *Nagmani* is an institution, which has promoted such literary concepts as *Nagmani* Library and *Nagmani* Evenings, a monthly meeting of writers where literary pieces are read and discussed.

Floated from Jalandhar by Prem Prakash (b. 1932), a famous Punjabi short story writer, *Lakeer* has had sporadic runs since its inception in 1970. Though essentially conceived as a monthly magazine, it changed into a quarterly for some time, before ceasing publication temporarily and being revived again. Until 2000, some 75 issues of this magazine had been brought out. *Lakeer* promotes the cause of avant-garde Punjabi literature, and shows a definite proclivity towards experimental and progressive writing. For years, it ran a column titled '*Patni De Jharokhe*' ('Through Wife's Eyes') in which famous writers and their writings were perceived exclusively from the point of view of their wives. Among others, Mohan Bhandari, Ranjit Dheer, Surjeet Kaur, Amarjeet Chandan, Prem Gorky and several others have published their writings in *Lakeer*.

Aks, a monthly, started in 1975 from Delhi by Amarjit Singh, was conceived as a literary magazine. But after 1984, having lost its distinctive literary character, it seems to have become more of a political broadsheet. However, literary pieces continue to hog most of its space. One of the conspicuous features of this magazine is that it takes special interest in serialising novels by well-known Punjabi novelists. So far, among others, it has serialised Baldev Singh's *GT Road*, Baljeet Sing Raina's *Yathaarth* (Reality), Pargat Singh Sidhu's *Apni Miti Di Saajish* (Conspiracy of One's Own Soil) and Jaswant

Singh Virdi's *Varkha Wali Raat* (The Rainy Night). Besides, it publishes articles on subjects as diverse as science, health, culture, sports and humour.

Samdarshi, a quarterly, was started by Punjabi Akademi, New Delhi, in 1985, once again, under the editorship of Amrita Pritam. There was a time when people like Balwant Gargi, Kulwant Singh Virk, Wanjaara Bedi and Harbhajan Singh were members of its editorial board. Since 1992, Satinder Singh Noor has been editing this magazine, and this change of guard has certainly brought about changes in the editorial policy as well. *Samdarshi* has lost its exclusive character and like any other literary magazine, it offers an odd assortment of poems, stories, articles, news items and research-based essays. One of the consistent features of *Samdarshi* is that, from time to time, it does bring out theme-based issues on extremely provocative and meaningful subjects.

Janakraj Singh started *Sirnavaan*, a monthly magazine, from Chandigarh, somewhere in 1987. This magazine gives ample space to both poetry and short stories. On the one hand, it has showcased a number of contemporary poets such as Manjit Indra, Amar Jyoti, Sidhu Damdami, Ajmer Rode and countless others, on the other, it has brought into critical attention short story writers such as Baldev Singh, Sharan Makkar, Narinder Bhullar, Jinder, Tarlochan Tarsi, etc. Bhushan Dhyanpuri has been successfully running a humour column called *Mooh Aai Baat* in this magazine. *Sirnavaan* also publishes Punjabi translations of literatures from other languages.

Though *Kahani Punjab* is a late entrant into this extremely competitive field, it has already created a secure niche for itself. Started as a quarterly in 1993 by Ram Sarup Ankhi (1932–2010), a famous Punjabi novelist and short story writer, *Kahani Punjab* is devoted exclusively to the promotion of Punjabi short stories. In one of its regular columns, Gurbachan Bhullar, a renowned Punjabi writer, offers critical commentaries on various aspects of some of the well-known Punjabi stories that are considered to be modern classics.

Pancham is the only little magazine in Punjabi that claims to support the cause of Dalits. Started in 2002 as a monthly and brought out from Jalandhar, this magazine not only publishes writings by Dalit writers in Punjabi, but also offers liberal space to those who write in a manner sympathetic to the marginalised and the oppressed. Without restricting itself to any specific genre, *Pancham* offers a diverse range of reading materials, including thought-provoking essays, research-based articles, short stories, poems, etc.

From this survey, it is evident that little magazines in Punjabi have had a fascinating journey down the decades. In over 120 years of their existence, these magazines have been through several incarnations and reincarnations—from religious to secular and from secular to purely 'literary' and/or 'semi-literary'. Despite the constraints of funding, and their limited readership and circulation, these magazines have managed to survive and flourish, through dogged perseverance, determination and the personal commitment of writers and workers. The ideological spectrum that these magazines represent has been truly astonishing and in historical terms, it helps us understand the rise and fall of various literary trends, impulses and movements in Punjabi literature/culture. While rendering a yeoman's service to the cause of *Punjabiat*, these magazines have enriched both Punjabi language and literature in ways that are hard to quantify. One could also suggest that, historically, it is the short story that has emerged as the most favoured, if not the privileged, form in these little magazines. And this points to the simple fact that, in the ultimate analysis, short story is the representative genre of our times and that the genre is flourishing in our languages.

References

Atari, Ishaar Singh. 1987. *Bharat Wich Patarkari Da Itihaas*. Patiala: Punjabi University.

Khera, Surinder Singh. 1983. *Punjabi Patarkari*. Patiala: Sukhraj Prakashan.

Singh, Megha. 2001. *Punjabi Patarkari Da Itihaas*. Chandigarh: Lokgeet Prakashan.

Singh, Suba. 1973. *Punjabi Patarkari Da Itihaas*. Chandigarh: Punjab State University Text Book Board.

Walia, Harjinder. 2003. *Patarkari Ate Punjabi Sahitik Patarkari*. Delhi: National Book Shop.

CHAPTER SIXTEEN

Class, Ideology and Politics of Globalisation: A Case Study of Aravind Adiga

More than a decade after Arundhati Roy won the Man Booker Prize (in 1997) for *The God of Small Things*, the prestigious honour went to another debut effort by an India-born author when Aravind Adiga's *The White Tiger* made the cut in 2008. (*The Inheritance of Loss* for which Kiran Desai won the Man Booker in 2005 was her second novel.) Apart from the fortuitous first letter of the alphabet which they both share, there is very little that is worthy of comparison between these two Booker sensations. Roy's was undoubtedly a rites-of-passage novel, whereas Adiga's work is not even remotely connected to his personal life and/or milieu. Roy turned to journalism only after her resounding success as a novelist, whereas Adiga ventured into writing a novel after many years as a working journalist with *Time*. Somewhere, all of this is reflected in the way he has gone about crafting his novel—with a razor-thin prescience and clinical objectivity. Roy found inspiration in her Syrian Christian background and the childhood days spent in the backwaters of Kerala, whereas Adiga descends into the dark alleys of Delhi and Mumbai, to create a story of India, which is at once disturbing and fascinating. It is no wonder that Michael Portillo, the head of the Booker jury, went so far as to say that Adiga's novel had literally 'pulled his socks off'.

Once the Booker was announced in October 2008, Adiga was almost instantly hailed as a literary icon. Scott Medintz of *The New York Sun* (29 April 2008) literally drooled over the novel, saying, '[A]t once a fascinating glimpse beneath the surface of an Indian economic "miracle", a heart-stopping psychological tale of a premeditated murder and its aftermath, and a meticulously conceived allegory of the creative destruction that's driving globalization … That may sound like a lot to take in, but *The White Tiger* is unpretentious and compulsively readable to boot.' The reviewer of *The Economist* (11 September 2008) went a step further, comparing Adiga to Dickens, saying, 'In creating a character who is both witty and psychopathic, Mr Adiga has produced a hero almost as memorable as Pip, proving himself the Charles Dickens of the call-centre generation.' Akash Kapur, in his review of the novel published in *The New York Times Book Review* (9 November 2008) was no less euphoric: '*The White Tiger* is a penetrating piece of social commentary, attuned to the inequalities that persist despite India's new prosperity. It correctly identifies—and deflates—middle-class India's collective euphoria.' In his review published in *USA Today* (23 April 2008), Deirdre Donahue declared, 'Aravind Adiga's *The White Tiger* is one of the most powerful books I have read in decades. No hyperbole. This debut novel from an Indian journalist living in Mumbai hit me like a kick to the head … This is an amazing and angry novel about injustice and power.' It is quite apparent that the newspapers were almost vying with each other to fill their columns with articles on Adiga's novel and the reviewers were jumping over each other's head in their bid to canonise him. Of course, the gaze of his publishers, like that of the eternal watchers of the 'sensex', had been constantly riveted on to the soaring sales figures, both in India and abroad. These are, after all, some of the professional hazards of being famous overnight and Adiga must have by now got used to his share under the sun.

In the midst of all this whirling confusion his novel had then generated, it is important to look beyond the glare of publicity and ask some serious questions. We must ask ourselves, for instance, what kind of future does this Booker augur, not only for the author—which is a purely speculative enterprise—but for Indian fiction in general, and/or Indian English fiction in particular? We must also ask ourselves: Is Adiga charting a new territory or breaking some fresh ground in his novel? Or is he simply returning to the well-trodden, over-beaten path that so many of his predecessors, both in Indian English and regional languages, have traversed already? And, what kind of impact is this overvaluation of the Booker—the media suddenly goes into an overdrive each time this award is announced, hailing it as a 'global event'—likely to have upon the growth and potential of Indian fiction, both in English and regional languages?

It has been argued by a good number of reviewers/media critics of *The White Tiger* that its main strength is in the way in which it puts the question of 'class' back on our 'literary plate'.[1] While some would have us believe that this is where the novelty or originality of Adiga's novel lies, others are willing to push the point further by claiming that the question of 'class' has surfaced in our literary imagination, perhaps, for the first time ever. A reviewer has compared the novel to 'the rooster coop', about which his protagonist says, '[It is] the greatest thing to come out of this country in the ten thousand years of its history.' Does it not then sound somewhat like Salman Rushdie's notorious comment on the 'poverty of Indian fiction'? A media watcher has gone to the extent of suggesting that 'the book has won all round applause for its political position—that of pointing to the anger of the Indian underbelly of 400 million and the contempt, at least, the disregard the Indian middle class has for this lot.'[2] Such claims may, undoubtedly, prove to be preposterous, as they rest upon a blinkered view of history. Once we invoke history and its multiple burdens, such claims begin to fall apart sooner than we expect them to. For as long as one can remember, Indian English fiction has prospered, thanks to the exclusive patronage of the middle-class readers and has enjoyed an equally exclusive affiliation with the bourgeoisie ideology. This was partially so, owing to the fact that the novel has everywhere been regarded as a genre closely tied to the apron strings of the bourgeoisie.

Rarely do we come across such avant-garde novelists as Mulk Raj Anand (1905–2004), who in *Untouchable* (1935), *Coolie* (1936) and *The Village* (1939), portray the downtrodden and rural poor with both compassion and sympathy. Most of these novels are dictated by a conscious impulse to overturn the bourgeoisie ideology, so that fictional space for the lower classes or the marginalised groups could effectively be created. In a way, it was the residual effect of the Marxist ideology and its strong hold over Indian literary imagination that had initially propelled it towards the question of class and/or ideology. As far as Indian fiction in regional languages is concerned, this process started somewhere in the early 1930s. That is when the progressive movement was getting off to a start, slowly seeping through various regions, luring scores of writers into its seductive fold. Much before this question could leap into Indian English fiction, Munshi Premchand (1880–1936), Phanishwar Nath 'Renu' (1921–77), the pioneer of *anchalik upanyas* in Hindi, and several others had already projected it through their fiction. One is reminded of Premchand's 'Kafan' and several similar stories that deal with the plight and sufferings of the landless peasants in a predominantly feudal Indian society. This was the phase of critical realism, and the portrayal of the peasants, workers and/or the poorer sections of society was largely a matter of personal conviction, ideological preference and a cultural necessity (this era being the high-water mark of nationalism).

In the context of Punjabi fiction, the phase of progressive writing started much later around the 1950s, with the novels of Sant Singh Sekhon (1908–97), Narinder Pal Singh (b. 1923) and Amrita Pritam (1919–2005). However, the real concern with the twin questions of class and ideology did not enter the lexicon of Punjabi fiction until Gurdial Singh (b. 1933). It was in his person that Punjabi fiction acquired a true representative, a forceful, genuine advocate, of the subaltern and the oppressed. *Marhi Da Deeva* (The Last Flicker), published way back in 1964, was hailed as a landmark novel precisely because it sought to push the socially and economically challenged common men and women to the centre stage of fiction. By doing so, Singh not only energised Punjabi fiction but also paved the way for re-examining the history of Punjabi society and culture from below.

Those times were different, and so were the impulses behind such efforts. Such works of fiction were mainly the outcome of a society in the throes of change and transition, poised delicately between the pulls and counter-pulls of tradition and modernity. The overarching context of socialism, which had flourished within such stories, has now long ceased to exist, both as a seductive idea and an impinging reality. It was the growing awareness of human dignity, freedom and personal worth coupled with a political consciousness generated by Nehruvian socialism that ultimately brought Dalit writings to the fore in the 1960s. And it was through Dalit writings that class and caste entered into an entirely new sociological equation—perhaps, for the first time ever. Though Dalit writings are known to have flourished in other Indian languages too, it was Marathi language and culture that emerged as its nodal epicentre.

Unlike the works of novelists such as Anand or Premchand—who chose to focus on the problems of the marginalised, despite belonging to the middle-class milieu themselves—Dalit narratives are characterised by an inwardness and an exclusiveness that make it truly pungent, and even distinctively authentic. Such writings were an attempt to reclaim Dalits' true voice and idiom, a form of articulation that enabled them to represent themselves, rather than being represented by the 'other', as had happened earlier. It is no wonder that it was in this form of writing that the 'subaltern' truly began to rip apart the facetious, bourgeoisie logic of Gayatri Spivak's rhetorical question, 'Can the subaltern speak?' In this respect, one may think of the significant contributions made by Dalit writers such as Baburao Bagul, Daya Pawar, Namdeo Dhasal in Marathi, Om Parkash Balmiki in Hindi and Prem Gorky in Punjabi. All of these are vibrant, strong and assertive voices, which have not only challenged the limits of societal and political conventions, but also the literary and cultural norms. Moreover, they have created new literary landscapes and a new aesthetics that lie beyond the ken of our middle-class sensibility, much in the manner Balzac, Maupassant and Charles Baudelaire had done in the middle of the nineteenth century. That is how Dalit writers have managed to re-inscribe the rules of what it means to be human in an unequal, unjust, exploitative and repressive world.

Significantly, most of these voices have emerged in regional languages, not in Indian English narratives. One may ponder over this question: Why does Indian English fiction choose to construct its sociology differently from the other Indian languages? Why has it not dealt with the issues and problems that perennially engage writers in regional languages? Could it have something to do with its inherent dominant ideology per se, or its peripheral engagement with Indian social reality, or its nagging anxiety to target an audience out there in the West? It is against this backdrop that Adiga's novel must necessarily be seen or read. He certainly constructs the sociology of his novel very differently from the way it is being done by most of his contemporaries, especially in Indian languages. But the question is this: Could there be a hidden agenda, or a definite ideology or politics, behind it?

Of course, it is for the readers to ponder some of these questions as they pore over the pages of *The White Tiger*. But while doing so, they must remember that we are yet to witness a literary movement supporting the working-class ideology in Indian English fiction—something comparable to what British literature witnessed in the post-War period. Even at the risk of sounding presumptuous, we can assume that despite all the hype and hoopla, Adiga's novel is unlikely to trigger off one such movement at this stage. If we do understand the history of Indian English fiction, we will know that it has hardly ever had a perceptible, identifiable movement, but only short-lived trends that come and go. We have writers who either plough their lonely furrows or just keep up with the Joneses, doing what is trendy or t(r)opical. Perhaps, we are not really as fortunate as some other cultures that have had the benefit of such thinkers as Georg Lukas, Walter Benjamin, Raymond Williams or Frederic Jameson. Critics of such stature alone could have lent credibility to our literary causes, turning them into self-sustaining literary movements. In the 1960s, if Richard Hoggart, Raymond Williams and several others were around to theorise on the working-class culture; John Osborne, Arnold Wesker and Alan Bennett were there to inscribe this culture into their works. In our context, apart from Dalit writings, which definitely did evolve into a full-scale literary movement, with its own historical and political logistics, our literary concerns with the working-class ideology have been, at best, only perfunctory, and, at worst, fitfully sporadic.

This is where Adiga's story gains its literary and historical edge. He has chosen to focus his attention on the Marxist notions of class and ideology in an era of hard-core globalisation. This is where the politics of globalisation or that of the insidious market forces essentially takes over. To some of us, the magical sales figures may appear more seductive than the actual content of the novel. Besides, let us not delude ourselves into thinking that Adiga's novel sets out to critique the invasive forces of globalisation—instead, one can argue that his novel seeks to legitimise their pervasive sweep, power and influence. The content of the novel speaks for the vicious hold that the forces of globalisation exercise over the imagination of the masses. Even a small-time driver, Makhan Lal, born and brought up in Bihar (the underbelly of India), develops a strong yearning to participate and even capture the mirage/illusion of success and glory that these forces prop up. That he happens to nurture this dream in the times of 'global meltdown' is only one of the several ironies that this novel gets tinged with. Variations apart, Makhan Lal's story does throw us back to the dark days of the Great Depression, reminding us of Fitzgerald's famous novel *The Great Gatsby* (1925).

However, the final answer to all our queries is provided by the symbolism of the title itself. It nudges us into believing that regardless of how we choose to look at the Indian reality—as an area of darkness (with its definite resonance of Naipaul's anti-India bias) or as a continent of light (not 'Circe' as Nirad C. Chaudhuri saw it)—everyone, including Makhan Lal, simply wants to ride this 'white tiger' called 'globalisation'. And the only rule for riding this tiger is that there are no rules. This is a 'white' tiger (with all its racial and hegemonic overtones) precisely because it will not allow us any longer to retain our distinct cultural identity, stripes and all. In the context of the recent global meltdown (which coincided with the publication of the novel but certainly predates its conception), this 'whiteness' acquires a totally new signification. This 'tiger' has been as ruthlessly bleached white as the American economy, thanks to its unreliable financial institutions and wayward 'sub-prime borrowers'.

Our altered economic realities lend to Adiga's novel a sense of urgency, and a poignant topicality and immediacy. The extent to which Makhan Lal shows a typical picaro's unconcern for ethical norms in his search for personal success and glory, this novel almost ends up valorising the dubious ethics of universal capitalism that sustains itself on the predatory principle of 'foul is fair and fair is foul'. And why not—especially when it offers such an alluring, albeit deceptive, promise of upward social and economic mobility? For all Adiga's disclaimers, this novel fails to become 'a potent instrument of social dissent and protest', and remains a status-quoist novel. One really wonders what is it that Adiga is actually protesting against when his complicity with the politics of globalisation is near total. For Adiga, globalisation is not so much of an exclusionary choice as the only choice available to most of us, even to those residing on the periphery or in the backwaters of India. Only if one were to read this novel along with the Human Development Index (2007)—which paints a hopelessly grim picture of rural India where 47 per cent of all Indian children suffer from severe malnutrition and three fourths of its population still survives on an income of ₹25 a day—would the complete picture of contemporary India emerge before us. And needless to say, such a realisation makes this novel truly an over-hyped celebration as well as a lamentation of our times. Of course, the paradoxes never cease to surprise us. Whoever said that India is a land of gloomy, not groovy, paradoxes perhaps knew it better than most of us!

Notes

1. See, for instance, Krishna Singh, 'Aravind Adiga's *The White Tiger*: The Voice of the Underclass—A Postcolonial Dialectics', *Journal of Literature, Culture and Media Studies* I, no. 2 (2009); or Uma Mahadevan-Dasgupta, 'The Voice of Dark India', *Frontline*, 7 November 2008.
2. Sanjay Suri, 'Foreign Correspondent', *The Outlook* 48 (27 October 2008): 61–62.

References

Adiga, Aravind. 2008. *The White Tiger*. New Delhi: Harper Collins.

Berberoglu, Berch. 2009. *Class and Class Conflict in the Age of Globalisation*. New York: Lexington Books.

Donahue, Deirdre. 23 April 2008. Review of *The White Tiger* by Aravind Adiga. *USA Today*.

Friedman, Jonathan. 1994. *Cultural Identity and Global Process*. London, Thousand Oaks, New Delhi: Sage Publications.

Friedman, Kaisa Ekholm, and Jonathan Friedman. 2008. *Modernities, Class and the Contradictions of Globalisation*. California: AltaMira Press.

Gelinas, Jacques. 2003. *Juggernaut Politics: Understanding Predatory Globalisation*. London: Zed Books.

His Master's Voice. 11 September 2008. 'New Fiction: Aravind Adiga', *The Economist*.

Kapur, Akash. *The New York Times Book Review*, November 9, 2008.

Mahadevan-Dasgupta, Uma. 7 November 2008. 'The Voice of Dark India". *Frontline*.

Martell, Luke. 2010. *The Sociology of Globalisation*. Cambridge: Polity Press.

Medintz, Scott. 29 April 2008. 'Adiga's *The White Tiger*'. *The New York Sun*.

Munch, Ronaldo. 2005. *Globalisation and Social Exclusion: A Transformationalist Perspective*. Bloomfield: Kumarian Press.

Nordtveit, Bjorn Harald. 2009. *Constructing Development: Civil Society and Literacy in a Time of Globalisation*. New York: Springer.

Ritzer, George, and Zevnep Atalay, eds. 2010. *Readings in Globalisation: Key Concepts and Major Debates*. Oxford: Basil Blackwell.

Rupert, Mark, and Hazel Smith. 2002. *Historical Materialism and Globalisation*. London and New York: Routledge.

Rupert, Mark. 2000. *Ideologies of Globalisation: Contending Visions of a New World*. London and New York: Routledge.

Singh, Krishna. 2009. 'Aravind Adiga's *The White Tiger*: The Voice of the Underclass—A Postcolonial Dialectics'. *Journal of Literature, Culture and Media Studies* I, no. 2.

Suri, Sanjay. 27 October 2008. 'Foreign Correspondent'. *The Outlook*: 61–62.

Rediscovering Humanities in Life and Literature

We are poised at a critical juncture in our history. The twentieth century was a century of world wars, an extended Cold War, the Holocaust, partitions, ideological collisions, the death of imperialism and birth of neo-imperialism, collapse of the erstwhile Soviet Union, and the triumph of market-driven capitalism and American globalisation. In a way, we have experienced so much in our recent history that it may take us several generations to absorb and assimilate the impact of what we have collectively been through. One of the most obvious inferences we can draw from this situation is that the world around us has changed at a frenetic, maddening pace, so much so that it has left most of us reeling under the shock, quite disoriented, even off-centered. In his book *Future Shock* Alvin Toffler says that one of the defining words of our contemporary reality is 'change', and that this change is likely to take place at such a staggering pace that it would leave most of us in the middle of a maelstrom, swirling like leaves in a whirlpool.[1]

One of the ways in which this frenetic change has impacted our lives is that it has given us a permanent sense of living with multiple crises. Be it the Great Depression or economic recession, failure of the ruling elite or the rights of the marginalised, oppressed minorities, political corruption or bureaucratic indifference, we no longer talk now in terms of finding a remedy or a solution. Instead, we discuss how we can 'negotiate', 'circumvent' or 'manage' these crises. This is one of the ways in which the twentieth century has changed our perception of our situation, milieu and circumstances: we invariably talk in terms of a 'management approach' over a 'diagnostic approach'. Until the end of the nineteenth century, it was the diagnostic approach, supported by medical sciences, which held sway over human imagination. But somehow, the swirling changes in the twentieth century compelled human beings to re-examine their approach to problem solving. From attempting to find abiding, permanent solutions which were nowhere to be found—as the problems far exceeded the limits of human understanding—to 'managing' or 'containing' or 'cohabiting' with the problems, there has been a great leap forward.

Before we start outlining the exact nature of the 'crises' (the plural form is used here deliberately and self-consciously) confronting the 'humanities', let us raise a few semantic questions, which may even appear rhetorical. Let us first go into the history of the term 'humanities' and see the implications it has for the subject under discussion. The term derives itself from the root word 'human' and is ideologically linked to the philosophy of 'humanism' that, we all know, gained currency in the West during the Renaissance. This essay does not have the scope to discuss the social, political or cultural practices that supported, endorsed or legitimised humanism during the Renaissance. However, if I have to historicise this idea or concept, it may safely be traced back to the fourth century BCE, a period in history that saw the emergence and consolidation of Greek language, literature and civilisation.

The ideas propagated by Socrates, Plato and Aristotle were closely tied to the philosophy of humanism. Despite their apparent differences, all the three great philosophers, in their own distinctive ways, promoted the humanistic tradition. However, humanities, as a discipline, is a later invention, whose contours had begun to emerge around the sixteenth and the seventeenth centuries and coincided largely with the project of Enlightenment. The Enlightenment project represented the triumph of scientific reasoning and progress, and concerted efforts to build a material culture around these principles.

Humanism represents a philosophy centred around 'Man', and here, 'Man' is not used in its 'gendered' sense, but in its 'generic' sense. It has nothing to do with the primacy of man over woman. It does not see women as inferior to men or take any such ideological slants that our postmodernist/poststructuralist theorists often attribute to it. Somehow, humanism has been made into such a pariah term these days that often we end up celebrating anti-humanism, without realising its deeper implications. It is one thing to question the assumptions of humanism or the project of Enlightenment that derived itself from it, but it is quite another to denounce it, lock, stock and barrel. In a way, the decline of humanism started with the arrival of 'theory', which has apparently knocked humanism out of the reckoning. Ever since Jacques Derrida challenged the notion of the 'metaphysics of presence' and the rationale behind logo-centric 'subject' in the 1960s, not only has humanism become a bad word for most of us, but those of us who do believe in humanism are constantly on the defensive.

Ever since the moment of theory arrived, we have stopped thinking of 'Man' as a unified being and have increasingly begun to think of ways in which we can possibly split, divide, and fragment his (again, used as a generic term) identity. The marker of Man's identity is no longer his ability to either 'be' or 'become'. It has been 'contaminated' or marked by race, gender, nation, class, caste, ideology, etc. This is not to suggest that theory has not served much purpose. It certainly has, and that purpose is to make all those classes that have been marginalised, oppressed and colonised through history to reclaim their identity, and provide them with a framework within which they could create their own narratives of liberation. But has it really happened? Are the blacks in America or South Africa in a much better position today than they were in, say, the 1960s? Have the colonised nations been able to work towards their 'narrative of emancipation' by overturning colonial practices/institutions or by recreating the indigenous ones? Have women across the world become freer and reclaimed their dignity after all the efforts made by the First World and/or the Third World feminists? As a result of theory, our hermeneutic and textual practices may have changed, but our economic, political and cultural practices have largely remained unchanged. If theory has only given rise to another kind of neocolonialism or neo-imperialism, or a new logic for the sustenance of globalisation (another unequal economic/political order), one should certainly prefer to side with the age-old, time-tested notions of humanism, even at the risk of being labelled a dinosaur.

Now we come to another dimension of the problem. It is quite easy for one to support the return of humanism in some form, but things are not as simple as they appear to be. Having been viewed with suspicion and distrust over the years, humanism is certainly in a state of deep crisis today. There are three possible ways in which we may configure this crisis. At this point, one could raise an important question: When we talk about the 'crises' (the plural version) in humanities, what is it that we are really talking about? Are we talking about the crises 'in' humanities, crises 'of' humanities or crises 'for' humanities? Though it might appear that it is just another linguistic game which has to do with the arbitrary change in the 'middle term' or the preposition of the proposition, it is not quite so. With each semantic shift, you would concede, a concurrent lexical shift would occur and our understanding of the problem would alter and shift—qualitatively and substantively—acquiring very different contours. For instance, if it is conceived as the crises 'in' humanities, it would possibly mean that there are crises everywhere, and so also in humanities, where the latter is merely a shadow or a reflection of the former.

However, if one insists upon perceiving it as the crises 'of' humanities, somewhere the assumption is that these crises are peculiar to humanities, a particular branch of knowledge or discourse and, therefore, deserve to be viewed in isolation. But in case, we choose to formulate it as the crises 'for' humanities, one of the direct implications would be that these crises have been created, even manufactured, for humanities by forces inimical to it. I do not know if you, as readers, share this understanding of these propositions, but if you do, then it certainly gives me the legitimacy to proceed further, and if you do not, some more clarification may be needed on the subject. The point is very simple: there are only two ways of looking at any crisis; either we see it in relative terms or in absolute terms. Further, we may perceive it either as a by-product of both internal and external factors or merely as the result of the factors extrinsic to it. My understanding is that the crises in humanities is the result of both external and internal factors, and that it is not peculiar to humanities but is an expression of much larger crises. They confront, on the one hand, other allied disciplines such as natural sciences, pure sciences and social sciences, while on the other, our own culture. In other words, we are hinting at our preference for a relativistic, holistic approach, not an absolutist, segmented one.

The frame of reference for discussing these 'crises' is strictly native and Indian, not Euro-centric, circumscribed as it is by our understanding of our own context and milieu, with culture (in its broadest sense possible) being its overarching expression. At this stage, it might be argued that humanism, as a philosophy and ideology, is Euro-centric and that it has a definite context (of European Renaissance) within which it originated, flourished and finally decayed. It may be further argued that, given these constraints, it is impossible to make a distinction between two variants of humanism—Indian and Euro-centric. The popular perception of humanism, undoubtedly, brackets it with European Renaissance, and to that extent, it is perceived as a European or Euro-centric notion, though Europe had experienced humanism much before the Renaissance actually dawned. The first flush of humanism in Europe, as we have seen, coincided with the early phase of Greco-Roman civilization, when Socrates, Plato and Aristotle held sway over human knowledge and thought. Humanism has a history that goes as far back as the fourth century BCE. If this was the case with European history, what was the situation in the Indian context?

In the Indian context, the concept of humanism has, from the ancient times, been closely tied to the notion of *dharma* and is perhaps as old as the history of *dharma* itself.[2] One of the questions worth raising here is this: Did the notion of *dharma* emerge with the *Manusmriti*[3] or does it predate it and has its beginnings elsewhere? The notion of *dharma* can be found in our myths and legends, especially in our epics—the *Ramayana* and the *Mahabharata*—where it exists either as a normative principle or as an exceptionalism. As it happened in Europe centuries later, the notion of humanism took its roots in the Indian context in our philosophical system, our structures of thought and feeling, our cultural matrix. To a large extent, it drew its main stimulus from the theological framework of Hinduism, though in its long journey through history, it became secular in nature as it sought synthesis with theological frameworks other than those of Hinduism, such as Buddhism, Jainism, Christianity, Islam and Sikhism. It is a sheer quirk of history that so many world religions found their homes in India, had interface and dialogue with other religions, and ultimately helped in consolidating, redefining and challenging the limits of humanism from time to time.

Quite clearly, our concept of humanism is much more comprehensive, composite and synergetic/hybridised than the European notion could ever hope to be. It is not simply a case of scoring brownie points, but a way of suggesting that our history has been much more inclusive than European history. In any case, inclusivity, catholicity and comprehensiveness could easily be isolated as specific markers of Indian humanism. While in the West, the whole grid of humanism hinges upon the notion of existential, philosophical dualism, or what often passes off as 'self–other' differentiation; in the Indian context, humanism bases itself on the all-inclusive, monotheistic notion of the 'Cosmic Self'—which assimilates and is assimilated, absorbs and expands, recognises no 'other' except as an expression of the 'self'. Besides, in the West, humanism is broadly seen as a god-centric or a man-centric philosophy, but in India, humanism is a *dharma*-centric philosophy. The notion of *dharma*, as it is understood in the *Mahabharata*, is something that pre-existed man and shall also exist after the generic man has ceased to exist on the face of this earth. In other words, *dharma* is said to be the unchanging, immutable reality that is neither born nor dies, neither increases nor decreases, quantitatively or qualitatively. It is something that supersedes the temporal existence of man or men, and so acquires an eternal, universal form and/or character.

In the penultimate chapter of the *Mahabharata*, when Yudhisthira had finally decided to renounce the world and embark on his final journey to heaven, he was accompanied by his wife, brothers and a dog. As the journey progressed, his wife and brothers fell by the wayside, but the dog continued to bring up the rear. When the moment came for him to enter the portals of heaven, Lord Indra offered Yudhisthira a choice between his faithful dog and heaven, saying, 'Heaven has no arrangement for people with dogs. Think it over, good Yudhisthira. My suggestion is, you forget the dog. No wrong will be done if you do.' Yudhisthira said, 'To abandon anyone who is devoted is immoral. It is as immoral as killing a Brahmin. Great Indra, I'll not abandon this dog even if it means losing heavenly bliss.' As the story goes, that very moment, the dog transformed himself into the god of *dharma* and began to sing Yudhisthira's praises. Nowhere is the concept of *dharma* enunciated better than in the last chapter of the *Mahabharata*, where the significance of the epic is finally summed up in these words:

> Vyasa condensed the *Mahabharata*
> for the sake of *dharma* . . . .
> . . . .
> From *dharma* comes success and pleasure:
> Why is *dharma* not practised?
> Never reject *dharma* – not for pleasure, not from fear,
> Not out of greed either.
> *Dharma* is eternal. Discard life itself,
> but not *dharma*.
> Pleasure and pain are not eternal,
> The soul alone is eternal.[4]

It is this equivalence between *dharma* and 'soul' that needs to be examined somewhat critically if the true meaning of *dharma*, enunciated as it is in our ancient texts, is to be grasped in its totality. The notion of *dharma* is not only a moral precept or imperative that guides our path of life in this world, but a governing principle that determines our position in the 'other world'. The notion is not simply a regulatory principle of social engineering, as we often take it to be, but also a way of enlarging our consciousness and expanding our soul and spirit. In other words, *dharma* is the only connecting link, a bridge across this world and the world hereafter, the world of materiality and that of spirituality. *Dharma*, at once, offers deliverance from this world and from the next; a way of imposing order on the worldly life and also a way out of this world into a state of transcendence that *moksha* promises. The *Mahabharata* also reminds us that the performance of *dharma* is a sacred duty, enjoined upon every living being, especially in critical junctures when adherence to *dharma* becomes a pretext for self-questioning or a calculated personal risk. Even in the face of a Nietzchean nightmare, when one has lost the last vestiges of love and hope or faith in the legitimacy of human bonds, *dharma* stands firm as the sustaining, if not the guiding, principle of our life and existence.

This discussion of *dharma* should not mislead the readers into believing that we are trying to give the notion a specifically Hindu orientation. Instead, the discussion shows that though it may have originated in Hinduism, it certainly has undergone several changes and modifications through history, especially as it was, from time to time, incorporated into and reinterpreted by exponents of Buddhism, Jainism, Christianity, Islam and Sikhism. The concept of *dharma*, as it either exists or is practised today, is neither pure nor uncontaminated, as it does not belong to a particular religious denomination or group, but over the centuries, it has truly become a hybridised, indigenous form of humanism that is truly Indian in character, form and spirit. This shows that, when in India we speak of the 'crisis in humanities', it is this absence of *dharma* in our emotional, social, political, religious, intellectual and cultural life that we are essentially trying to bemoan.

At this juncture, another question arises: Are there any solutions to this state of affairs, this absence of *dharma* and the consequent threat to our humanity, our very existence? We are living through the times when diagnostic approach has already been abandoned in favour of a management approach. Does it mean we should now stop talking in terms of abiding solutions, permanent cures or prescriptive remedies? In a way, yes, but to accept it in totality would mean that we are walking into the trap of Euro-centrism. When it comes to a crisis, nothing works better than our home-grown prescriptions, our own remedies. Often, in the times of crises, borrowed ideas fail to work for indigenous problems. So, if we can allow ourselves to step out of Euro-centrism, for some time, we may be able to work our way around our crises. In the nineteenth century, the West (read Nietzsche) had already proclaimed that 'God is dead' and now it has declared (read Derrida and company) that the quintessential 'Man' in the sense in which we have always understood him, is now a 'decentred subject'. The death of God and the decentring of 'Man' have left them in a situation where they are busy rewriting 'histories' and rereading 'textualities'. The 'author' of their lives is dead and now they want the reader (read consumer) to step in and start playing an active role in scripting meanings. As far as they are concerned, there is perfect symmetry of thought and action. With the triumph of capitalism and globalisation, markets have multiplied and so have the consumers. In that context, it makes sense to search for the plurality of meanings, which creates more and more fissures and internal divisions.

But can *we* afford to abandon our God? Can we afford to ignore our dialogic tradition, our composite culture and our plurality that celebrates difference? More than ever before, it is now that we need to revisit our *Bhakti* poets, revive interest in the Sufi tradition and look for other similar paths that reinforce our faith in both God and Man. This is where the management, not the solution, of our crises lies, and this is where the ultimate redemption of our divided culture also lies. We have somehow lost our inheritance—the composite culture and the dialogic tradition—and because of which we too often feel lost as a generation. Jalal al-Din Rumi, the great Sufi saint, says,

> Try and be a sheet of paper with nothing on it.
> Be a spot of ground where nothing is growing,
> Where something might be planted,
> A seed, possibly from the Absolute.[5]

We do not have to look for solutions in Western traditions. We will find answers in our own traditions—for instance, in our own version of Sufism, available in Punjabi language and culture. As Baba Farid says,

> O Farida! Why do you wander through the dark forests
> Pushed back by the thorns, pricking your tender toes
> Why don't you return to the silent corners of your heart,
> Where your *Sain* resides, unbidden, waiting to greet you.[6]

Of course, not to forget Baba Bulleh who says,

> I am neither hungry nor satisfied;
> I am neither naked, nor am I covered.
> I do not weep; I do not laugh.
> I am not settled; I am not homeless.
> I am neither a sinner nor a saint;
> I know not the path of vice or virtue.
> O Bulleh! If in their hearts dwells the Lord,

They renounce duality, be they Hindu or Muslim.
I am neither a Hindu nor a Muslim.[7]

Let us bring back this humanism, which is already there in our blood and in our culture. Let us not fall back on borrowed, alien notions that have no connection either with our life or our literature. Once that happens, we would have taken care not only of our classrooms but of our society as well. It is the return of this kind of 'humanism' that can help us rediscover ourselves as human beings, negotiate the multiple crises we are facing today, or pave the way for our emancipation, at both individual and collective levels.

Notes and References

1. Alvin Toffler, *Future Shock* (New York: Random House, 1984).
2. The notion of *dharma* denotes 'law' or 'natural law' (as in 'the natural order of things') and is a concept of central importance in Indian philosophy and religion. In the context of Hinduism, it refers to one's personal obligations and duties, and a Hindu's *dharma* is determined by the person's age, caste, class, occupation and gender. In modern Indian languages, it can refer simply to a person's religion, depending on the context. The idea of *dharma* as duty or propriety derives from an idea found in India's ancient legal and religious texts, the idea that there is a divinely instituted natural order of things. Justice, social harmony and human happiness require that human beings discern and live in a manner appropriate to the requirements of that order. According to various Indian religions such as Hinduism, Jainism, Buddhism and Sikhism, beings that live in accordance with *dharma* proceed more quickly towards *dharma yukam*, *moksha* or *nirvana* (personal liberation). In traditional Hindu society, *dharma* has historically denoted a variety of ideas—Vedic rituals, ethical conduct, caste rules, and civil and criminal law. Its most common meaning, however, pertains to two principal ideals: that social life should be structured through well-defined and well-regulated classes (*varna*), and that an individual's life within a class should be organised into defined stages (*ashrama*). The antonym of *dharma* is *adharma* which means 'unnatural' or 'immoral'. *Dharma* also refers to the teachings and doctrines of the founders of Buddhism and Jainism—the Buddha and Mahavira. In Buddhist philosophy, *dhamma/dharma* is also the term for 'phenomenon'. 'Dharma', Wikipedia, http://en.wikipedia.org/wiki/Dharma (accessed November 12, 2011).

3. *Manusmriti* has been extensively translated into English. One of the earliest translations was attempted by William Jones, the famous orientalist scholar and was later redone by G. Buhler, an Indologist from Oxford. One of the recent translations is by Wendy Doniger and Brian K. Smith, trans., *The Laws of Manu* (London: Penguin Books, 1991).
4. P. Lal, trans., *The Mahabharata of Vyasa* (New Delhi: Vikas Publishing House, 1980), 369–70.
5. Jalal al-Din Rumi, *The Essential Rumi*, trans. Coleman Barks (New York: Harper One, 1995), 15.
6. This is the nineteenth *shloka* of Baba Farid from *Shlokas of Baba Farid* (translation mine).
7. Bulleh Shah, 'Kalam-i-Bulleh Shah', in *Bulleh Shah*, trans. J.R. Puri and R.T.R. Shangari (Beas: Radha Swami Beas Satsang, 2010), 313.

Index

Aarsi, xxiii, 249
Addh Chanini Raat, 82, 86, 87
Adiga, Aravind, xxiii, 253–55, 257–61
Aks, 250
Alkazi, Ebrahim, 52
alterity, xxv, 91, 95
amnesia, 92, 99, 175, 197
Anand, Mulk Raj, xxiii, 41, 255, 257
anchalik upanyas, 72, 83, 256
Anglicists, 13
Anhe Ghore Da Daan, 82, 87
'anxiety of influence', 2, 3, 6, 7, 9, 11, 26, 28, 169, 232
Aristotle, 13, 16, 263, 266
Atwal, Harjit, 77, 154–55
avant-garde, 8, 42, 53, 71, 250, 255
Babur, 178
Baghri, 185, 186
Bakhtin, Mikhail, 3, 4, 10, 117, 118, 197, 198, 201
Batalvi, Shiv Kumar, 70, 74, 98, 247
Benjamin, Walter, xi, 163, 190, 258
Bhabha, Homi, 32, 174, 191
Birk, Harbhajan Singh, 112
Bloom, Harold, 26, 35, 209, 237
Boli Dharti, 123
'Bondage', 130–32
Brecht, Bertolt, 59, 61, 62, 213, 214
Buber, Martin, 110, 120
carnival, xvi
Chatrik, Dhani Ram, 73, 246
Chatterjee, Upamanyu, 39, 40, 41
Christian, Barbara, xviii, 29, 139, 162, 173
Cohen, Robert, xvii, 138
Commission for Racial Equality, 147
cultural dislocation, 186
cultural memory, xvi, 81–104
Dalit writing/writers, xxiii, 251–52, 256, 257, 258
Dard, Giani Hira Singh, xiii, 76, 246–47
Das, Gurcharan, 53–55
Dattani, Mahesh, 53, 56–58
de-culturation, 117, 191
Derrida, Jacques, 1, 3, 12, 16, 173, 264, 269
Descartes, Rene, 229, 236
desi, xviii, 140, 143, 146, 148
Devi, Mahasweta, xx, 216–20, 222–23
Dhah, Jagtar, 112
Dhand, Raghbir, xvii, 122–24, 130–38, 152
dharma, xxiv, 85, 90, 100, 107, 266–69, 271
Dheer, Darshan, 152
Dheer, Santokh Singh, 74, 181, 247
Dhooaan, 154
diaspora, xv, xvii, 78, 125, 126, 128–30, 137, 140, 145–48, 151
dispersal, xv, xvii, 124–28, 130–37, 145
Diwana, Mohan Singh, 246
Doabi, xvii

Duggal, Kartar Singh, 76, 78, 248
'Dustbin', 132
Eliot, T.S., 5, 37, 99, 106
'Eye of a Serpent', 133
Farid, Baba, 65–67, 69, 96, 98, 177, 270
Forbes, 238, 240
Foucault, Michel, 3, 16, 92, 105, 196, 198
foundationalism 10, 12
Freud, Sigmund, 229
Frye, Northrop, 10, 16
Fukuyama, Francis, 195–98
Ghadar Movement, 149, 178
Ghosh, Amitav, 39, 40
globalisation, xxiv, 195, 198, 258–60, 262, 264, 270
Goswami, Kishori Lal, 199
Gupt, Babu Ganga Prasad, 200
Gurbani, 27, 29, 89, 245
Hajar Churashir Ma, xx, 216–24
Hegel, Georg, 4, 14, 118, 229, 230
heteroglossia, xvii, 117
Hinduism, 69, 163, 207, 209, 232, 266, 269
Hindutava, 232
humanism, xxiv, 7, 16, 22, 77, 124, 134, 263–67, 269, 271
humanities, viii, xxiv, 263, 265, 269
Husserl, Edmund, 229
hybridisation, 7, 8
Imroz, 250
itihasa, 2, 13
Jameson, Frederic, xiv, 4, 14, 22, 23, 29, 258
Jungnaama, 67, 150, 179
Kabir, 37, 69
Kahani Punjab, 251
Kakhan Kanian Da Ghar, 152
Kamloops Dian Macchian, xvi, 110, 111, 113, 114, 117, 118, 120
katha, xviii, 139, 140, 143
kavya, 2, 13, 65, 79
kaya kalp, 162, 163, 165, 166, 168, 170
Khalsa Panth, 178
Khalsa Samachar, xxiii, 245
Kuka Movement, 149
Kuwela, 82, 85, 87
Lakeer, 250
Lasch, Christopher, 234–35
Last Flicker, The, 82, 182, 186, 256
Lebedev, Gerasim, 48
Libri Hoi Chaddar, 155
Locke, John, 229
Lyotard, Jean Francois, 196
Macauliffe, Max Arthur, 183
Mahabharata, 2–3, 13–15, 47, 76, 101, 105, 108, 163, 173, 208, 266–68
Mahir, Mohan Singh, 247
Majhi, xvii, 119
Malwa, 83–84, 86, 94, 188
Malwai, xvii, 83, 185, 188–89
Man Booker Prize, xxiii, 41, 253–54
margi, 146
Marhi Da Deeva, xix, 82, 84–85, 87, 104, 182, 186, 256
Marx, Karl, viii, xxi, 5, 123, 230, 236
Marxism, 14, 33
Marxist, 5, 72, 77, 85, 97, 107, 123, 137, 196, 197, 202, 247, 255, 258
masnavis, 180
'Matching Horoscopes', 136
media projections, xxii

'Meeting Point', 136, 217
Midnight's Children, xiv, 38, 39, 40, 41
modernism, 8–9, 16, 29, 32, 71
mofussil, 142–43, 148
Mohammed, Shah, 67, 150, 179
multiculturalism, xvii, 115, 124, 136, 147, 151
Nagmani, xxiii, 249–50
Nanak, Guru, 29, 67–69, 96, 98, 177–78, 180, 193
Nanda, Ishwar, 77
Narada (as messenger across different worlds), 162, 166
narrative of healing, xx, xxvii, 216–17, 224
Narula, Surinder Singh, 72, 83
Nath *jogis*, 66–67, 80
Nath, Gorakh, 66–67, 80
National School of Drama (NSD), 52
Naxalite movement, 74, 90, 97–98, 218
New Criticism, 9, 16
'No Exit', 134
Nooyi, Indra, xxii, 240
orientalism, 13, 237
orientalism-in-reverse, 172
orientalists, 2, 13
Pancham, 13, 251–52
Panj Darya, 82, 247–48
Parsa, xv, xvi, xvii, 81–82, 85–88, 91, 94–95, 98, 100, 103–105, 107, 164–65
Parsi Theatre, xiv, 49, 51–53, 60
Pattar, Surjit, 75, 98
Phulwari, xxiii, 246–47
Plato, 3, 6–7, 11, 81, 103, 263, 266
Poetics, 2, 6, 10, 13, 16–17, 60
polyphony, xvi, xvii
postcolonialism, xv, 23, 33, 140, 145, 176
postmodernism, 8, 9, 14, 21–23, 29, 32, 33
Prakash, Prem, 250
Preetlari, xxiii, 82, 247, 249
Premchand, xxiii, 123, 200, 256–57
Pritam, xxiii, 246
Pritam, Amrita, 72–74, 83, 247, 250–51, 256
Punjabi diaspora, xv, 78, 128–30, 140, 145–48, 151
Punjabi immigrants, xvi, 111–12, 119
Punjabi journalism, 245–46
Punjabi Sahit, 248–49
purana, 2, 13
qissa-kavya, 65, 79
'Race for Theory, The', 29, 39, 135, 162, 173
race riots, 147
Ramayana, 47, 108, 163, 266
rasa, 13, 201, 229
rasika, 201
Ravi, Ravinder, 75, 112
readerly, 168, 214
Renaissance, 7–8, 15–16, 118, 168, 192, 263, 266
Renu, Phaneshwar Nath, 72, 256
Richards, Norah, 77
Rode, Ajmer, 112, 186, 251
Roy, Arundhati, 39, 43, 253
Rumi, Jalal al-Din, 270, 272
Rushdie, Salman, xiv, 10, 33, 39, 40, 41
rustic dowdy, 188
Saaddhi Kahani, 248

Sahni, Balraj, 247
Sahni, Bhisham, xix–xx, 202–204, 207–210, 212–14
Said, Edward, 126
Samdarshi, 251
Sekhon, Sant Singh, 35, 72, 76, 78, 83, 104, 181, 248, 256
Sen, Amartya, 37, 45
Seth, Vikram, 42, 43
Shah, Bulleh, 66, 70, 89, 96, 272
Shah, Waris, 27, 66, 70, 79, 96
Shan-e-Punjab, 124
Sharma, Pratap, 53, 61
Shastri, Acharya Chatursen, 201
Shiromani Gurdwara Prabandhak Committee (SGPC), 184
Sikh Religion, The, 183
Singh Sabha Movement, xxiii, 71, 76, 149, 193, 245
Singh, Atamjit, 78, 110, 111
Singh, Bhai Veer, xxiii, 71, 73, 83, 180, 193, 245, 246
Singh, Gopal, 183–85, 248
Singh, Gurbaksh, 76, 82, 181, 247
Singh, Gurdial, xxiii, 72, 78, 81, 89, 91, 103–107, 168, 181, 256
Singh, Guru Gobind, 69, 105, 178
Singh, Labh, xxiii, 246
Singh, Maharaja Ranjit, 55, 148, 178
Singh, Nanak, 71, 76, 83
Singh, Narinder Pal, 72, 83, 256
Singh, Puran, 73, 246
Singh, Raghbir, 249
Singh, Sardar Manmohan, 184
Sirjana, xxiii, 249
Sirnavaan, 251
'Snowbound in London', 135
'sphere of influence', 239
Spivak, Gayatri Chakravorty, 191, 217
Sri Guru Granth Sahib, xix, 5, 69, 182–85
structuralism, 9
Sufi, 65–66, 70, 75, 79, 89, 96, 101, 177, 180, 270
Talib, Gurbachan Singh, 185
Tamas, xix, xx, xxvii, 195, 198–214
Teesri Jaat, 179, 193
Tempest, The, 141
Temple, R.C., 180
'third space', 164, 174
Toffler, Alvin, 262, 271
Toonda Jat, 150
'translating consciousness', xi, 132, 133
Trishanku, 163–64, 166
Trumpp, Ernest, 183
underclass, xxiii, 260, 261
Unhoye, 82, 86–87, 185
urban rowdy, 188
Us Paar, 123
Vaid, Mohan Singh, 70, 246
varaans, 65, 67–68, 180
Verma, Veena, 77
Verma, Vrindavan Lal, 200
videshi Punjabi short fiction, xviii, 139, 157
Virk, Kulwant Singh, 76, 181, 251
Vyasa, 2, 170, 268, 272
wa Thiong'o, Ngũgĩ, 10
White Tiger, The, xxiii, 253–55, 258, 260
women's empowerment, xxii, 243
world literatures, xv, 25, 65
writerly, xx, 133, 214
Yayati, 163, 166, 173